THE TASK OF THE CLERIC

Cartography, Translation, and Economics in Thirteenth-Century Iberia

The Task of the Cleric

Cartography, Translation, and Economics in Thirteenth-Century Iberia

SIMONE PINET

UNIVERSITY OF TORONTO PRESS
Toronto Buffalo London

ISBN 978-1-4426-4993-4

Library and Archives Canada Cataloguing in Publication

Pinet, Simone, author

The task of the cleric : cartography, translation, and economics in thirteenth-century Iberia/Simone Pinet.

Includes bibliographical references and index.
ISBN 978-1-4426-4993-4 (cloth)

1. Libro de Alexandre.   2. Alexander, the Great, 356 B.C.–323 B.C. – Romances – History and criticism.   3. Romances, Spanish – History and criticism.
4. Geography and literature – Iberian Peninsula – History – 13th century.
5. Cartography – Iberian Peninsula – History – 13th century.   6. Politics and literature – Iberian Peninsula – History – 13th century.   7. Economics and literature – Iberian Peninsula – History – 13th century.   8. Clergy – Iberian Peninsula – History – 13th century.   9. Iberian Peninsula – Literatures – Translations – History and criticism.   I. Title.

PQ6411.L32P55 2016   861'.1   C2016-900259-4

This book has been published with the help of a subvention granted by the Hull Memorial Publication Fund of Cornell University.

University of Toronto Press acknowledges the financial assistance to its publishing program of the Canada Council for the Arts and the Ontario Arts Council, an agency of the Government of Ontario.

**Canada Council
for the Arts**

**Conseil des Arts
du Canada**

ONTARIO ARTS COUNCIL
CONSEIL DES ARTS DE L'ONTARIC
an Ontario government agency
un organisme du gouvernement de l'Ontaric

Funded by the   Financé par le
Government   gouvernement
of Canada   du Canada

Canadä

Contents

Acknowledgments   vii

Illustrations   ix

Introduction   3

1 The Cleric's Compass   13

2 Bricks and Mortar   59

3 Coins on the Desk   95

Afterword   134

Appendix   137

Notes   143

Bibliography   173

Index   185

Acknowledgments

As books tend to do, this one acquired debts to a large number of people. I would like to thank especially Emily Apter, Henry Berlin, Josiah Blackmore, Diane Brown, Marina Brownlee, Joshua Clover, Jean Dangler, María Judith Feliciano, Michelle Hamilton, Elisabeth Hodges, Jacques Lezra, Albert Lloret, Julia Lupton, Oscar Martín, Ignacio Navarrete, Ken Reinhard, Jesús Rodríguez-Velasco, and Michael Solomon. I also thank the students of two iterations of the course I taught in which I rehearsed the ideas for the book. I am fortunate to have had brilliant students in both; the finished piece of writing does not do justice to their insight, creativity, and spontaneity. I have presented arguments from this book at different professional conferences and colloquia and am grateful for comments and suggestions from my always generous colleagues, especially Frank Domínguez, Emily Francomano, Clara Pascual-Argente, and Barbara Weissberger. At Cornell I thank my friends and colleagues for their wit, rigour, and laughter, especially, in no particular order, Cynthia Robinson, Rachel Prentice, María Fernández, Liz Anker, Jeannine Routier, Pedro Erber, Richard Klein, Jonathan Culler, Edmundo Paz-Soldán, Laurent Dubreuil, María Antonia Garcés, Laurent Ferri, Pietro Pucci, Brett de Bary, and Tim Murray.

Generous support for research and writing came in the form of a fellowship from the John S. Guggenheim Foundation and a grant from the Program for Cultural Cooperation of Spain's Ministry of Education. I am grateful for the erudition and helpfulness of the staff of the Real Biblioteca del Escorial, especially José Luis del Valle Merino, its director; the Biblioteca Nacional de España; the Archivo de la Corona de Aragón; and the Real Academia de la Historia. A fellowship from the

Society for the Humanities at Cornell provided the intellectual energy and time for researching and writing chapter 2 in particular. From that wonderful group I'd like to especially mention Chris Nealon, Meg Wesling, Charles Kronengold, C.J. Wan-ling Wee, and Rachel Prentice.

Lucas and Manu walked La Rioja with me looking for arches and ghosts, and waited outside libraries (and churches, and monasteries), always asking the right questions and demanding simple answers. To them is owed any clarity this book has to offer. My parents listen patiently and encouragingly to what I inevitably lecture them on. As always, I thank them for their support.

Very preliminary or exploratory versions for what would become chapters 1 and 2 were presented at conferences in Spain and published in the proceedings ("Será todo en cabo a un lugar: Cartografías del *Libro de Alexandre*," in *Actes del X Congrés internacional de l'Associació Hispànica de Literatura Medieval*, ed. Rafael Alemany, Josep Lluís Martos and Josep Miguel Manzanaro [Valencia: Institut Universitari de Filologia Valenciana, 2005], 1321–34; "Babel historiada: Un episodio del *Libro de Alexandre*," in *Literatura y conocimiento medieval: Actas de las VIII Jornadas Medievales*, ed. Lillian von der Walde, Concepción Company, and Aurelio González [Mexico City: Universidad Nacional Autónoma de México, Universidad Autónoma Metropolitana, El Colegio de México, 2003], 371–89). A partial version of chapter 3 appeared as "Between the Seas: Apolonio and Alexander," in *In and Of the Mediterranean: Medieval and Early Modern Iberian Studies*, edited by Michelle M. Hamilton and Nuria Silleras-Fernández (Nashville: Vanderbilt University Press, 2015), 75–98; an early partial version appeared as "Towards a Political Economy of the *Libro de Alexandre*," *diacritics* 36.3 (2006): 44–63. I thank the editors for their kindness in allowing their use here. Finally, I thank Suzanne Rancourt, whose guidance and sense of humour have been unexpected gifts.

A Bruno, siempre.

Illustrations

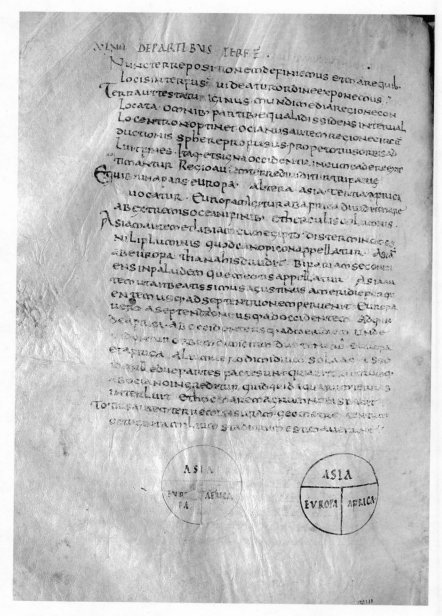

1. Two Isidorian or T/O maps. The oldest map is on the left. Escorial r.II.18, f. 24v, 7th c. © PATRIMONIO NACIONAL

DE ASIA

2. T/O map: A cross marks the Orient above, on the ocean ring, while underneath it a circle maps Paradise as origin of the four rivers. Escorial p.I.8, fol. 187r, 9th c. © PATRIMONIO NACIONAL

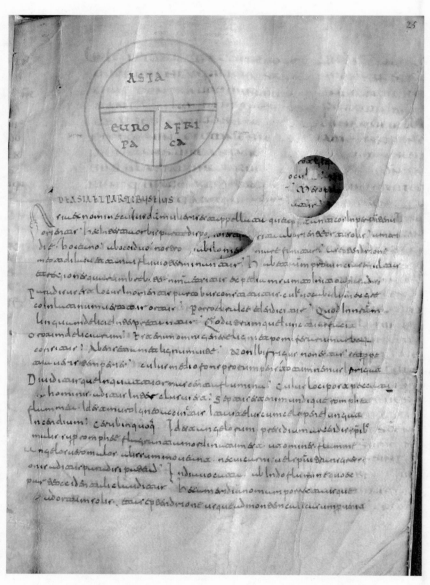

3. T/O map: The first sign of the Christianization of the map is in the annotation of Noah's sons to the outside of the circumference. Isidore of Seville, *Etymologies*, Escorial r.II.18, 25r, 9th c. © PATRIMONIO NACIONAL

4. Isidore of Seville, *Etymologies*, detail. Escorial r.II.18 25r, 9th c.
© PATRIMONIO NACIONAL

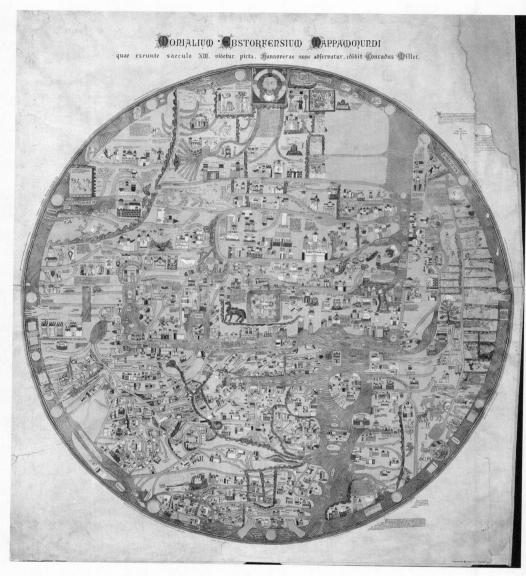

5. The world as Christ, or Christ as the world. The original (ca. 1239), one metre in diameter, was destroyed in World War II by the Allies' bombing of Hanover. Facs. Ebstorf mappamundi. BnF Cartes et Plans, Ge AA 2177. With permission from the Bibliothèque Nationale de France.

6. Continents, cardinal points, waterways are noted in Latin, and the names of the continents are also added in Arabic. Escorial t.II.24, fol. 175r, late 9th c. © PATRIMONIO NACIONAL

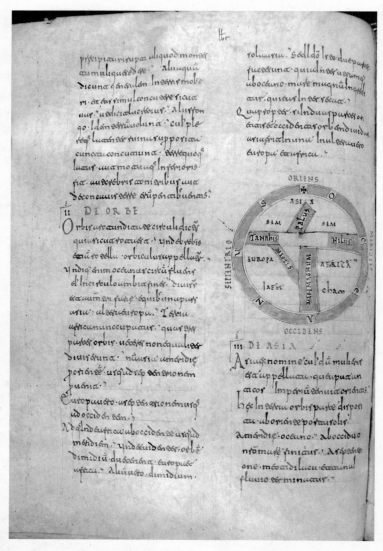

7. A variant of the T/O map, it changes its shape to include the sea of Azov;
the map here includes the names of the continents next to the sons of Noah.
The four cardinal points have been added to the exterior of the circumference,
naming also the waterways and marking the east above with a cross on
the surrounding ocean. Escorial p.I.7, fol. 222v, late 9th c. © PATRIMONIO
NACIONAL

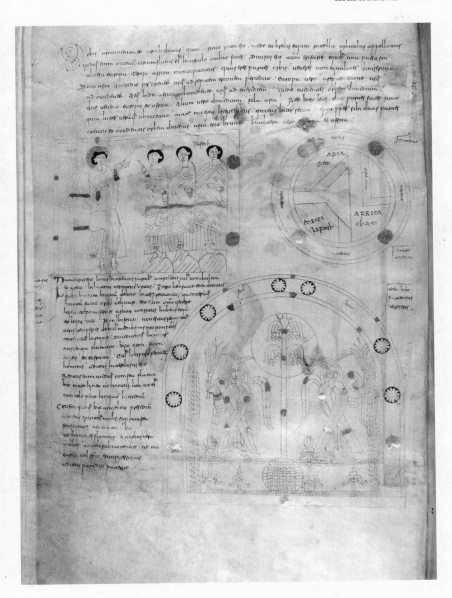

8. Modified T/O: Escorial d.I.1, fol. 14v, drawn in 992 or 994. © PATRIMONIO
NACIONAL

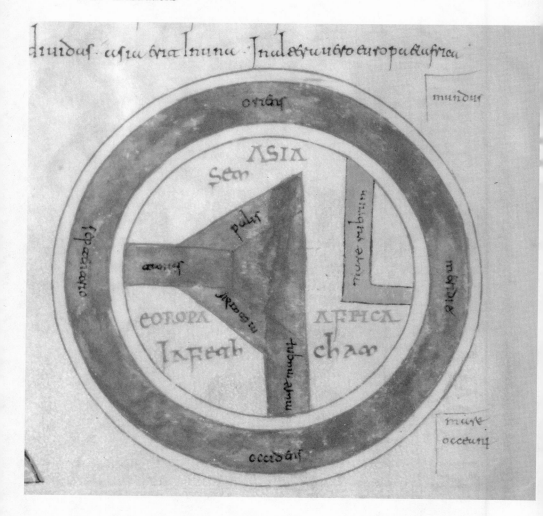

9. Modified T/O: Escorial d.I.2, fol. 17v, drawn in 976 (detail).
© PATRIMONIO NACIONAL

10. Paradise and the *fons paradisi*, Noah's sons, provinces, cities are listed. RAH cód. 76, fol. 108r, drawn in 954. © Real Academia de la Historia

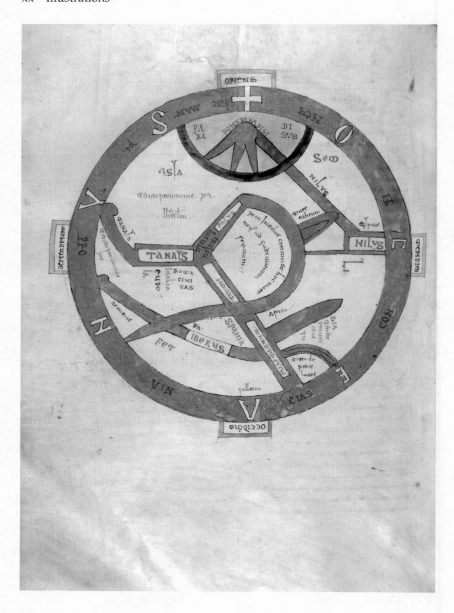

11. In a luxury codex for Queen Sancha, the map signals a transition in the relation between map and text, taking up a full folio. Escorial &.I.3, fol. 177v (detail), drawn in 1047. © PATRIMONIO NACIONAL

12. *Itinerarium*. Escorial r.II.18, fol. 67r, 7th c. © PATRIMONIO NACIONAL

13. *Itinerarium*. Detail: map of the Strait of Gibraltar. Escorial r.II.18, fol. 67r, 7th c. © PATRIMONIO NACIONAL

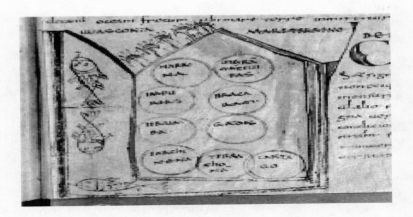

14. Schematic map of the Iberian Peninsula. España. Ministerio de Cultura. Archivo de la Corona de Aragón, Ripoll 106, fol. 82v. Reproduced with permission of the Ministerio de Cultura.

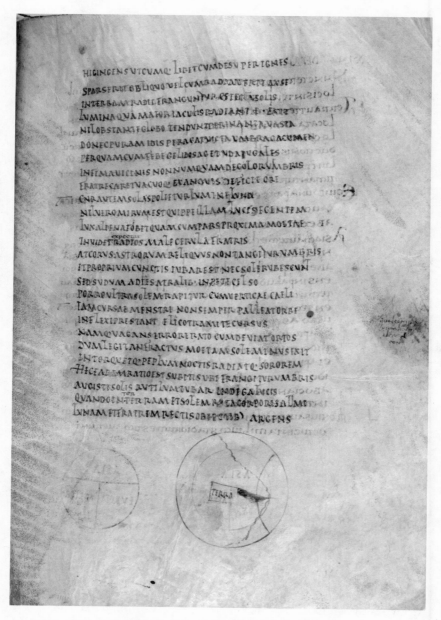

15. Eclipse. Escorial r.II.18, 24r. © PATRIMONIO NACIONAL

16. Cosmological map. Escorial r.II.18, 14r. © PATRIMONIO NACIONAL

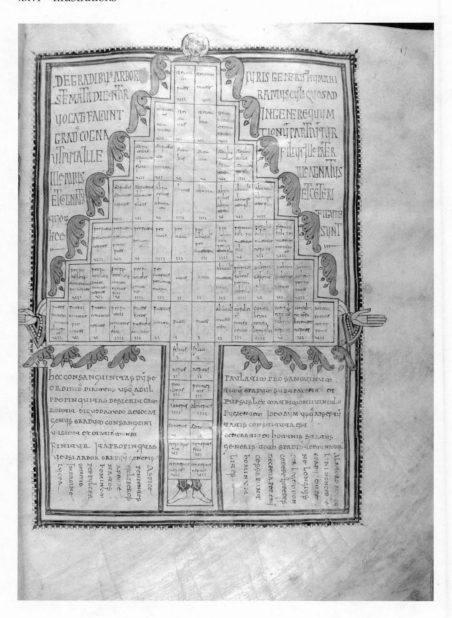

17. Map of consanguinity. Escorial d.I.2, 15r. © PATRIMONIO NACIONAL

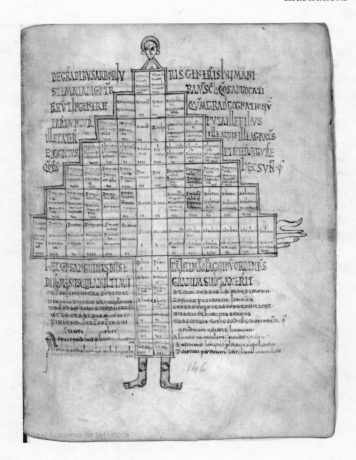

18. Map of consanguinity. RAH cód. 25, 146r. © Real Academia
de la Historia

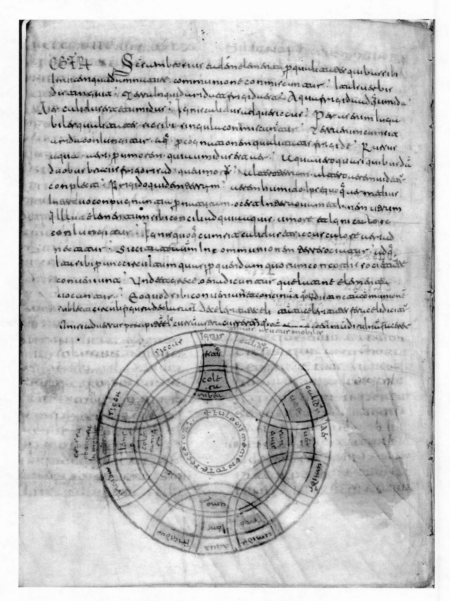

19. *Rotae* with note on Eulogius at centre. Escorial r.II.18, 6v.
© PATRIMONIO NACIONAL

20. *Rotae* organizing chapters, RAH cód. 25, 17r. © Real Academia
de la Historia

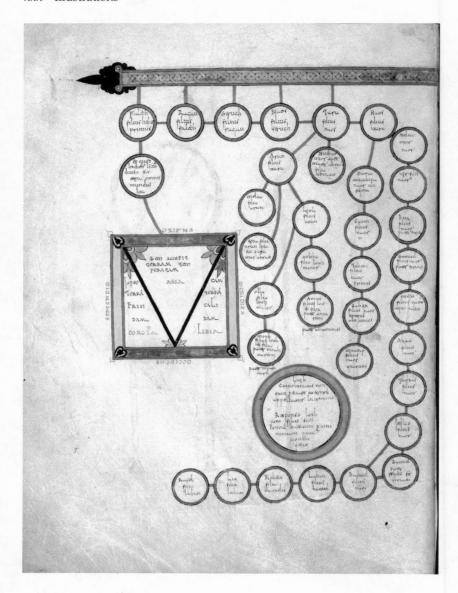

21. Square map on left; *rotae* organizing information. BNE Vit 14-2, f. 12v. ©
Biblioteca Nacional de España

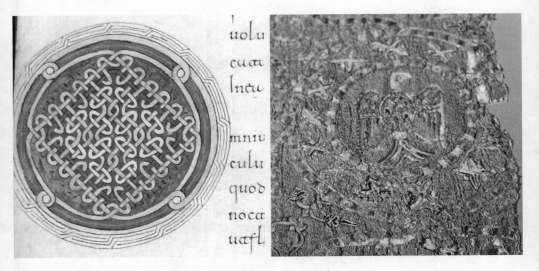

22. *Rota* in manuscript (Escorial &.I.3 fol. 198v) and textile rondel (fragment of the Oña textiles). © PATRIMONIO NACIONAL

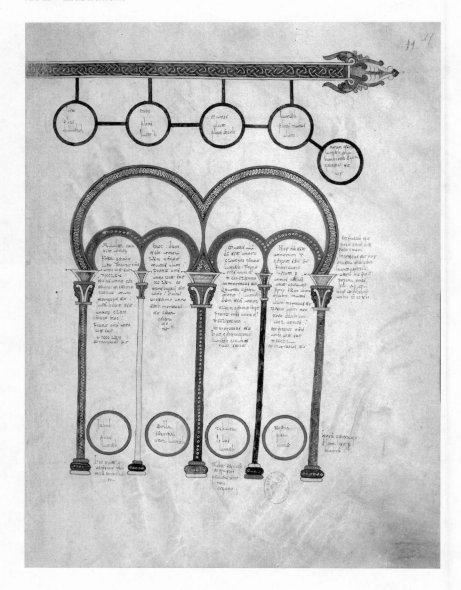

23. *Rotae* and horseshoe arches function as organizers of the page, as spatial markers of memory. BNE Ms. Vit. 14-2, f. 11r. © Biblioteca Nacional de España

24. Horseshoe arches distribute information on the page. RAH cód. 25, 28v. ©
Real Academia de la Historia

25. Façade and interior of San Millán de Suso (5th–11th centuries).

26. Fortress of Clavijo, 10th c.

27. Diagram on the classification of animals in Calchidius, *Commentary to the First Part of the Timaeus*. Escorial s.iii.5, fol. 134r, beginning of 12th c. © PATRIMONIO NACIONAL

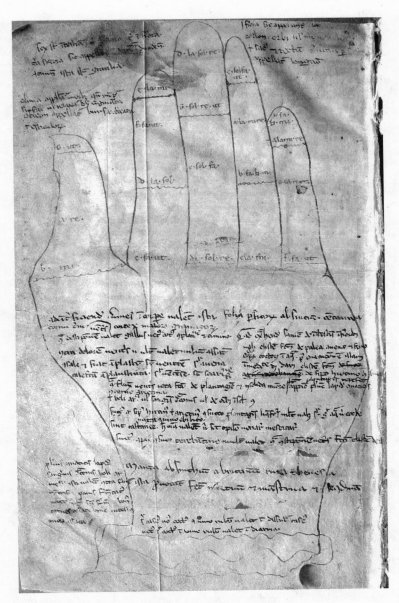

28. Guidonian hand drawn in interior back cover. Escorial s.III.5
(last folio). Composite codex, 12th and 13th centuries. © PATRIMONIO
NACIONAL

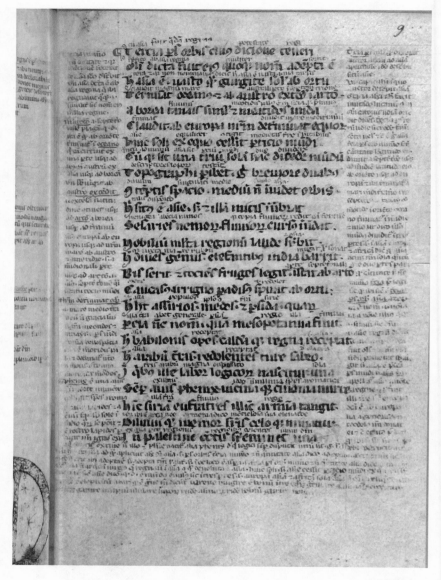

29. Extensive gloss triggered by Alexander's arrival in Asia: *Tertia pars orbis.*
Alexandreis. España. Ministerio de Cultura. Archivo de la Corona de Aragón,
Ripoll 137, fol. 9r, 14th c. Reproduced with permission of the Ministerio
de Cultura.

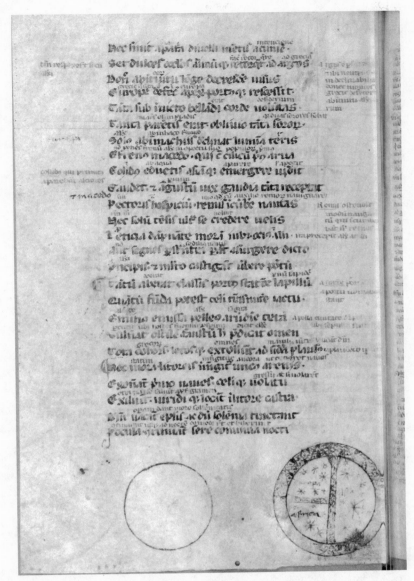

30. Map (and rehearsal on the left?), oriented north, naming the continents. *Alexandreis*. España. Ministerio de Cultura. Archivo de la Corona de Aragón, Ripoll137, fol. 8v, 14th c. Reproduced with permission of the Ministerio de Cultura.

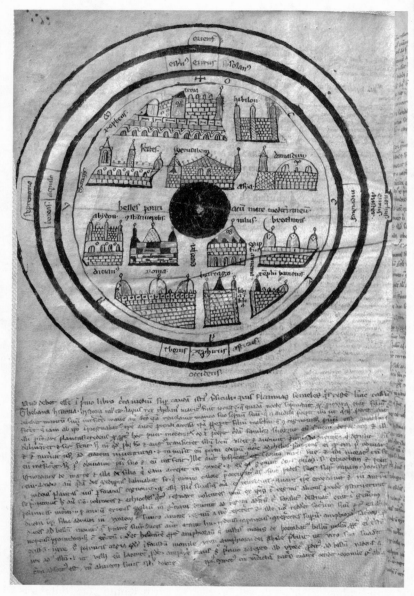

31. Map and text: geographic gloss as appendix. *Alexandreis*, BnF Latin 8352 fol. 100v, 13th c. With permission from the Bibliothèque Nationale de France.

THE TASK OF THE CLERIC

Introduction

Devising Language

In the northern half of the Iberian Peninsula, in the age framed for the Christian kingdoms by Alfonso VIII's defeat at Alarcos to the armies of al-Mansur in June of 1195 and his subsequent victory over al-Nasir (known to the Christians as Miramamolín) at las Navas de Tolosa in July 1212, clerics articulated a literature that would buttress the prolonged military and political effort by providing it with an imperial imaginary and a language in which to rehearse it. Spain's version of the Alexander legend, the *Libro de Alexandre*, is the first among these works of cleresy, aware of itself as a distinct mode of composition and performance, that uses and presents itself as a mastery over rhetoric, as a task of the cleric. Uniquely within this varied and vast group of texts, these fictions also work as a tool for sovereignty, most explicitly the *Libro de Alexandre*, *Libro de Apolonio*, and *Libro de Fernán González*.[1]

The task of the cleric, as the *Libro de Alexandre* details in its beginning stanzas, is a *service* undertaken in favour of those who are willing to be an audience for it, an audience that will obtain from this experience both entertainment and knowledge. The poem's emphasis on the transmission of knowledge as it is received explicitly expects others to continue this process, pointing to the potential recreation of the pedagogical exercise of composition. It is this process of composition as part of the didactic project of *mester de clerecía* – understanding that task as a duty, as a craft, and as an opportunity for self-fashioning – on which this book will focus.

While considering the modes of transmission and reception of *mester de clerecía* as mainly oral, and mostly as reading out loud (as opposed

to recitation or memorized declamation), the chapters that follow are
motivated by the task of writing as part of the process of composition
of these works and the context for this process as an archive of knowledge in the making.[2] Without excluding the complementary part of
these works, profoundly bound up with orality and aurality, this book
focuses on a "poetics of writing and textuality" that, I argue, is carefully
crafted and thematized in these works as a project in and of itself.[3] As
Pablo Ancos argues, "to say that the authors of *mester* considered their
task as labour essentially based on writing reflects well the reality that
examples offer," without excluding the role of orality or, especially, of
memory in the creative task.[4]

The interwoven analyses in this book reveal the task of the cleric,
understood within this poetics of writing and textuality in thirteenth-
century Iberia, to be a conscious crafting of an intellectual project for a
political period marked by engagements with the vernacular, whether
in law or poetry, well before the Alfonsine period. In this sense, the clerics' fictions, popularly seen as curious by-products of devoted minds,
will be revealed to be *also* exercises of power, attempts at deciding the
relations between aesthetics and politics, rehearsals for the imagination of empire, drafts for the self-definition of an ambiguous, imperiled
task of the cleric. I detail these processes of the invention of a vernacular learned fiction by way of three converging threads, cartography, language, and political economy, by proposing their common articulation
of a rhetoric for learned fiction. By investigating cartographic and economic discourses as they take part in the configuration of this fiction, a
literature both self-conscious and prescriptive, I illuminate the process
of translation and language consciousness in medieval Iberia from a
radically new perspective. Studies on translation in Iberia tend to focus
on either the corpus of materials being translated, recently with a special eye to intercultural or interfaith translation, and most frequently
they focus on the projects of the Toledo school of translators and specifically on the practices surrounding the period and court of Alfonso X.
The Task of the Cleric displaces the question of translation geographical-
ly, turning north; chronologically, it chooses to begin in a slightly earlier
period; and in terms of practices, it traces a general, far more common
form of translation within scholarly life as a translation between disciplines and discourses both inside and outside the *studium*. As a slightly
different take on translation, this book also moves out of a strict focus
on literature and language to seek in parallel fields ways of thinking
about problems in vernacular translation, and of the new solutions and
proposals this translation presents for its own future.

The Task of the Cleric focuses on texts that overlap in terms of composition, at times in terms of genre, type of protagonist, links to historiography, and modes of diffusion and/or reception. Their contexts of production are what most interest me, in that this particular moment of Iberian history saw the emergence of a specific model of heroism that mobilizes a precise rhetoric for and by clerics and sovereigns in northern Iberia. This context of production has become emblematized in the events leading up to and unfolding from the battle of Las Navas in 1212. In a remarkable special issue of the *Journal of Medieval Iberian Studies*, a number of important scholars debate and nuance the role, uses, and effects of the 1212 victory of Alfonso VIII. The editors carefully relabel this the "age of Las Navas," in order to account for the number of processes that predate and follow, enable, or at times contradict the general interpretation of the effects of Las Navas in the later history of interfaith relations in the peninsula. In that complex set of processes we call the age of Las Navas, then, this book seeks to emphasize the role clerics in close relation to the royal sphere had, contemporaneous to the events, in the changing articulation of the relation between the battle, a desired or hoped for fate, and the credit given to or taken by the different players, as Miguel Gómez details. The role of writing in the hands of those courtly clerics producing history, such as Lucas de Tuy or Rodrigo Jiménez de Rada, runs parallel to my goals in looking at the production of fiction in this same period. I want to inscribe the analyses detailed in this book in the processes that underlie the age of what would in Las Navas "become an icon, a cliché, that represents and summarizes with extraordinary simplicity and effectiveness a long and complex historical process,"[5] particularly as to how fiction, as part of the rhetorical exercises of a cleresy invested in the reconfiguration of sovereignty and the creation of a place for the cleric in its sphere, was invented as a learned literature that was both the result and the origin of this age.

While the book mostly focuses on the first of works of *mester de clerecía*, the *Libro de Alexandre*, perhaps the one that engages most overtly with a large variety of discourses, I also read texts that share with it a certain context of production, circumstances, and intentions. Texts such as the *Poema de mio Cid*, the *Libro de Apolonio*, and the *Libro de Fernán González* highlight similarities and differences with the *Libro de Alexandre* in solutions chosen, in dead ends and novel answers. In the short period one can comfortably wedge in between the first vernacular hero, the Cid, followed by the two pagan heroes, Alexander and Apollonius, and finally that mythically Castilian Fernán, a number of conceptual instruments are invented with monstrous bibliographical effects: Alfonso X as institution, of course; Gonzalo de Berceo as author-corpus-figure; but mostly the great hermeneutic tool of the *reconquista* that has plundered both the *Poem of the Cid* and the *Fernán González* for evidence. It is beyond the scope of this work to recover the many nuances or to undo the bonds that have been constituted between this interpretive paradigm and the history of Spanish medieval literature in general, but by introducing a change in perspective on how to study these texts I seek to amplify, deepen, and in some cases contradict the accepted roles of these texts in the narrative of contemporary debates on literary canons, national literatures, and disciplinary restrictions or freedoms. The critical possibilities stemming from the decidedly less studied *Alexandre* and the inconspicuous *Apolonio* will be projected onto the scholarly charged *Fernán,* using the ideological project delineated by the first two – centred on the role of the cleric – to suggest an appropriation (and deviation) of the clerical project in the *Fernán.*

The *Libro de Alexandre* and the *Libro de Apolonio* were composed, read or performed, and listened to during one of the most exciting, turbulent, and contradictory moments in medieval Iberian culture, within what is perhaps the most revolutionary period in the medieval West. Their relatively marginal status within Hispanomedievalism has always baffled me, especially when we consider their originality as a project of aesthetic, political, and ethical dimensions in the strongest terms. The period, of course, has received not only significant but brilliant attention to its intricate and multiple explosions, commercial, scientific, and linguistic, which undergird my analyses. Thus, my task in writing this book imitates that of the clerics I study, being one of compilation, elaboration, verification, and assemblage of the different discourses it seeks to bring together: history and economics, cartography and meditation practices, translation and rhetoric, literary criticism and theory.

Inventing Fiction

I first read the *Libro de Alexandre* in a seminar with the erudite Francisco Márquez-Villanueva, who complained that editors left the reader *con los toros en la plaza,* "with the bulls in the ring."[6] There are, however, many simultaneous rings and bulls in this lengthy poem, and while scholars have sectioned off many of the main issues – most notably, genre and sources – a wider look at the poem in its totality has remained, understandably, elusive. This might be why, within the larger, generally well-known European corpus of Alexander romances, the *Libro de Alexandre* has not found a place.[7] The *Libro de Alexandre*, dated to the first third of the thirteenth century, contains in its first stanzas a series of compositional, performative, and reception principles that will be reaffirmed by other works of *mester de clerecía*, principles that will reappear in the context of courtly culture and royal authority.[8] These are to be read as rearticulating rhetoric as an art of language that teaches how to speak, recite, enunciate, and pronounce as elements of the discipline of grammar and, especially, through the process of translation. As Rita Copeland has argued in a groundbreaking book, if grammar was the core of clerical linguistic knowledge, translation offered the possibility to recuperate classical notions of rhetoric within scholarly practice, thus appropriating political and ethical dimensions that had pertained to rhetoric until Late Antiquity and that had been slowly incorporated into grammar as a discipline in the first centuries of the Middle Ages as a pedagogical curriculum developed.[9] The process by which vernacular translation reappropriated the ethical and properly political dimensions of rhetoric within the discipline of grammar, minutely analysed by Copeland, is the immediate backdrop to clerical composition in Spain in the thirteenth century, and its effects are the focus of my research on the *Libro de Alexandre* in this book, as those effects anticipate the complex production and articulation of culture and politics in the Alfonsine period.

I am especially interested in how the cultivated vernacular that is *invented* in the *Libro de Alexandre* draws on different disciplines outside of literature; that is, beyond a concern with sources and influences, I am intrigued by how the poet looks to the margins or even outside of his texts, his library, to configure what will be a blueprint for the composition of learned literature in the vernacular in Castile. This book offers some hypotheses on how in the *Libro de Alexandre* a particular vernacular learned rhetoric is invented. In these pages, I understand *inventio* as *creative thinking* by drawing on Mary Carruther's reflections on monastic thinking practices, in its rhetorical meaning, and I understand rhetoric to be part of the grammatical curriculum, as detailed by Rita Copeland, and documented specifically in Iberia for the period of the *Libro de Alexandre* by Peter Such.

Spain's first vernacular Alexander is an early thirteenth-century version that takes its basic structure and content from Gautier de Châtillon's *Alexandreis*, supplemented and complemented by the usual suspects, the *Roman d'Alexandre*, the *Historia de Preliis*, the *Ilias latina*, Isidore's

Etymologies, Quintus Curtius, Flavius Josephus, Ovid, Cato, and so on. Beyond a concern for sources, in the only two extant manuscripts of the *Libro de Alexandre* there are curious digressions and original elaborations that have not been traced back to a specific source, and there is in general a free manipulation of sources that allows for constant and extensive rewriting. These authorial interventions, along with the expected Iberization, linguistic formulas, and a special emphasis on the sin of pride tied to the role of monarchy that the Castilian poet exercises on the translation, give the text its most interesting and timely qualities.

If Alexander's territorial conquests defied the limits of the epic hero, his travels to the bottom of the sea and up into the sky defied the imagination and the very notion of the human. A military mindset guides all movement, however, for after the sea creatures bow to Alexander as he invades their kingdom in a sort of submarine, the hero goes back to his quarters and draws a map – *compassó el mundo,* writes the Spanish poet – in order to know how to reach all of its borders, in a plan of global domination. A few stanzas later, Alexander wishes to see the world for himself, through his own eyes, and thus devises a flying machine. Numerous medieval artists devoted themselves to depicting this culturally specific aircraft, and many scholars have analysed its technological claims and details. Few, however, have wondered what exactly it was that the poet imagined that Alexander saw from above.

In chapter 1, "The Cleric's Compass," I show, on the basis of extensive archival research, how cartography served as a source not only for the descriptive details of the numerous cartographic moments in the *Libro de Alexandre,* but for the rhetorical invention of fiction, its troping. Through cartography, chapter 1 looks at questions of representation and the role of the visual within verbal composition; it also reflects on the articulation of a nascent university curriculum beyond the arts of language and in the context of meditative and pedagogical practices. While in my *Archipelagoes: Insular Fictions from the Chivalric Romance to the Novel* (University of Minnesota Press, 2011) I argued for structural links between cartography and literature, I here investigate cartography as one of those disciplines that supply this newly minted vernacular writing with strategies and operations – indeed, a rhetoric – with which fiction could *invent* itself in the *Libro de Alexandre.* The presence of maps, both verbal and visual, in works such as the *Libro de Alexandre* – thought of as pertaining to both history and fiction, to the past and to the active imagining of the present and future – suggests a more porous consideration of the role of cartography in clerical culture, one that, as the corpus I have compiled suggests, is not strictly bound by disciplines. Here, maps are weighed not only for their scientific information or their capacity for the location of events but also for their rhetorical roles. In contact with cartography through study and investigation of other subjects, such as geography, the clerics of this period would not only have been familiar with maps as devices within those disciplines, but as I argue, would have incorporated the different functions of the map as tools to engage with other subjects. Both as gloss and as interpretation in relation to the text, the "main" content, maps engage in different operations that are properly rhetorical, such as the map's specific actualization of *deixis*, techniques of *digressio* and *abbreviatio*, allegory and figural language, which are at play not as pictorial companions to the Alexander legend but as integral parts of the text, as elaborations that are often revealed to be the original contributions of the poet to his work of translation. It is only, however, because cartography is here conceived as a general tool of the period's curriculum, a constant and pervasive presence in the most basic understanding of glossing, illustration, and supplementation, that we can begin to consider the sharing of operations or tropes with the composition of fiction.

This section of the book incorporates extensive archival materials into a corpus of cartographic images frequently present within complex diagrammatic programs. I use this corpus as a framework to analyse in detail the verbal maps of the *Libro de Alexandre*, attending especially to cartography's role in the rhetorical invention or troping of fiction, and in the configuration of a cartographic rhetoric to be used as a blueprint for *mester de clerecía* in general. Through these close readings I expose not only the sharing of rhetorical strategies between fiction and cartography, but also a literal form of translation as displacement or re-placement (*translatio*), and as transfer (*transferre* or *vertere*) from marginal glosses to the body of the text, from the visual to the verbal, that can be used to think not only of cartography but of many other disciplines as working their way in the discourse of *mester de clerecía*. The focus on translation as a question of *space/place* puts an emphasis on translation between disciplines, as an exchange or negotiation not (only) of meaning but of context, where the dis- or re-placement of cartography from the margins to the centre serves as transition to the next chapter.[10]

Chapter 2, "Bricks and Mortar," considers rhetoric and translation through the metaphor of Babel/Babylon dear to the poet of the *Libro de Alexandre*. Babel, from Augustine to Benjamin to Steiner to Derrida, is of course not only the figure of linguistic difference but also the figure of its counteraction, whether taken as a reflection on a lost pure or natural language, an unfinished or unfinishable project, or the restoration of a divided community. The recurrent motif of Babel in the *Libro de Alexandre* serves to underpin the narrative, predictably, with a reminder of pride and its punishment. In its different emphases throughout the poem, Babel also serves to negatively characterize Darius's lineage and to anticipate his defeat, to imbue passages with biblical content, or to provide a geographical-historical setting for Alexander's conquests. Cumulatively, however, as I detail in this chapter, the passages articulate a role of translation in a specifically political context that must be interrogated theoretically. Thematizing confusion through construction, and thereby explicitly relating languages and craft, I argue that the Spanish poet is claiming as his own task a craft of language that has to do not only with a specific, divided labour, but with the work of language as figural, as saying something else than itself, a *technè*.

Rita Copeland's *Rhetoric, Hermeneutics, and Translation in the Middle Ages* provides the theoretical backdrop for this development, along with James Murphy's account of rhetoric in the Middle Ages, while the work of Isabel Uría Maqua, Peter Such, and Charles Faulhaber on the specific development in Iberia of a grammatical and rhetorical curriculum contextualizes these developments within the peninsula. The process by which vernacular translation reappropriated not only the ethical but, crucially, the properly political dimensions of rhetoric within the discipline of grammar is at the core of clerical composition in Spain in the thirteenth century not only as an effect of translation and the rearrangement of disciplinary hegemonies, but as a strategy within translation for the recasting of the task of the cleric within the sphere of sovereignty. First rehearsed in the *Libro de Alexandre*, these rhetorical exercises in fiction anticipate the complex elaboration of culture and politics in the well-studied period surrounding Alfonso X's numerous intellectual projects.

Chapter 2 thus investigates the task of the cleric as one bound with translation as a practice that bridges the text and its outside, language and its others; it does so by closely studying passages in the *Libro de Alexandre* that thematize translation to suggest its potential impact on sovereignty and political discourse in general. This reflection suggests lines of thought on a reconfiguration of the figure of the writing and performing cleric in the sphere of influence of a new model for sovereignty that is being proposed by figures such as Rodrigo Jiménez de Rada or Lucas de Tuy, incarnated in the later figure of Alfonso X, of course, but also in those of Ferdinand I, Sancho IV, and especially Alfonso VIII, whose reign is both conjured up and restrained within the *Alexandre* – in contrast with the alternative model proposed by the *Libro de Apolonio*. After a contextualization of rhetoric in the clerical world of thirteenth-century Iberia, the chapter turns to the recurrent story and image of the Tower of Babel as a point of entry in the discussion of translation as a practice related to labour, visual culture, and urban architecture, but especially to the political potential in the figure of the cleric as translator in the sphere of this new model for sovereignty as one intimately bound up with languages.

The task that the title of this book refers to mimics the genre's *mester*. *Mester* can be translated not only as "mastery" or "craft" but also as "task" or "technique," including the ancient sense of *technè*. Such *technè* as *mimesis* is intimately related to the new regime of the vernacular – an effect in the thirteenth century of the Latin renaissance of the twelfth – and to the transition from a gift economy to a profit economy that had profound effects on all levels of medieval culture. Grappling with these new conditions, Spanish clerics had to improvise new solutions by incorporating operations and materials from elsewhere, by translating rhetorical strategies learned from other disciplines, such as cartography, in their literary compositions, and by rehearsing novel figures of language inspired by recent rapid economic changes.

An emerging vernacular, monetary culture, in which the definition of the task of clerics was to be crucial for their survival as elite, required clerics not only to master the arts of language but also to link this mastery to royal power and to articulate ways to benefit from the new exchange systems that subverted the established social relations through new mintings, inflationary practices, and the rise of commercial culture. In the final chapter, "Coins on the Desk," I look at how contemporary practices and linguistic registers belonging to the sphere of economics enter the learned rhetoric that is invented for the translation of the *Alexandre* poem and aimed at a particular courtly politics. In a close comparison with the language of politics as economy that is presented in the *Poem of the Cid*, where a gift economy not only structures political relations but serves as the narrative structure of the poem, this chapter analyses the differing projects in economic language that the later *Libro de Alexandre*, the *Libro de Apolonio*, and the *Libro de Fernán González* rehearse as literary strategies, moving from a gift economy to a profit economy in a rapidly changing political and economic landscape. Taking as a conceptual framework Marcel Mauss's and Georges

Bataille's theories of expenditure, this chapter exercises a comparative figural analysis of these texts to bring out the different operations they propose. Together, they offer a striking view of how clerics in thirteenth-century Iberia saw themselves and their tools in a changing economic environment. As Alexander wagers a life in this story, so the cleric coins a language to mirror history in his present, a hero with the figure of the Castilian king.

The investigations into the *Libro de Alexandre* this book details address three problems that produce interlacing sets of questions: those of translation, cartography, and political economy. Through cartography, in chapter 1, this book looks at questions of representation, of the role of the visual within verbal composition, at the articulation of a nascent university curriculum beyond the textual and in the context of meditative and pedagogical practices. Through specific passages in the poem I want in chapter 2 to illuminate different facets of the task of the cleric as related to translation, passages that thematize translation to suggest its potential impact on different spheres. This reflection is also intended to suggest lines of thought on a reconfiguration of the figure of the writing and performing cleric in the sphere of influence of a relatively new political figure in Castile, that of the learned monarch, inspired in some ways in Arabic and Hebrew sapiential literatures and conflated with the figure of the philosopher king.[11] Finally, through political economy, this book considers in chapter 3 at how contemporary practices and linguistic registers belonging to the sphere of economics are translated into a rhetoric that can negotiate increasingly complicated courtly politics. Through the examination of different texts and by looking beyond disciplinary boundaries, this book joins the rhetoric of cartography with the economics of translation. Moving from a very detailed archival study of maps in Iberia up to the end of the twelfth century, through a detailed rhetorical analysis of the *Libro de Alexandre*, to a highly speculative reading of four canonical texts of the period, *The Task of the Cleric* also offers new methodologies and perspectives on each of the books addressed, and on medieval Spanish fiction in general.

1 The Cleric's Compass

Writing has nothing to do with meaning. It has to do with land surveying and cartography, including the mapping of countries yet to come.

Gilles Deleuze, *A Thousand Plateaus*

As Alexander goes up in the air in his flying machine, the reader is astonished not only by what seems to be a predating of Leonardo Da Vinci's imagination by a few hundred years, or by the technological detail offered to mask a credibility issue for the poet, or by the striking differences between cultures and media in their rendering of the contraption.[1] For one is most struck by the inevitable question of what it was that Alexander saw from above. His perspective is God-like, to be sure, but added to the curiosity of aircraft technology is the question of how the medieval mind imagined this view, how through writing the poet mapped what could be nothing but an imagined country composed of bookish fragments, a world of fiction. In the Spanish version, Alexander looks down and, turning a figure of speech on its head – "man is a world" – sees the world in the shape of a man. The literary source for this particular passage in the *Libro de Alexandre* has remained elusive, and one of my goals in this chapter is to consider instead cartography itself as a source, here and elsewhere, multiple times, for the poem. Alexander's world vision is one that offers immediate knowledge, contrasting the gifts of simultaneous vision with the delayed relaying of information that conditions verbal accounts, for the poet claims here that what Alexander saw in one hour could only be half-told in a full day. It is the map as instrument of knowledge and as tool of the cleric that places cartography in this book as counterpart and accomplice to literary production in medieval Iberia. The development of cartography before the period and its relevance for the study of literature will serve as a frame for a more detailed argument on cartography in the medieval curriculum and its relation to the production of fiction. The last part of the chapter takes a close look at how cartography, thus presented, is instrumental to the composition – and interpretation – of the thirteenth-century *Libro de Alexandre*.

Maps in the Syllabus

Cartography shares all of the advantages and disadvantages of representation. This is the first "way of knowing" cartography offers that I want to emphasize, its confluence with visual representation. Early on, the overlaps with language from its most material or graphic to its most rhetorically complex operations are explored from within both literature and cartography, testing the porosity and limits of this relationship.[2] The fifteenth-century idea, for instance, that the graphic interpretation of the main dividing lines of the maps known as T/O maps are letters that form the acronym for *Terrarum Orbis* follows and complements the earlier idea that the *T* should be read as a figure of the Crucifixion, making the map an essential symbol of sacrifice and salvation.[3] This kind of map, though inherited from the classical world, has its earliest extant version in Isidore of Seville's *Etymologies*, following Isidore's description of the division of the earth in book 14.2 of that work. The earliest surviving example of this type of map is in an Iberian composite codex that binds together maps from the seventh and ninth centuries (Figure 1). On the lower margin of the last folio of the seventh-century part of the codex there are two maps. The oldest, on the left, was drawn just a few years after Isidore's death in 636. The one on the right imitates the lines of the lefthand map, as if practicing how to draw a T/O. This ninety-five-folio codex, known as the *Codex Ovetensis* because it came to belong to the cathedral of Oviedo, is copied in several hands, and it has been argued that folios 1–8 might be in Saint Eulogius of Córdoba's own hand. Eulogius, as is well known, was at the centre of the martyr movement in ninth-century Córdoba and his travels to the Pyrenaic area, Gonzalo Menéndez Pidal argues, might explain the movement of scientific-geographic texts such as this one to the northern part of the peninsula. The codex has been augmented with materials of unknown origin that were added to an original Iberian centre.

It bears numerous marginal annotations, some in Arabic, adding to the intriguing collection of historical, scientific, and especially geographic works it compiles.[4]

The circular shape of the T/O map, representing a sphere (and not a disk, as is sometimes claimed) in a bidimensional medium, gains symbolic force from its gestures at totality and at concentration, generating spatial oppositions within its frame that in turn produce hierarchies within the map. However, the divisions within the circle – the *T* – suggest an opposite symbolic dynamic at work, a fragility, the loss of unity or the possibility of dispersal that is only reinforced when the Earthly Paradise is represented within that circle.[5] This is what the very small and simple map drawn in Escorial p.I.8, f. 187r, barely 3.4 cm. in diameter points at when, in a few lines, drawing a cross marking the Orient and, beneath it, within the circle of the surrounding Ocean – within the Earth – it inserts a semicircle figuring the isolated or closed Paradise from which the four rivers flow. The fragility suggested by the memory of Paradise and its loss is unwittingly reinforced by the fragmentation of knowledge that the structure and text of the *Etymologies* themselves underline (Figure 2). This manuscript of Isidore's *Etymologies* is also dated to the ninth century and has likewise been linked to the Pyrenaic region, in parallel with the first Isidorian map mentioned a few paragraphs above. These manuscripts are part of Gonzalo Menéndez Pidal's theory of the recuperation of Isidore within Mozarabic communities moving north. Menéndez Pidal's theory has interesting implications in terms of the social conditions of dissemination of knowledge, the transmission of different cultural elements, and of manuscript transmission in a time of flux and the reconfiguration of polities in Iberia.[6]

The association of the three continents with Noah's three sons, Shem, Cam, and Japheth, was often layered with information brought in to T/O maps from other types of medieval maps, such as Macrobian or zonal maps. These maps, also called climatic, divide the world according to five zones classified by temperature and habitability. The division of territory among Noah's sons also called forth the assignation of provinces to each, indexing yet other types of information, provided elsewhere, which begin to populate those internal divisions of the map. These divisions also have social and political implications that will be of interest to us later in both this chapter and the next, especially the spatial distribution of labour. The continental division of the world that is also a distribution between sons was to become standard in descriptions of the Earth, producing novel associations: in his *Imago mundi* (12th c.), Honorius of Autun explicitly associates the division of the earth among the sons precisely as a division of labour, and Alfonso X's *General estoria* (second half of thirteenth century) does the same in the chapters devoted to Noah and the Ark. I want to underline how there is, in this map, a primary gesture of adding information that is extraneous to the cartographic representation (Figures 3 and 4). Copied in the folio that binds together a ninth-century quire with the earliest surviving example of a T/O map is a map that reflects the supplementary information T/O maps would tend to absorb. To the minimal abstraction of the purely geographical information of the division of the world in three labelled continents, separated by the Mediterranean and the rivers and surrounded by the ocean, are added, to the margins of the map, as if self-conscious that this information is extraneous to the text to which the map serves as supplement, the names of Noah's son's, Shem (the eldest, linked to Asia and thus written above the map), Cam (or Ham, the youngest, linked to Africa), and Jafeth (or Japheth, the second son, linked to Europe). This intervention is a first sign of the Christianization of cartography. As the names of Noah's sons are inscribed at the edges of the map, they signal the erasure – or the porosity – of those presumed boundaries between the geographic, the historical, and the spiritual that will become a staple of medieval cartography. In terms of the arts of language, this is also a rhetorical move on the part of the scribe, who here incorporates within the map (and implicitly the text the map is dependent upon) information that is brought from elsewhere, and is thus a gesture of *amplificatio*.

The two examples I have discussed, one bringing in information in visual form as elaboration of the map in its graphic dimension – Escorial p.I.8's addition of Paradise and its four rivers – and a verbal elaboration one – Escorial r.II.18's addition of Noah's sons to the margins of the map – put forward medieval cartography's first engagements with rhetorical gestures or operations. The incoporation of maps into the general economy of diagrams in medieval pedagogy, as the frequency of maps in different contexts conveys, will also include the exploitation of rhetorical possibilities of mapping, becoming a sort of *habit*, an intrinsic part of mapping. This first gesture of *amplificatio* will only multiply and expand in the following centuries as scribes continue to add information to the margins of the map to then, moving this content to the interior of the map, transform the relation between map and text, and the role of cartography itself within clerical discourses. If we have here pointed to a first rhetorical figure in cartography, the example also highlights another, perhaps more essential rhetorical operation of cartography, even if it seems invisible or obvious: *abbreviatio*, cartography's capacity for holding information in spatial form in a contained, efficient set of lines.

Medieval maps are about the organization of knowledge on the basis of geography and spatial relation in varying degrees of complexity. The geographic framework that thus comes to house or place overlapping layers of knowledge in terms of space is a receptacle, a reservoir, but more remarkably, it is a machine for the production of knowledge that works with these layers.[7] As content migrated from the margins of the map to its interior, the map, of course, became fat, full of the most diverse materials, cannibalizing content. While the simple T/O used an outside voice, that of the cleric, to enact possible discourses abstracted or *abbreviated* in its lines, the sheer density of the new, fat *mappaemundi*'s contents would require a different approach to actualize its content. If the diagrammatic T/O – silent maps, as Christian Jacob calls them – presupposes a cleric who can summon from memory the information the map is there to merely *index*, the elaborate *mappaemundi*, eloquent in their accumulation of texts, require a sort of pathfinder to carve an itinerary through this information overload, a guide who was, in both instances, the cleric: either silently and individually involved in private meditations or the performing cleric acting as teacher.

In the thirteenth century this elaborate type of T/O map, which responded to the increasing interest in the accumulation of knowledge in simultaneous presentation, has its most famous examples in the excruciatingly detailed and very well known Ebstorf, Hereford (both thirteenth century), and Fra Mauro 1459 *mappaemundi* (Figure 5). The Ebstorf's massive 3.6 metres in diameter represented the world as overlapping or as embodying the metaphor of man as a world, except that the man represented in the Ebstorf is not only human but is the Christ as human, that is, it is God's mortal body that is figured as the Earth. The head, coinciding with the east, was drawn at the top, while his hands hold the north and south and his feet, as if stepping or standing on the west, complete the figure. The world as crucified Christ thus proposed a knowledge produced by accretion, where both material and spiritual meanings were elicited, from the materiality of parchment representing divine skin rematerialized on the world's surface, to the sacrifice of divinity that is the embodiment of mortality, the wor(l)d made flesh, offered to the viewer as object of knowledge by identification and through meditation.[8]

While the relevance of portulan maps or sea charts, as they are sometimes referred to, contemporaneous to *mappaemundi*, is indisputable in the story leading to late-medieval commerce and exploration, for the history of cartography in medieval Iberia up to the thirteenth century it is really the T/O and its story that is the most important, and I will focus on this type of map. In its movements between a silent, diagrammatic T/O and the more eloquent, content-filled *mappaemundi*, which often if not always include information from zonal maps in their distribution, legends, or graphic disposition, the T/O's place in the cleric's set of instruments merits a closer look.

One might speak of individual maps, but to speak of a cartographic *culture* before the thirteenth century in Iberia is a prickly question, mostly because a vast majority of medievalists would see the emergence of the elaborate *mappaemundi*, such as Hereford's or Ebstorf's in the thirteenth century, as inaugurating the tradition of an encyclopedic approach to the depiction of the world, represented monumentally in those examples but also in manuscripts, such as the well-known Psalter maps. To speak of a cartographic culture would entail the continued and somewhat popular dissemination of a series of traits, of given content and form, one that would need much evidence. On the other hand, the sheer beauty and variety but especially the detail or abundance of information in the thirteenth-century *mappaemundi* render any prior example one might offer for consideration a poor relative. The well-known *mappaemundi* of the Beatus manuscripts, copies spanning the ninth through the eleventh centuries and often studied as a separate phenomenon, are treated, if not as anomaly in the narrative progression of cartographic mastery, then as a brilliant but isolated and exceptional phenomenon.[9]

Bringing together scattered pieces of information, references, and evidence from a variety of sources, I have assembled what I want to posit as a cartographic culture that builds up in Iberia *before* the thirteenth century. Such cartographic culture is to be found always embedded within other discourses that it is intended to sustain, confirm or, more simply, teach. That is, maps may serve specific text-related purposes, such as illustrating holy sites or rendering visible the apostolic diaspora as Beatus *mappaemundi* do, but they also serve general historical, geographical, and spiritual didactic purposes, often simultaneously.

Emphasizing the *cultural* over the cartographic, I am attempting to paint a picture of disciplinary interaction and permeability.

Because this is a cartographic culture that will be presented to contextualize the emergence of a series of interactions between cartography and literature, and especially because this is Iberia, a brief note on Islamic cartography is necessary. While European interest in Arabic scientific writing favoured Islamic calendars, horoscopes, and star tables, materials that may appear next to cartographic ones, there were a few exceptions in favour of specifically geographical materials. Geographical materials are known to have been commissioned and produced in Baghdad, especially around the Balkhi school of geography. Cartographic examples dating to the period in question are scant, however, and their dating much debated; to my knowledge, none of them are extant in Iberian libraries. Among well-known examples, al-Idrisi's tablets and smaller *mappamundi* have been extensively studied; however, there is no evidence of a contemporary influence on the peninsula that can make them part of the corpus studied here.[10] Only two Islamic maps, as Patrick Gautier Dalché has argued in a recent article, might have been copied in the Latin West in this period.[11] In terms of maps, however, he writes, "barring the probable discovery of a Latin translation of al-Idrisi's oeuvre, the contact between the two cultures on Sicily or on the Iberian Peninsula had no net effect on the terrain of cartography." Relative to geographical oriented texts, moreover, the evidence we do have up to the twelfth century speaks to an influence in the Latin-Arabic direction, centred on figures such as Orosius and Isidore and, most interestingly (if predictably), closely linked to historiography.[12]

Cartography – that is, the verbal and visual representation of the medieval world in a geographic framework, to borrow Woodward's concise formulation – informs the general knowledge of clerics as they produce the first learned romance literatures in the Iberian Peninsula. As share of the basic curriculum, linked to rhetoric and the study of history, as part and parcel of scientific discourse, and as aide to the reading of ancient poets and the understanding of the Bible, cartography is central to the preservation of knowledge and thus at the core of memory and its role in medieval pedagogy and culture in general. It is this coincidence in time, this sharing of process and tropes between cartography and literature at the turn of the thirteenth century that particularly interests me. If cartography's accessibility was somewhat restricted to the student in the emerging and changing monastic and cathedral schools, this milieu paradoxically also guaranteed its dissemination and reproduction beyond the learned debates of natural philosophers via the figure of the cleric. Cartography, slightly shifting in this period from its role of mnemotechnical mechanism – the diagrammatic T/O – to one of archive of knowledge – the encyclopedic *mappamundi* – evidences a series of operations that can be related to the emerging tools in the *inventio* or creative composition of learned vernacular fiction in Iberia. Geography as one of the discourses of literature – that is, cartography in and as fiction – is ultimately my main interest in documenting an environment in which the practices of cartography and fiction share a series of traits as tools of the cleric.

Memory, central to the cleric's craft in his many capacities, was carefully cultivated and buttressed by a number of devices, whether verbal or visual, as detailed by Mary Carruthers first in *The Book of Memory* and in expanded form in *The Craft of Thought*. In its most schematic form as a speedy organization of the world, or as a more elaborate but easily accessible *aide-mémoire*, was the map. For even if their support, format, and intention may differ, maps, memory, and rhetoric are three ways of referring to very similar practices, from very early on.

The tale of the invention of mnemotechnics illustrates this relation of overlaps and shared processes. The story goes like this: Simonides of Ceos, in the shocked aftermath of a banquet hall that crumbled around him leaving him as the only survivor, lists in sorrow his dead friends, lying around him beneath the rubble. His observation that he remembers exactly who had been sitting where around the table reveals the basic tenets of classical memory techniques. For memory is built of *loci*, of places, places that are collected in buildings, spatial backdrops, the memory palaces that Francis Yates studied and that, from classical times through today's memory champions, are still used.[13] In medieval times, these techniques of memory, built on the storage of knowledge in places in the mind, in the association of particular bits of information with specific spaces, were studied within the discipline of rhetoric.

As intrinsic to these arts of memory, the map in the text shares a number of traits with rhetoric, most basically in that it organizes discourse (*locus*, *loci*, commonplaces as the most basic building block of discourse, for instance). Curiously, even though Quintilian mentions the possibility of "placing memory images along an itinerary," classical rhetoric never seems to have applied the model to geographical maps.[14] Nevertheless, this does not mean that the paths of maps and memory did not cross. The crux of my argument here is that as a result of the continued cartographic culture that I have documented for Latin Iberia, cartography, as organizer of discourse, as classification device, as tool for distribution and composition, would not only have been part of the cleric's mnemotechnics but, as a habitual tool of the task of the cleric, would have also served as a source for the invention of a literary language, the troping of fiction itself. What was the context in which a cartographic culture is to be understood as part of clerical knowledge in Iberia? After sketching this intellectual landscape, the chapter will look at the *Libro de Alexandre* to show how cartography serves not just an illustrative or mnemotechnical role but, crucially, a thematic and structural one as well, that evidences this sharing of operations, this tropic interaction between disciplines.[15]

Curriculum and Corpus

The study of geography as part of the general curriculum of university studies in the Middle Ages is well documented. Cartography, however, is rarely considered in this discussion, since geography as a discipline was studied as a verbal, written discourse, transmitted and preserved mainly in writing. The medieval image of the world, one would have to say, is less likely a visual one than one brought about by narrative, description, and lists, though there are many examples both of verbal/written maps and of illustrations, visual glosses to verbal descriptions of the physical world that we can ultimately link to didacticism, as in Charlemagne's call for the illustration of useful surfaces of churches for the instruction of the faithful, following Gregory's famous and debated pronouncements on the use of pictures.[16] It is thus that we must look to the basic geographical curriculum to find the first contexts for maps.

The first and perhaps most important source on geography known directly and widely during the Middle Ages was Macrobius's *Commentary* to the *Dream of Scipio*, the last part of Cicero's *Republic*. The commentary is much longer than the *Dream* (over fifteen times longer), and though it is mainly an exposition of Neoplatonism, it digresses into cosmography, dreams and dream theory, numerology, and geography, all topics dear to the medieval mind, which assured its popularity and its transmission, often bound separately with other bits and pieces of astronomical information as if a separate work. The *Commentary* was frequently accompanied by a zonal map in its margins, with different levels of elaboration.[17] Next in the medieval curriculum on geography came Calchidius, whose extensive commentary and almost complete translation of Plato's *Timaeus* was to be one of the most important cosmological treatises up to the twelfth century, and was often bound together with Macrobius, thus sharing the zonal map as visual gloss to its content. The zones, determined as to their effects on the habitability or inhabitability of the lands associated with them – *frigida* and *calida* are inhabitable, and the *temperata* zones are the only ones where life is possible – are one of those contents that will migrate to other types of maps, maps glossing texts that are *not* Macrobius or Calchidius.

In this basic context, Isidore of Seville's works added, in the words of Edward Grant, "a more practical method of presentation." *On the Nature of Things (De natura rerum)* devotes its last chapter to the parts of the earth (chapter 11, though titled as on the parts of the world, is on the four elements). *Etymologies (Etymologiae)*, the encyclopedic work composed much later, and of greater length, deals with cosmography and geography in books 13 and 14, books that were extremely influential throughout the medieval period, often copied separately and independently.[18] These two texts by the bishop of Seville house the largest number of maps from the medieval period, ranging from the most diagrammatic to very complex ones with numerous place names and details.

The twelfth century, right before the most important wave of translations of Greek and Arabic scientific texts, saw important figures emerge in the study of natural philosophy that also bear weight on the study of geography in the period that interests me here. Among the many figures that radically changed the way knowledge was taught and learned, institutionally or in terms of method in the period leading to the thirteenth century, was Hugh of Saint Victor. His *Didascalicon*, which functioned as a sort of student guide or survey manual for teachers, serves as emblem for how changes in the scientific curriculum might be interesting to the study of literature. Written in the tradition of didascalic or didactic literature concerned with how and what a man should study – a tradition that encompasses figures such as Socrates and his attacks on the sophists, Aristotle and Plato on education, Cicero and Quintilian, Martianus Capella and Augustine, among others – the *Didascalicon* appeared at a moment when education itself was undergoing what we might call infrastructural changes, moving from rural monasteries to urban cathedral schools, and within its institutions the benefits of specialization were debated, questioning the abilities of masters, and asking how devoting oneself to intellectual life might want or be able to adapt to the demands of secular life. At the heart of this discussion was, Chenu has argued, not merely the relation between faith and reason, but that between nature and the divine, nature and grace.[19] This basic problem seen in a new light – the demarcation and mediation between the worldly and the transcendental, between the physical, mortal body, and the time of salvation, particularly when linked to the figure of the cleric and its task – is one that medieval cartography takes up by infusing the spatial with the symbolic. Bridging natural philosophy and the study of geography, and functioning as an instrument for the organization of knowledge, cartography was thus a most appropriate form to be integrated to and to incorporate within it other disciplines.

Parallel to this discussion that pertains both to natural philosophy and cartography, central to the emergence of learned romance fiction in Castile, is the relation between orality and written culture. While I will not rehearse here a period characterization of these relations, which has been done expertly elsewhere, it needs to be emphasized that as part of this emerging way of composing/writing that is known as *miester de clerecía*, the codependence between the textual and the performed is mirrored in the map's elicitation of both writing and enunciation, to which I will turn below.

Through the study of geography and, indirectly, of natural philosophy and history, but especially as a tool for the classification and memorization of information of different kinds, as a tool for the cleric, cartography would have ensured its continued place in the curriculum. Within this context, I want to emphasize its didactic role, a didacticism that characterizes the first learned literatures in romance and works as a basic link with cartographic operations.[20] This didacticism may also point to a particular operator, that is, to the student experimenting to perfect his exercises in grammar and rhetoric, and to the basic building blocks of medieval pedagogy: classification and memory. If cartography entered the university curriculum via the study of geography – mostly in verbal form as gloss or as description, but also graphically, as many of these examples convey – it is its principal didactic role in intimate relation to a text, a relation established early on, that I turn to now in order to illuminate cartography's intimate role in clerical life.

Cassiodorus, the sixth-century monk and statesman, recommended that monks study geography and history along with the liberal arts, referring explicitly to cartography as an aide in such an enterprise. Gautier Dalché concludes from his reading of Cassiodorus that the map, clearly distinguished from the text it accompanies as its representation, is

> destined to clarify the descriptive text, but remaining very often in a relation of subordination. This situation does not fundamentally change if, deviating from the model proposed by Cassiodorus, the cartographic

representation is situated not separately but to the interior of a codex. Confirmation is provided by the fact that descriptive geographies, whether autonomous or within compositions of a different nature, are generally devoid of maps.[21]

This basic relation of dependence, moving towards codependence and cannibalization between image and text, is one that we have to take into account first, and one that I illustrated as already happening in a first imitation of a map in the ninth-century Isidorian manuscript (Figure 1). If with Cassiodorus we can already see how rhetorical operations in cartography might begin to be identified beyond the basic *abbreviatio* and *amplificatio*, in a *second* early medieval source that details the use of maps, Jonas of Bobbio's *Life of St. Columban* (7th c.), it is not only the mention of a map, or the connection between maps and dreams or prophecy, but specifically the reference to the map not as an exceptional but as a *common* type of illustration, a habitual one for monks, that I find most striking. Jonas of Bobbio has a vision in which the Lord shows him a map as a tool for the evangelization of the Slavs. He goes on to specify that this image of the world, this map, is such as those "we are *in the habit* of representing the inhabited earth in ink, drawing a circle on a page" (my emphasis). The characterization of the drawing of maps by monks as a habit, as a common tool for clerics, intimates how cartography was seen and used by those clerics who inherited such a tradition.

From Bobbio's reference to cartography, Gautier Dalché underlines a most obvious but often overlooked function of maps in medieval culture: beyond instrument of assemblage or device for containment of information, the map works as a support for *different* types of knowledge – it is not tied to a particular discourse. This versatility is one whose importance needs to be reassessed, most especially for the early medieval period, for which numerous maps must still be catalogued.[22]

As luck would have it, a (probable) map of Hispania – a partial and incomplete map of the peninsula, not a *mappamundi*, and the only available painted fragment of a papyrus intended to be a luxurious edition of Artemidorus of Ephesus's *Geography*, written before the last quarter of the first century BC – is among the few remnants of classical cartographic culture, and the oldest.[23] The ninety-centimetre map is drawn in the large empty space the calligrapher left between the proem, which dwells on the importance of geography as equal to philosophy, and the beginning of the geographical verbal description of Spain. Here one can see how the map functioned as gloss or complement of the verbal in a geographical and historical context.[24] The map is what fills in the blank spaces of the verbal, in a relation of dependence to the text, a "silent" complement to the eloquence of the verbal that it illustrates. This, we will see, is in opposite relation to what will happen thirteen centuries later as *mappaemundi* expand, and legends, stories, and written language come to fill in those spaces, freeing the map from the text it had depended on by appropriating that text.[25]

It was in Iberia, the Hispania of the Romans, that two of the most important figures for geographic literature in Western Europe throughout the Middle Ages emerged, Orosius and Isidore, who provided not only the texts that will bear the most numerous cartographic depictions before 1200, but also the flexible contexts for the plays between the graphic and the verbal that can allow for a fuller appreciation of the interpretive dimensions of cartography in this period. After these figures, but central to this brief summary of cartographic considerations for Iberia, is the Beatus *mappaemundi* tradition, the single most important cartographic event before the thirteenth century, which focuses on cartography as meditative practice. The two cartographic traditions I have thus referred to – an Isidorian and a Beatus one – have been studied in conjunction as a sort of progression by the eminent Gonzalo Menéndez Pidal, who follows and speculates on the movement of two series of manuscripts from southern Iberia to the Christian kingdoms of the North via Mozarabic culture, a particular take on *translatio* (and one that is most common in the study of material culture in medieval Iberia, shuttling between notions of spatial displacement and linguistic and cultural translation). Menéndez Pidal studies these codices because they are the longest extant series of the Iberian High Middle Ages, traceable at times not only to specific scriptoria, but even to scribes and glossing hands.[26]

There is evidence outside manuscript culture, even if little, that supports the idea that a pre-thirteenth-century cartographic culture in Iberia extended beyond the space of the *scriptorium*, evidence that can only hint at the examples we have might have lost to fire, the elements, looting, war, and the like.[27] The mural painted in the left chapel of the monastery of San Pedro de Rocas, for instance, shows the last traces of a map, probably painted in the last quarter of the twelfth century. This is the oldest monastery in the region known as the Ribeira Sacra in Galicia, allegedly founded at the end of the sixth century, abandoned due to Muslim advance on the peninsula in the eighth century and rediscovered in the ninth century by the knight Gemodus who, according to legend, stumbled upon the construction while hunting and, suddenly struck by devotion, decided to become a hermit in that place. Others, moved by his devotion, later joined him, and the monastery was granted donations and privileges by Alfonso III.[28] This mural map, with thematic connections to the Beatus tradition as it is a map of the apostolic diaspora, can be also contextually linked to a larger tradition of commissioned mural maps beginning with that made under Agrippa that hung in the Porticus Vipsania or Porticus of the Argonauts under Augustan rule according to Pliny's account in his *Natural History* (book 3).[29] Later examples of this mural map tradition include fourth-century Gaul, where the orator Eumenius lectured on a world map suspended from a balcony at the academy at Autun; and well throughout the medieval period maps, now lost for the most part, painted on walls or on vellum or as floor mosaics, are known through their literary descriptions to have existed, such as the one at the Lateran Palace under Pope Zacharias, the painted tablets of Charlemagne, and the one in the palace of Orléans under Bishop Theodulf.[30] A map similar to our Galician one, painted on the walls of a monastery, is the lost *mappamundi* of Chalivoi-Milon, dated as well to the twelfth century, studied by Marcia Kupfner. And finally, there are those we know only from their verbal memory or confabulation, such as Baudri de Bourgueil's imagined floor mosaic as an emblem of power for Adela, countess of Blois.[31] Within this last category, but linked in their possible materiality to those on walls or on parchment, I would include the verbal *mappamundi* that Hugh of Saint Victor provides instructions for drawing, those described in the *Libro de Alexandre*, or the one we can speculate on as a likely companion to the *Semejanza del mundo*, different genres that evidence a clerical culture that draws from its many disciplines the architecture of its writing.

What would be the contexts for a cartographic culture in the twelfth century that would serve as ground not only for the connections and transitions between the San Pedro de Rocas and Hereford *mappaemundi*, between the Beatus and Hugh of Saint Victor maps, but for the rhetorical manipulation of geography in texts such as the *Semejança del mundo* and the *Libro de Alexandre*? How does the cleric in his rehearsing of a learned vernacular build on cartography's tropes? In order to tease out the different relations between these disciplines, it is necessary to first establish a corpus – which may very well be expanded – and a number of hypotheses on the roles of cartography pre-1200 in Iberia.[32]

I have assembled a working corpus of pre-thirteenth-century maps in Spanish archives for which a series of general traits can be discerned, from *amplificatio* to intertextuality, allegorization and symbolization, to eschatology and moralization. A continental organization of the world can add information on population through the names of Noah's sons, for instance, or incorporate the data offered by zonal maps.[33] The same tripartite division may be read as a symbol of the Passion, in which the cross, either marking the Orient as origin or as guiding the eye to the East on the Ocean ring, or superimposed to the orb of the world, marks the earth as the place for salvation (and the space outside the border of the earth as the *time* for salvation). In strict relation to their staging of political power, *mappaemundi* also represent the world as the backdrop for vanity, for futile glory, discursively represented in the trope of *contemptus mundi*.[34] In this corpus, the elaborate *mappamundi* is not represented. The vast majority of the examples here are simple T/O maps, with varying degrees of decoration, though a few do include a more elaborated toponymy and incorporate details. Some merge information from zonal maps into T/O maps, and most are to be read not only along with the text they gloss or supplement, but also within the corpus of diagrams that weave through the text. The ability of diagrammatic maps to actualize/perform all possible discourses, such as those I have just listed, does not reside solely within the text the maps gloss and rely upon: it is dependent on the master, the teacher, whose performance of the map's potential contents will actualize these possibilities, many times unrelated to the glossed text, adapting them to different situations, providing verbally from memory that content the diagrammatic map summarizes.

Related thus to the general curriculum of the period, I have found in peninsular codices from the seventh through the twelfth centuries[35] maps that exhibit the very operations I have detailed – subordination, conventionality in the sense of habit, and a structural support for different types of knowledge – a corpus from which new operations might be drawn.[36] There are over thirty maps in total in this working corpus: most of them have been copied on the peninsula, and some are associated with specific monasteries and scriptoria in the area of La Rioja. A good number of them present other diagrams, especially *rotae* and horseshoe arches as tools for the organization of information; some share the use of windroses and genealogical diagrams. Some are clearly associated with royal circles, some are present in student manuals; some of these maps have been conceived along with the text from the beginning of the copy, some are additions in the margins or "on the go" drawings.[37]

Of these, one of a pair of maps in f. 24v of Escorial R.II.18, which I mentioned at the beginning of the chapter, represents the earliest example of an Isidorian T/O map, drawn only a few decades after Isidore's death, accompanying the *De natura rerum*, a manuscript that carries a lot of weight in Menéndez Pidal's tracing of the itinerary of Mozarabic culture into the northern Christian kingdoms (Figure 1). To its immediate right, an apparently later hand copies the map and in the facing ninth-century folio the manuscript shows a later hand and a new map (Figure 3). Williams, as Menéndez Pidal, points out the change of hands in the manuscript, not only in terms of the (re)drawing of the map but also in terms of the movement of the codex, for "when, in the ninth century, the Escorial manuscript fell into the hands of Eulogius and was supplemented, this precise text (*Etymologiae* 14.2.3) was placed on the page, folio 25r, facing the primitive map and was introduced by another small T/O map. To this later T/O diagram, however, were added the names of Noah's sons … outside the circle of the globe."[38] This is particularly interesting to me, since it joins two periods and two clerics through the drawing of slightly different maps that elicit new gestures from the cleric. The added information – the names of Noah's sons – is only implied in the Bible, but was made explicit by Josephus. That this manuscript contains face to face both the earliest example of an Isidorian T/O map and the first elaboration on it is of particular importance for two reasons. First, it points to what will become a continued supplementation of the map with information from other texts outside the specific one the map is illustrating or glossing – a gesture that will eventually lead to the elaborate monumental *mappaemundi* – both by Christianizing the map, which had no such content in its simple division of the earth, and by adding information. Second, by pointing to the superimposition of text on the map as a placeholder, as a "hyperlink" that brings to mind a number of other texts, this elaboration works as a rhetorical operation that inserts other texts within this one.

Two of the oldest of the T/O maps, later expanded to accommodate more information, and known as Y/O maps due to their change in drawing to include the Sea of Azov or *Meotis Palus*, are found in copies of the *Etymologiae* from the early tenth century, which Williams relates to the renewed interest in Isidore under King Alfonso III of Asturias[39] (Figures 6 and 7). Here we can see how this process of supplementation of the map with texts other than the one adjacent to the map has continued.

Still more examples, each gathering more information, are found in copies made in San Millán de la Cogolla of Isidore's *Etymologies*, and in another made for Queen Sancha of León in 1047, highlighting the movement towards the northern kingdoms traced by Menéndez Pidal (Figures 8 to 11). The presence of a map in these particular texts indicates not only a continued tradition, or a relation to the text that is illustrative, subordinate, or supportive of its verbal contents, but especially the tendency of the map to increasingly and simultaneously harbour and project the need for more information.

It is as if the articulation between a clerical need for the storage of information and the map's essential structure, which does not set limits on the amount or types of information that may be stored in it, were inherently to prompt infinite digression. For the map can, as if in a palimpsest, superimpose information from a variety of disciplines, unrelated, unbound by time or genre. It can, as in infinite bifurcations, detail a particular site into myriads of bits of data drawn from a variety of disciplines. It can establish a fundamental link, a basic thread of connection between all of this information by virtue of place. Set in practice, publicized, exteriorized, this internal possibility is enacted especially in pedagogy, for which the moment/place of enunciation will result in "localisms," ways of inserting the particular into the potential infinite digression of the map.

The presence of other types of cartographic devices in those codices, which house very early examples of Isidorian and Macrobian maps, is not analysed by Gautier Dalché, since his emphasis is on *mappaemundi*. In Escorial r.II.18, a miscellany binding together texts from the seventh, eighth, and ninth centuries of mostly geographical and historical texts, f. 67 introduces the very popular Antonine Itinerary (*Itinerarium provinciarum Antonini Augusti*) by way of a schematic map of the Strait of Gibraltar[40] (Figures 12 and 13). Regional cartography – the map of the Strait – is important here not only because it underlines a rhetorical possibility – for the map to include the local in the global, a form of synecdoche – but because it confirms an interest in "local" mapping within the very well known genre of the itinerary as an organization of space and state roads. This highlights the connection between different forms of the organization of (geographic) space, either through the distances marked in the itinerary or through the graphic disposition of places on the map. Another example of this local interest in mapping is a schematic map of the Iberian Peninsula that appears in a religious-scientific miscellany mostly copied in the eleventh century, closely guarded at the Archivo de la Corona de Aragón, specifically in a tenth-century *Ars gromatica "Gisemundi"* and in the context of numerous other diagrams and drawings (ACA, Colecciones, Manuscritos, Ripoll 106, 82r) (Figure 14).[41] The frame resembles a triptych or retable on whose central panel the names of the cities of Narbona, Impurias, Ierunda, Barchinona, Terrachona, Cartago, Gadis, Bracaram, and Vrigancia are written within circles.[42] On the left "panel" are two fish (and a third at the bottom), and place names – Wasconia, Mare Terreno (Medi Terraneo?) – at the top of the image. To the right, a silhouette of a "panel" has begun to be drawn, but it has been occupied by text. The circles resemble no geographic composition, but the map nevertheless exploits a spatial relation – the circles designate cities and the layout might be related to the sea, both the Atlantic and the Mediterranean.

Related to the flexibility of maps and especially to their tie with the arts of memory, and their function as organizers of knowledge and visual summaries of didactic intent, is their relation to the diagrammatic programs that maps are often a part of. While the scientific nature of many of these diagrams situates the map as a stage in a series, as an almost natural development in the progression from cosmology to geography, at other times the relation between map and diagrams is not as straightforward. The case of diagrams of the elements and their relation to cardinal points, the presence of cosmological spheres and diagrams of eclipses in the same visual program as maps, does not prescribe a macro-micro relation between diagrams and maps but suggests a disciplinary, thematic relation between them (Figures 15 and 16). Other manuscripts present less obvious connections, for instance, the relation of genealogical diagrams and diagrams of consanguinity to maps is less direct, or we might label it as oblique. Here, the capturing of the time of humanity in the image of the earth it occupies is what relates maps and diagrams. This symbolic relation of the map to the history of humanity suggests that the border of the map, the encircling ocean, the exterior limit, marks simultaneously both the end of the time of humanity and the beginning of the time of God, the end of history and the beginning of eternal life in a metonymic link (Figures 17 and 18). *Rotae* can be related to this function as well, but *rotae* in particular seem to connect to maps in multiple ways simultaneously: replicating the circular/spheric shape, they reinforce ideas of continuity, cyclic repetition, interrelatedness. They also set clear limits, thus serving well to set off chapter title, or to organize a table of contents. Alternately, these circles, linked intellectually to Isidore in particular, can be related to *rondels*, mostly used to address scenes inscribed within a circle in a number of artistic objects, particularly textiles. As a *contemporary* and equally interdisciplinary and intercultural form of the organization of decorative material on weavings, these rondels are useful as parallel visual cues to the use of *rotae* within these manuscripts (Figures 19–22) Most curiously, at times these *rotae* are used in conjunction with one of medieval Spain's dearest and most debated forms, the horseshoe arch.

Horseshoe arches as part of manuscript illumination programs are quite interesting, and they have received considerable attention from art historians. Beyond the discussion of whether these arches are Visigothic, Islamic, Mudéjar, or simply Iberian/Spanish elements, they decorate Christian, Islamic, and Hebrew manuscripts, both religious and secular. Katrin Kogman-Appel gives the examples of Bibles copied in Cervera and Tudela at the end of the thirteenth century, which echo the examples adduced by the Biblia Hispalense or the Bibles of León. While not wanting to repeat here the list of loans and borrowings between manuscript illumination and architecture, between the sacred and the secular environments, especially around 1200, that this particular element evidences, what I want to emphasize is that horseshoe arches not only decorate these manuscripts, they organize the entire space of the page and, ultimately, the knowledge inscribed within those pages (Figures 23 and 24).[43] If one considers that those palaces of memory in which monks organize their knowledge are to be structured upon the most familiar of places, the monastery itself, it should be no surprise that the contemporary examples one finds in the civil and religious architecture of the period, even this far north, exhibit the same horseshoe arch organization of space that the folio itself presents (Figures 25 and 26, which can be complemented by images of Las Huelgas, San Cebrián de Mazote, San Miguel del Escalada, Santiago de Peñalba, San Juan de Baños, and Santa María de Wamba, among others). To press the point: the horseshoe arches in these manuscripts are also part of a program of the classification and organization of knowledge in spatial form, echoing mnemotechnical practices and grounded in contemporary visual clues, and not merely or mainly decorations of the page. Much of this can also be said of *rotae*. In the spatial emphasis they exhibit, *rotae* and horseshoe arches can be said to be *also* maps because they perform a cartographic function.

Finally, a diagram of the classification of animals and the drawing of a Guidonian hand in the miscellaneous codex Escorial S.III.5 (figures 27 and 28) complete the catalogue of visual programs accompanying the maps in this corpus, from the most unquestionable *mappaemundi* to the most diagrammatical map in a dynamics of spatial organization through abstraction. This diverse catalogue of images coheres when we consider all of these as devices for the classification of knowledge in the broadest sense. The importance of the taxonomy of the sciences in the perception, preservation, and dissemination of knowledge in the Middle Ages cannot be overestimated, especially when we consider the sciences of language at the core of the medieval curriculum. Copeland and Sluitker, in the general introduction to their anthology of medieval rhetoric, write that "comprehensive accounts of the divisions of knowledge had a role akin to that of a world map or the modern atlas: to give visible contours to a vast inheritance about the very nature of knowledge itself, so that it could be at once externally systematized and internally assimilated."[44] To follow this train of thought, the many diagrams that configure a program in any given manuscript in which one finds a map are different schemata devised as if they were lockers or library stacks: "the classification scheme is used as a kind of library or other holding structure in whose empty compartments may be stored the archives of knowledge pertaining to each of the disciplines," continue Copeland and Sluitker, where horseshoe arches and Guidonian hands are both systems of classification and archives, devices that both separate and hold information as *rotae* organize and put together disciplines.[45] As mnemotechnics, as a machine of memory, the map, in its basic geographic proposal for classification, not only archives but also promises something that will happen; it is an archive and a device where a totality might be imagined, invented, or produced.

The Fiction of Maps

Maps, as has been noted for later works but not in this early corpus, appear not only in scientific works; they also gloss or illustrate works of fiction. Of unknown provenance, kept in the Ripoll collection of the Archive of the Crown of Aragon, is a copy of Gautier de Châtillon's *Alexandreis*, with an extensive gloss in f. 9r triggered by the beginning of the description of Asia as Alexander disembarks on its shores (Figure 29). The *Libro de Alexandre*, kept in only two copies but with an extraordinary life on the peninsula, as attested by numerous references to it from historiography, poetry, travelogues, and the like, is mostly a translation of this French work written in Latin in the twelfth century.[46] The *Alexandreis* was a textbook in medieval education principally used for the study of Latin, as many of the extant copies evidence through the extensive marginal and interlinear glosses, translations, and corrections they bear. On this copy of the *Alexandreis*, in f. 8v, the verbal gloss is supplemented by a map, a simple T/O oriented north noting the names of the continents (Figure 30). As Gautier Dalché has himself pointed out, one out of every four copies of the *Alexandreis* features a map – a frequency that speaks to the map's role in the legend's pedagogical dissemination. These maps display different levels of elaboration, and may be schematic, as the Archivo de la Corona de Aragón example, or function as elaborate appendices, as Bibliothèque Nationale de France, Paris 8352, f. 100v (Figure 31). This particular injunction of cartography and fiction in a pedagogical context marks our arrival at the centre of this articulation between cartography, pedagogy, and the invention of vernacular fiction in Castile.

The presence of maps in works that are considered as pertaining to both history and fiction, to the past and to the active imagining of a present and future, such as the *Libro de Alexandre*, suggests a more porous consideration of the role of cartography in clerical culture, one that, as this corpus suggests, is not disciplinarily bound. In this clerical culture, I argue, maps are considered not only for their scientific information, or their capacity for the location of events, or even their mnemotechnical properties, but also and perhaps mainly for their rhetorical roles. Both as gloss and interpretation in relation to the text, the "main" content, but also because of the map's specific actualization of *deixis*, techniques of *digressio* and *abbreviatio*, a use of allegory and figural language in general can be seen at play not as pictorial companions to the Alexander legend but as part of the text, as elaborations that are often revealed to be the original contributions of the poet to his work of translation.[47] It is only, however, if we consider cartography as a general tool of the period's curriculum, as a constant and pervasive presence in the most basic understanding of glossing, illustration, supplementation, and invention, that we can begin to consider the sharing of operations with the composition of fiction.

The *Libro de Alexandre*, the first Iberian vernacular version of the immensely popular story of the Macedonian hero, contains in its first stanzas a series of compositional, performative, and reception principles that will be reaffirmed by other works of cleresy, and that will also reappear in the context of courtly culture and royal authority. Cartography (and I will look at this same issue from different perspectives in ensuing chapters) is one of the disciplines that supply this newly minted vernacular writing with strategies, operations, and a rhetoric with which to *invent* itself in the *Libro de Alexandre*, operations that I have been gesturing at as part of cartography's role in the assemblage of a clerical education.

That the *Libro de Alexandre* as mostly a translation of Gautier de Châtillon's *Alexandreis* includes a verbal map as a geographic gloss in imitation or as translation of its source in stanzas 276–293, a diagrammatic description that can be paralleled to a T/O map, is but logical, given the *Alexandreis*'s previously mentioned role in the teaching of Latin in the Middle Ages.[48] In the Iberian poem, Alexander and his crew sail swiftly thanks to favourable winds that bring them to sight Asia in st. 276. As a sign of the violent possession of land that will ensue, Alexander sends a poisoned arrow as soon as they are at a stone's throw in a call for good fortune, confirmed by a crow flying on the right and the crew's general joy. The ships come into port and lower their anchors, and the poet remarks on the need and appropriateness of a cartographic digression:

> La materia nos manda   por fuerça de razón;
> avemos nós a fer   una desputaçión:
> cuémo se part'el mundo   por triple partiçión,
> cuémo faze la mar   en todas división.

(The subject-matter tells us by force of reason;/that we now must introduce a disputation:/how the world is divided in three parts,/how the sea makes in all of them a division.)

If the digression/disputation is motivated here by the subject matter – the sighting of Asia – it is prompted already in the Latin original. However, the map in this version is much more detailed than it is in the Latin: the *Libro de Alexandre* has brought into the translation, as I argue was the tendency of maps themselves, new information to inhabit within the limits of the verbal map.[49] The poem's added details include the description of Asia as occupying more than half of the representation, and the interpretation of the layout of the division of the continents by the waters orients the map and reads it as resembling the cross, an interpretation charged with being a warning or a sign of conversion:

> Más de la meatad   es contra Orïente:
> fízola una suerte   el Rey Omnipotente;

las otras dos alcançan   por medio Oçidente:
fiende la mar por medio   ad ambas igualmente
(...)
Qui asmar' cuémo yazen   las mares, de quál guisa
– la una que comedia,   la otra que quartiza – ,
verá que tien' la cruz   essa figura misma,
on' devién los incrédulos   prender la mala çisma.   (st. 278–80)

(More than half is towards the East;/that's how the Omnipotent King made it;/the other two reach the West in the middle:/the sea cuts them equally in half//... Whoever wants to judge how the seas lie, in which manner/– the one which halves, the other which quarters – ,/ will see the cross has this same shape,/where the incredulous should see their errors.)[50]

After this line, the verbal diagram leads naturally to a focus on Asia, organized in terms of geography, noting salient places such as Paradise and the four rivers and following up with related information, in this case the precious stones that come from there, for India its fertility and elephants, in the case of Babylon its wealth, for Armenia the landing place of Noah's ark, and so on. The digression ends on st. 294. Following the cues of the *Alexandreis* but adding information to the cartographic digression, what I want to underscore is how descriptive this version is, how it seems that what the poet is doing is not translating a verbal description but in fact describing a map itself, perhaps one in the margin of his copy, a description that has been validated as a geographic digression in the source itself. The translation here entails not merely the displacement from Latin to Romance but (also) a translation from the visual to the verbal, words supplemented by the information the cartographic device on the margin triggers in the memory of the cleric. If the cue for the cartographic is built in the source as text, the visual gloss on the margin provokes a series of operations in the mind of the cleric that supplements the translation and complements the knowledge of the verbal map in the *Libro de Alexandre*: the visual map is the architecture the *Alexandre*-poet uses to compose a new verbal map as he translates into this newly drawn Spanish.

But the *Libro de Alexandre* does not limit itself to this engagement with cartography. This map and gloss could have been attributed to scribes' digressive tendencies, for instance, a version of the *Alexandreis* that would have been supplemented here with numerous other materials taken from Isidore and the Bible, a digression perhaps motivated by cartography as visual cue in the margin. However, the presence of numerous other maps within the text itself, and perhaps more importantly, maps that can be related to different cartographic practices, suggest a much more structural role of cartography in the *Libro de Alexandre*. The first sequence I will discuss is the map on Alexander's shield, which can be related to the genre of the itinerary and has an extant example in the Dura Europos map. Related to this is another description of the world, an ekphrastic one, included in the description of Darius's tomb.[51] A second cartographic sequence in the *Libro de Alexandre* is the urban map of Babylon, and a third group is represented by four *mappaemundi*. These four include the T/O map that I have already introduced as gloss to Alexander's arrival in Asia, two *mappaemundi* related to Alexander's flight, and a last one painted on the walls of Alexander's tent at the end of the poem.

Shields and Tombs

As Alexander's investiture is narrated in the *Libro de Alexandre*, beginning in stanza 89, the equipage he receives is described in detail: the "camisa" (shirt), the "brial" (luxurious sort of silk, xamet, or *ciclatón* tunic that was worn by knights over the shirt and other tunics, with embroidered sleeves and a sort of skirt that was shortened over time to a shirt), the "manto" (mantle), the "çinta" (girdle), the "fiviella" (buckle), "zapatos" (shoes), "calzas" (chauses, or breeches), and "lúas" (gloves). Among these pieces is a shield, whose description extends from stanzas 96 to 98:[52]

La obra del escudo   vos sabré bien contar:
ý era debuxada   la tierra e el mar,
los regnos e las villas,   las aguas de prestar,
cascuno con sus títulos   por mejor devisar.

En medio de la tavla   estava un león
que tenié yus' la garfa   a toda Babilón:
¡catava contra Dario   semejava fellón,
ca vermeja e turvia   tenié su visïón!

Tanta echava de lumbre   e tanto relampava
que vençié a la Luna   e al Sol refertava:
¡Apeles, que nul omne   mejor d'él non obrava,
por mejor lo tenié   quanto más lo catava!

(I will tell you of the craft of the shield:/on it were drawn the earth and the sea,/the kingdoms and the villages, the notable waterways,/each with its legend to be better identified.//In the middle of the board was a lion/which had all of Babylon under its paw,/it glared at Darius and seemed in anger,/for red and blurred were its eyes.//So much fire and lightning its vision showed/it defeated the Moon and challenged the Sun;/Apelles, for there was no better artist,/the longer he looked at it it he admired it more.)

The last two stanzas repeat known themes in Alexander lore – the lion, the "blurred" vision – while praising the work of the shield itself, a recurrent gesture at artistry in the poem. The first stanza, however, provides us with different information: what is represented on this shield is a map, not only because land and sea are drawn on it or kingdoms and towns shown, but especially because the text points out that each of them bears an identifying title, a legend. Beyond this cartographic vocabulary, the shield can be read as (prophetic) itinerary of Alexander's life, introducing Darius and Babylon, which he will meet and conquer, symbolically representing the empire-to-be with this *abbreviated* image of Alexander's life and world.[53]

Written or narrative itineraries were of course central to the development of geographic maps and nautical charts, as O.A.W. Dilke reminds us, putting the relation between the verbal and the visual, narration and geography under scrutiny. If written or list itineraries from classical times were more common, used both for military and civil purposes and kept in multiple examples, surviving painted itineraries or maps proper from the Roman era amount but to one, the Peutinger Table, while a few add to this list the map of Dura Europos.[54] This last example is a parchment found in Dura Europos, on the Euphrates, in modern Syria, now kept at the Bibliothèque Nationale in Paris, dated to the year 260, measuring roughly 45 by 18 cm, with a west-southwest orientation. This map originally covered the shield of a Roman soldier. Depicted on it are the Black Sea and surroundings, especially the coastlines to the west and north. Two large ships and four heads peeking over the water can be distinguished, and on the coastline potential stops are marked with a building. After each place name, the number of Roman miles between them is duly noted, following a route to the north and then to the east (i.e., from left to right, then from top to bottom), perhaps depicting the way "home."[55] This military itinerary has a counterpart in pilgrims' itineraries, of which there are other examples varying in detail, audience, and destination. The best known to Iberianists are the materials included in the *Codex Calixtinus* or *Liber sancti Jabobi*, compiled in the mid-twelfth century around the subject of the pilgrimage to Santiago de Compostela. Iberian clerics would have been familiar with different types of itineraries, as the example of the Antonine Itinerary from Escorial r.II.18, discussed above, suggests. While Alexander's is not precisely, or not only, a *geographic* itinerary, but more of a *prophetic*, moral, Christianized one, hybrid possibilities were also in circulation, as the early thirteenth-century *Fazienda de Ultramar*, one of the earliest itineraries of the Holy Land, shows.

At a more basic level, the idea of the itinerary was built in the grammatical curriculum in the Priscian idea of the "road of reading," derived from an etymology of *litera* as *leg-iter-a*, an idea reiterated in Isidore that linked the study of language with the interpretation of literature, the principal motivator of this version of the life of Alexander.[56] It is this "road of reading" that links itinerary and literature in the ekphrasis of Alexander's shield at the beginning of the *Libro de Alexandre*, for it is an itinerary of his life and therefore of the book we ourselves are reading. Beyond geography, Alexander's shield holds within space prophecy and destiny:

> En medio de la tavla   estava un león
> que tenié yus' la garfa   a toda Babilón:
> ¡catava contra Dario,   semejava fellón,
> ca vermeja e turbia   tenié la su visïón!   (st. 97)

(In the middle of the shield was a lion/which had under his claws all of Babylon,/it looked to Darius, seemed angry,/for red and glassy were its eyes.)

At the centre of the map is Alexander figured as lion, his future summarized by his hold on Babylon, Darius as enemy, and the angry red eyes.

The description of the shield ends in stanza 98, noting that it is Apelles who has crafted the shield.[57] Apelles is responsible for many different works of art throughout the *Alexandre*, from Darius's wife's sepulchre to Darius's own tomb (stanza 1791ff.), to the Palace of Porus and Alexander's tent, described in the many ekphrastic excursus the poet engages in throughout the poem. Arizaleta has demonstrated in *La Translation* how the cleric/artist Apelles functions as a sort of alter ego of the author, and thus the artistic work by Apelles is a mirror of the poet's. Within these parallels, the inventive tools of the poet are, predictably, available to Apelles; therefore there are not only the fairly predictable cosmographic or geographic elements, but also instances that can be directly related to cartography as such.

The death of Estatira – Darius's wife – represents a challenge to Alexander's courtly upbringing, for he must render her homage in an exceptional way. Fifteen days of funerary rites are capped by the unveiling of a sepulchre sculpted once again by Apelles, and the poet describes the monument in detail, a description taken mostly from Gautier but, as usual, adding information of his own.[58] The details of Creation – Adam and Eve and the Fall, recalling their depiction in Beatus manuscripts but also the sepulchres that Iberian royalty produced for itself and exhibited – are followed by Noah's Ark (the Alexandre-poet elides the mention of drunkenness, present in Gautier) and his sons:

> Estava más adelant'   Noel el patrïarca,
> los montes de Armenia   do arribó el arca;
> Sem, Cam e Jafet, –   cadauno en su comarca;
> los Gigantes confusos   e la Torre que es alta.   (st. 1241)

(Further on was Noah the patriarch,/the mountains of Armenia where the Ark arrived;/Sem, Cam and Jafet, each in his province;/the confused Giants and the high Tower.)

The spatial representation and provincial attribution of Asia, Africa, and Europe to Noah's sons (Sem, Cam, and Noah respectively) is not present in Gautier. Tellingly, it is information that, as we have seen, was introduced early on in the margins of maps and then came to inhabit the continental masses as usual, habitual *cartographic* information. The description of *this story* ('estoria,' a visual narrative) sculpted in the sepulchre is followed by other episodes from the Old Testament – while Apelles's characterization as Jewish explains, in the poet's mind, his familiarity with the episodes – adding details that are not present in Gautier, to end in stanza 1244.

If Estatira's death was commemorated with such a wondrous monument, her husband Darius's death merits an even greater one five hundred stanzas later:

> Apeles, en comedio,   obró la sepoltura:
> la tumba de primero,   después la cobertura;

las basas en tres guisas,   de comunal mesura,
tant'eran bien juntadas   que non pareçié juntura.
     Debuxó el sepulcro   a muy grandes maravellas:
cuémo corre el Sol,   la Luna e las estrellas;
cuémo passan las noches,   los días en pues ellas;
cuémo fazen las dueñas   en mayo las corellas;
     quáles tierras son buenas   de panes e de vinos,
quáles pueblos son ricos   e quáles son mesquinos,
de quál lugar a quál   responden los caminos,
cüémo han d'andar   por ellos los peregrinos.
     Ý eran los griegos,   qué fazién los latinos,
e Saúl el vïejo   con todos sus veçinos;
cuémo yazién los mares   e los ríos veçinos,
cuémo sorven los ríos los grandes a los chicos.
     Libia era de miesses   rica e avondada;
la tierra de Amón,   de pluvia muy menguada,
riégala Egipto,   tiénela muy bastada;
el marfil es en India,   onde es tan nombrada.
     Es de piedras preçiosas   África bien poblada;
en ella yaz' Marruecos,   essa çibdat contada;
Greçïa, por Atenas   de seso alumbrada;
Roma yaz' sobre Tibre,   de buen muro çercada;
     los pueblos de España,   cómo son tan ligeros;
pareçién los françeses,   valientes cavalleros;
Champaña, que aqueda   los vinos delanteros;
Saba, do el ençenso   miden a sesteros; –
     cuémo se preçian mucho   por Artús los bretones,
cuémo son los normanos   orgullosos varones;
ingleses son fermosos,   de blandos coraçones;
lombardos, cobdiçiosos;   alemanes, fellones.   (st. 1791–8)

(Apelles crafted the sepulchre:/first the tomb, then the cover;/the bases in three forms, of great proportions,/were so well crafted no one could see the joint.//He drew the sepulcher with great marvels:/how the Sun runs, the Moon and the stars;/how nights go by, and days after them;/how ladies do the dances in May;//which lands have good bread and wine,/which people are rich and which stingy,/from where and to where roads lead,/how pilgrims must go about using them.//There were the Greeks, what the Latins were doing,/and Old Saul with all his neighbours,/how the seas and the neighboring rivers lay,/how the big rivers slurp up the small ones.//

Libya was rich and abundant in harvests;/the lands of Amon, lacking in rain,/Egypt waters it, has it well provided for;/ivory is in India, for which it is renowned.//Of jewels Africa is well populated;/in it lies Morocco, that famed city;/Greece, by Athens illuminated with knowledge;/Rome lies above the Tiber, surrounded by a good wall;//the people of Spain, how they are light;/there were also the French, brave knights;/Champagne, with the good wines;/Saba, where incense is weighed in sextarius; – // how the Britons prize themselves because of Arthur,/how the Normans are proud men;/the English are beautiful, of soft hearts;/Lombards are greedy; Germans, violent.)

The decoration of the funerary monument begins with a cosmographic scene, harnessing the scientific knowledge of the movement of the circles of the planets and layering this movement on the human calendar in 1792d with the reference to the month of May, bringing the time of the universe to overlap with the time of humanity. It is this allusion to the seasons, and specifically to spring, that determines the continuation of this spatial description in terms of fertile lands, the kindness of peoples, and the itineraries and routes of pilgrims. The description then, loosely following the *Alexandreis*, which in turn follows Isidore's *Etymologies* – notably, book 14, chapters 2–6, the usual emplacement of maps in *Etymologies* as chapter headings or in the margins – goes on to describe the spatial disposition of waterways and then of Libya/Africa. In Africa, our poet translates the *magne Kartaginis arces*, the cities of Carthage, as *Marruecos*, a translation explainable both by ignorance on the poet's part and by a desire to render these matters more familiar to the listener/reader. Through Morocco, as matter that lies next to each other in the ambulatories of memory, the poet enters Europe and mentions Spaniards, and lists a curious catalogue of stereotyped peoples, which Aníbal Biglieri studies as ethnography. The description ends in stanza 1799.[59]

After the cosmological description, the poet tells us that Apelles drew "Quáles tierras son buenas de panes e de vinos,/quáles pueblos son ricos e quáles son mesquinos,/de quál lugar a quál responden los caminos,/cómo han d'andar por ellos los peregrinos" (st. 1793, translated above), etc., before going on to the description of the world. The verses, it should be noted, signal stages in a pilgrimage road, *de quál lugar a quál responden los caminos, cuémo han d'andar por ellos los peregrinos*, that is, they are another itinerary, a pilgrim's itinerary in this case, the type of itinerary that a cleric would be most familiar with.[60]

The recurrence of Apelles's work in the text calls for at least some general reflections on the role of ekphrasis, not only because they are pertinent to all cartographic representations in the poem but because of the specific allusions to classical ekphrasis that a map on a shield brings into the discussion.[61] I am referring of course to Aeneas's shield in book 4 of the *Aeneid*, and to Achilles's shield in book 18 of the *Iliad*, both very close models to the Alexandre-poet. As a model for *digressio*, the description of Achilles's shield is the single most famous excursus in the *Iliad*.[62] The pretext for the introduction of this description as a plot element is the lending of Achilles's armour to Patroclus, followed by its loss to Hector, who claims it as booty. Patroclus's death anticipates Achilles's, whose death thus acquires the feeling of repetition, and it is also a rhetorical construction of fate, for we know Achilles will die; therefore when it happens, his death seems to fulfil a promise made with his friend's early death.

Alexander's fate is also written, known, and frequently anticipated, making of the poem's account of the past the narration of a future we can predict: Alexander's shield tells us what we know will happen, and what will be narrated – even if Alexander himself cannot know it yet, given the paradoxical fact that he is armed with the shield but cannot read it – making of a total vision, of knowledge of the road of reading, one that includes the future as well as the past, a key element of inter-pretation. As we visualize the shield, we anticipate narration. But this also adds something almost tragic and grandiose to Alexander's fate, for his ignorance of it corresponds to our foreknowledge.

Either as an element in the building of narration or as a competing strategy, ekphrasis holds the visual in strict relation to the verbal. Out-side narration, ekphrasis is important to Homer and Virgil, as it is for the poet of the *Alexandre*, because of the ways it underlines literary reflex-ivity, that is, because ekphrasis conveys an artistic self-consciousness, and that is where we can interrogate the *Libro* as *task* – a poetic and also a political one – through the visual.

In the *Libro*, Alexander is figured at the centre of his own shield. The shield is thus a symbol of his power in his military present and at the same time a prophecy of his imperial power. In the realm of the verbal, the inclusion through description of this visual summary of what is to come, that is, the narration of Alexander's conquests in the rest of the poem, forces us to reflect on the capacities and the limits of representa-tion of both the visual and the verbal media. In terms of composition, ekphrasis interrupts narration, delays or defers it, and has a series of stumbling effects on the text's momentum, but in so doing it adds to the effect of *summa*. Beyond the text, one must also ask what the role of the reader of these descriptions is, and what sort of visual literacy is expected of the audience. Alexander's shield, let us remember, is described by the poet in the past tense. It is a description that emerges not as a response to an urgency from the present of narration, but from the poet's desire to build the character and to create suspense for the story; it is a description meant specifically and solely for the audience, as are the rest of the objects that arm Alexander as knight: they do not serve the plot. The ideal reader of this image is thus not Alexander, but outside the text, residing both in *studium* and *court*, and within the court that reader is notably the king.[63] Anticipating the rest of the poem, the shield thematizes vision in a direct relation to empire. It does so through our – the listeners'/readers' – contemplation of what is to come, in that our "seeing" the shield allows us to compare it to our knowledge of the outcome; it also triggers a reflection on the nature of power that is tied to a vision of territory. This vision is balanced by Alexander's blindness, reinforced through the reference to his blurred or clouded vision: his lack of knowledge of his own future – which lies beyond the frame of the shield, for his demise, and his empire's, are not figured in it – is what engages our compassion, our identification with the hero.

Ekphrasis underlines point of view, perspective, and ways of looking as essential not only to interpretation but also to knowledge and the exercise of power and, especially, to artistic labour and its political role. Thus, when the poet of the *Alexandre* rewrites Homer in the long digression on Troy, he then describes Achilles's shield in ways similar to those he used to describe Alexander's at the beginning of his poem. This shield, Achilles's, also holds both past and future, history and promise. In anticipation of the *mappamundi* in the tent, which I discuss later in this chapter, the seasons are also painted, as are the stars and planets, linking once again the human and the divine, the geographical and the cosmographic, and at the end the poet places a particular emphasis on the viewer, a spectator who is converted by the vision of the shield into an ideal reader, a cleric:

> Non es omne tan neçio que viesse el escudo,
> que non fuesse buen clérigo sobra bien entendudo. (st. 659)

(There is no man so stupid who upon seeing the shield,/would not be a good cleric, with more than enough knowledge.)

The role of the cleric, extended well beyond the classification and preservation of knowledge to its rendering and interpretation, is put to the fore here, not only metaphorically through the figure of Apelles, but even as a knowledge and status that can be attained in this case through contemplation, through a vision of empire that relies repeatedly on *mappaemundi* to convey itself. This (imperial) vision evinces a clerical culture that seeks to bind epic hero and the task of the cleric, suturing royal power to clerical skill; subtly, it is one produced verbally for us by a cleric himself.

Urbs *versus* civitas

In the *Libro de Alexandre*, Alexander's army surrounds Babylon towards the middle of the poem in stanza 1456, whereupon Maçeo, Darius's son-in-law, surrenders the city and all it contains to the hero in haste – in fact only three stanzas later. The poet then announces that he will leave the story aside to tell of Babylon, of how it lies in a noble place, abundant of rivers and with easy access to the sea. Babylon is minutely described in the following sixty-two stanzas, moving from landscape to catalogue of spices, to a lapidary and a zoological inventory that bring in a variety of sources.[64]

After the reference to the city's many sweet springs, cold by day, lukewarm by morning, pure and healthy, the poet writes of the paradisaic abundance of bread and wine, of the game-filled forests surrounding the city, open to all, providing Babylon with singing birds and talking birds, to finally begin to describe its people. Gautier's *Alexandreis* is here supplemented by another, unknown source, which provides the author the information of the maritime commerce reaching the city from Africa and Europe, structuring the pretext through the height of the city walls, towers, and doors for introduction of the longest narration on Babel in the entire poem.

Framed by the description of Babylon as region – a digression that is doubly spatial because it embarks on a description of a *locus amoenus* – the story of the construction, sin, and punishment of Babel contains a linguistic catalogue, which is simultaneously a catalogue of nations, themes to which I will return in the next chapter.[65] After the enumeration of these, the poet abruptly shifts back to Babylon's specific history.

Semíramis, he writes as a way of reintroducing the historical narrative, a wise queen, founded the city. The poem goes into some detail as to how this was done:

> Tantas calles ý fizo   como son los linajes;
> fízolas poblar todas   de diversos lenguajes:
> los unos a los otros   non sabién fer messajes,
> – los unos a los otros   teniènse por salvajes –.
> Qualesquier' de las calles   es sobre sí çibdat:
> non sabrién contra otra   aver comunidat.
> La más pobre de todas   serié grant heredat,
> a un rëy podrié   sacar de pobredat.
> Qui todos los lenguajes   quisiesse aprender,
> allí podrié de todos   çertedumbre saber;
> mas ante podrié viejo   desdentado seer
> que la terçera parte   podiés'él aprender.
> Por quanto es la villa   de tal vuelta poblada,
> que los unos a los otros   non se entienden nada,
> por tanto es de nombre   de confusïón dada,
> ca Babilón *confusio*   es en latín clamada.   (st. 1519–22)

(As many streets as lineages she built there;/had them inhabited by diverse languages:/they did not know how to address each other,/– they took each other for savages –./Any of the streets is in itself a city:/they would not know how to be with another a community./The poorest among them would be a great inheritance,/bringing a king out of poverty./He who wanted all languages to learn,/could there certainly learn all of them;/but he would be old and toothless before/he had learned a third of them./Because of the mixed way it is inhabited,/the village cannot understand each other,/that is why it was given the name confusion,/for Babylon is in Latin called *confusio*.)

The ensuing description of the city then tells of the surrounding wall and the city's location on a rock with an encircling moat of such great engineering that ships can sail through it, emphasizing again the city's links to commerce; we are told of the height of the wall and the strength of its materials, of its width and ensuing safety. The great number of towers impresses the poet, and he tells of the variety of materials and shapes, of the doors guarded by the sculptures of kings, the royal encampment or seat in the middle decorated with the sun, moon, and stars, mirrors on its columns for all women to admire themselves in. The baths, aqueducts, and general waterworks are complemented by the vigilance and safety of citizens guaranteed by four crystal towers from where any crime within can be detected, and an approaching enemy readily seen (stanzas 1523–31).

The passage in its entirety has no parallel in the *Alexandreis*, except for some common details, mere mentions in Gautier that are expanded upon and reinterpreted in the *Libro de Alexandre*, for the episode is quite brief in the *Alexandreis*.[66] Raymond S. Willis suggests the passage's links with the description of Babylon in *Flores y Blancaflor*, and with the description of the palace in the *Epistola Presbiteri Iohannis*, which Alfred Morel-Fatio had pointed out earlier, and which led to the B manuscript of the *Roman d'Alexandre*, also known as the Venice manuscript.[67] The differences between the texts can be explained in a number of ways, but in any case our own author indicates that he is "abreviando," that is, summarizing his source.[68]

The tendency of the Spanish author to condense or eliminate materials he (idiosyncratically) considers digressive could explain the absence in the *Libro de Alexandre* of materials found in *Roman d'Alexandre* B and, on the other hand, the peculiar version of the Babel episode.[69] In the *Alexandre*, the tower is identified with the city on a number of occasions, but the identification in this particular elaboration is made part of the narrative structure, as the Babelian episode is here framed or encapsulated within the long episode of the description of Babylon. The encapsulation of the Babel episode reinforces its establishment as a commonplace, for Babel is mentioned nine times in the poem,[70] emphasizing different aspects of pride through associations with characters, or granting biblical authority to historical episodes. In the second of these allusions to Babel, Darius's shield depicts the deeds of the Babylonian kings alongside the memory of the giants who built the Tower:

> Avié en el escudo   mucha bella estoria:
> las gestas que fizieron   los reys de Babilonia.
> Yazié de los gigantes   ý toda la memoria,
> quando de los lenguajes   prisieron la discordia.   (st. 990)

(The shield had many a beautiful story,/the deeds achieved by the Babylonian kings;/the entire memory of the giants lay there,/when from the languages they were separated.)

Darius himself roots his lineage in Babel-as-Babylon by claiming to be heir to the warrior power of the builders of Babel:

> Yo só de los guerreros   que la torre fizieron,
> que con los dios del çielo   la guerra mantovieron!
> Vuestros grieves pecados   mala çaga vos dieron
> quando en la frontera   de Geón vos pusieron!   (st. 1369)

(I am from those warriors that built the tower,/who with the gods from heaven had a war;/your grave sins gave you bad luck/when they placed you in front of Geon.)

Here, the immediate function of Babel is to originate Darius's lineage and characterize it with both strength and a moral history, structurally anticipating Darius's death as a mark of destiny. But beyond this, Babel-Baylon also reinforces the theme of wealth and luxury that has enveloped Darius from the beginning of the poem, characterizing him negatively at the same time as it elicits the greed of the audience, who anticipate Alexander's appropriation of Darius's possessions as booty.

In the long passage describing Babylon that encapsulates the Babel narration, original to the *Libro de Alexandre*, the materials and elements the poet chooses to identify are yet again tower and city, particularly through the two powerful motifs that made Babylon part of the medieval imaginary: diversity and wealth. In the *Libro de Alexandre*, diversity and wealth are inextricably linked by making of urban architecture a sign, an effect, or a pattern that follows lineages and languages. Urban sprawl is made equivalent to linguistic difference, spatializing and materializing this difference. There, the inability of these different populations to communicate with each other leads to mutual consideration as savages. Thus, it is literally the city that *is* Babel in its confusion, a result of its variety. But not only that, every street is in itself a Babylon, rich to the point that it can make of any great king a very rich man. Despite this wealth or perhaps as a consequence of it, every street's strong urban identity prevents it from forming any kind of community with another, that is, every street is *also* Babel. The city is a wondrous resource of linguistic wealth, a treasure of languages, appropriate for the most ambitious of learning enterprises, but its sheer diversity, density, and inability to comprehend itself is what grants it its confusion.

Flight: Visions of Totality

Alexander was known for his military power, to be sure, but he was famous because of his fantastic feats, adventures that make of Alexander the Great not only a figure of empire or of philosophy but a figure central to the very stuff of magic and wonder. Alexander undertakes fantastic travels that take him across the lands to the Tree of Prophecy, to the bottom of the ocean in a submarine of his own invention, and up to the sky in a flying machine.

After the submarine exploration, and just as the Devil himself, through Nature's insistence and God's permission, has sent treason in the shape of Antipater to murder Alexander, the king considers his imperial achievements and further expansions. In stanza 2459 Alexander measures or traces the world in its three parts, each with its diverse regions, ways, and languages, literally drawing a map:[71]

> Ordenó sus faziendas   con sos buenos varones,
> compassó todo'l mundo,   cómo son tres quiñones,
> cómo son cadaúno   de diversas regiones,
> de diversas maneras,   de diversos sermones.
>
> Asmó de la primera,   mas non le valió nada,
> tornar en Babilonia,   essa çibdat famada,
> ordenar toda Asia,   la que avié ganada,
> que, si se fuesse ende,   estodiés' recabdada.
>
> Troçir luego ad Africa,   conquerir essas gentes,
> Marruecos con las tierras   que le son soyazientes;
> ganar los Montes Claros,   logares convinientes,
> que non son mucho fríos   nin son mucho calientes.[72]
>
> Desque oviesse Africa   en su poder tornada,
> entrar a Ëuropa,   toda la mar passada;
> empeçar en España,   una tierra señada,
> tierra de fuertes gentes   e bien encastillada.   (st. 2459–52)

(He ordered his things with his good men,/he measured the entire world,/ how there are three parts,/how each has diverse regions,/of diverse ways, diverse languages.//He judged the first, but it was not worth it,/ to go back to Babylon, that famed city,/to order all of Asia, which he had won,/for had he gone there, it would have been done.//He then considered Africa, to conquer those peoples,/Morocco with the lands that lie beneath it;/to win the Montes Claros, convenient places,/for they are not very cold nor very hot.//Once he had Africa in his power,/to enter Europe, a land of legend,/land of strong people and well castled.)

Contemplating the first of the regions, he judges he will one day return there, to Babylon in Asia. He then turns his gaze upon Africa, thinking of conquering Morocco *and the lands that lie below it*, describing a spatial representation of the world, along with the Montes Claros, convenient due *to their temperate climate*, joining once again zonal information to a T/O disposition of the continents (most probably a T/O oriented north, just like the one in the margins of the ACA copy of the *Alexandreis*)[73] (Figure 30). After conquering Africa, the king judges, he will cross the sea to enter Europe, beginning in Spain. This is a reference of course to the Strait of Gibraltar, and after pointing out the strong people and good castles of Spain, the poet goes on to describe France and other peoples of Europe to end in stanza 2463 in Greece.

What the poet is describing here is Alexander looking, drawing, tracing – *compassó* – a map of the world and triggering a geographic reverie that wanders through the desire to know the world and conquer it. Immediately after, the poet in his own voice quotes Solomon to dwell upon the vanity of men, who judge within them, who think their own will to be so much greater and powerful than what reality will prove to be true. The next time the verb *asmar*, to judge, to know, is used in 2496 is when Alexander has the idea of wanting to know how the entire world itself lies, that is, when the plan for the aerial enterprise begins to take shape, joining the theory – the visual cue of the map – to the practice – viewing the world for himself.

In the Spanish version, Alexander flies up in a culturally specific aircraft, a sort of soft leather carpet to which he is sewn (as opposed to the cages or thrones of French versions), but what is interesting to me here is how what he sees from above is described.[74] Alexander's flight in the Spanish version and its ensuing description of the world as seen from above, that is, from a godly perspective or Apollonian gaze, has been interpreted until now within the frame of the micro and macrocosmos, which Francisco Rico has detailed in various texts for the Iberian tradition. This critic particularly makes of the flight a figure of vanity, echoing comments by the poet, in which the hero is able to see the world but ultimately unable to understand it, is unable to *understand* himself,[75] thus prefiguring his spiritual fall and death, in parallel function to the shield I described before, and echoing debates on *mirrors* and vision. But I argue there is also something else going on:

> Tanto pudo el rëy a las nuves pujar,
> veyé montes e valles de yus de sí estar,
> veyé entrar los ríos todos en alta mar,
> mas cóm yazié o non, nunca lo pudo asmar.
> Veyé en quáles puertos son angostos los mares,
> veyé grandes peligros en muchos de lugares,
> veyé muchas galeas dar en los peñiscales,
> otras salir a puerto adobar de yantares.
> Mesuró toda África cómo yaz' assentada,
> por quál parte serié más rafez la entrada,
> luego vío por Siria aver mejor passada,
> ca avié grant salida e larguera entrada.
> Luengo serié de todo quanto vío contar,
> non podrié a lo medio el día avondar;
> mas en un ora sopo mientes parar
> lo que todos abades non lo sabrián asmar.
> Solémoslo leer, dizlo la escriptura,
> que es llamado mundo el omne por figura.
> Qui comedir quisier' e asmar la fechura,
> entendrá que es bien razón sin depresura.
> Asïa es el cuerpo, segunt mio esçïent;
> Sol e Luna los ojos, que naçen de Orient,
> los brazos son la cruz del Rëy Omnipotent',
> que fue muerto en Asia por salut de la gent'.
> La pierna que deçende del siniestro costado
> es el regno de África, por ella figurado.
> Toda la mandan moros, un pueblo muy dubdado,
> que oran a Mafómat, profeta muy honrado.
> Es por la pierna diestra Ëuropa notada.
> Esta es más católica, de la fe más poblada,
> ésta es de la diestra del obispo santiguada:
> tienen Petrus e Paulus en ella su posada,
> La carne es la tierra, espessa e pesada;
> el mar es el pellejo que la tiene çercada,
> las venas son los ríos que la tienen temprada:
> fazen diestro e siniestro mucha tornaviscada.

Los huessos son las peñas   que alçan los collados,
cabellos de cabeça,   las yervas de los prados;
crían en esta tierra   muchos malos venados,
que son por majamiento   de los nuestros pecados.
    Desque ovo el rëy   la tierra bien asmada,
que ovo a su guisa   la voluntat pagada,
senestroles el çevo,   guïolos de tornada,
fue en poco de rato   entre la su mesnada.

(So much did the king push into the clouds/that he saw mountains and valleys below him/He saw rivers entering the open sea/but how it lay or not he couldn't figure out. // He saw in which ports the waters were narrow,/saw many great dangers in many places,/saw many galleys crash into cliffs/others arriving at port, finding provisions. // He measured all of Africa, how it lay,/from which part the entry would be harder/he then saw how through Syria he could enter it/for it has a larger exit and longer entry. // Long it would be if I were to tell all he saw/I wouldn't be able to tell half in one whole day/but in one hour he found out more/than all abbots together could know. // We are used to reading, for books tell us,/that man is called a world figuratively./Whoever would wish to measure and guess its making/will understand this to be in good reason. // Asia is the body, as far as I can tell,/the sun and the moon eyes, born in the East,/the arms are the cross of the omnipotent King/who was killed in Asia for the health of mankind. // The leg that descends on the left side/is the kingdom of Africa thus figured,/commanded all by Moors, a feared people/who pray to Mohammed, an honoured prophet.* [The P ms. version of this verse is very different.] // On the right leg Europe is drawn,/this one is more Catholic, populated by the faith,/blessed by the bishop's right hand,/Petrus and Paulus have their residence there. // The flesh is the earth, thick and heavy/the sea is the skin that surrounds it,/the veins are the rivers that temper it,/they turn about left and right. // The bones are the rocks that make the cliffs,/the hairs on the head are the grass in the fields,/many bad deer pace on these fields/they are there as punishment of our sins. // Once the king had known the earth/and his will was satisfied to his pleasure/ he lowered the bait, guided them back/and was among his troops in no time.)

Alexander has his men sew him up face down on a type of carpet, in which he has cut a hole for his face to look downwards. In the meantime he has baited four griffins, which, lured by a piece of meat placed at the end of a pole that Alexander uses to guide this aircraft, will fly and thus raise the carpet and Alexander by the ropes that attach them to it. That is when the cartographic passage begins, as he looks down on the world and contemplates it. He sees the rivers, the ports and the seas, ships at risk and boats loading provisions. He measures Africa and does a sort of military survey, figuring out how to enter it. Here, the poet links this cartographic digression explicitly to rhetoric, as he says that it is as figure, as *rhetorical* figure, that man is sometimes called a world: *solémoslo leer, dizlo la escriptura, que es llamado mundo el omne por figura*. Alexander, turning this figure on its head, sees then the world as a man, as a body with eyes, arms, legs, flesh and veins, and bones and hair.

It has been noted, but not problematized, that this passage substitutes the source in Gautier de Châtillon's *Alexandreis*, the Pseudo-Callisthenes, with a vision of the world as body whose source has not yet been identified. While keeping in mind this symbolic dimension of man as figure of the world, what I want to emphasize is that it is not just any man that is here the body of the world, but Christ himself whose body is offered as material and spiritual matter for contemplation by Alexander and, ultimately, by the reader as well. Verse 2509c, *los brazos son la cruz del Rey omnipotent*, makes this very clear, and also makes a direct reference to an Isidorian-type map, a T/O map.[76]

The Ebstorf *mappamundi*, dated to 1235 and measuring 3.56 by 3.58 metres, mentioned above, represented the world precisely as the body of Christ, with an eastern orientation and Jerusalem as centre, collapsing divine skin and manuscript parchment, the border of the world with the limits of humanity (Figure 5). The description of Alexander's flight in the *Libro de Alexandre* seems to support this interpretation, for this flying machine envelops the king with a skin, thus duplicating the reference to mortality. The leather cover that envelops him has been cut to the size of precisely one man, and he has had himself sewn to it with his face uncovered, materials that remind one of parchment and binding, materials that support a *mappamundi*. There are many other diagrams that I think can be related to this one, which I studied earlier in this chapter, genealogical and consanguinity diagrams in particular, which figure the body as a space for writing (Figures 17 and 18). Like Ebstorf's, Alexander's vision of the world in the Iberian version offers a human history embodied in Christ, containing all, history and geography, marvel and legend, the time of mortality and the time of salvation. As Eucharistic symbol, this map in the *Libro de Alexandre* underlines salvation through Christ, the Christ of the Passion. Beyond that, the frame of this map, the border of the world, coincides with the limits of Christ as human, that is, Christ is there also as a symbol of humanity's mortal limitations, introducing the theme of Judgment, and therefore also becoming a symbol of *vanitas mundi*.

This cartographic passage elaborates on the relation between the body and its connotations in relation to time and geography, as advanced by Rabanus Maurus, for instance, who puts together not only the ends of the earth with the limits of the body, but also binds these to the limits of internal thought.[77] It is impossible to establish a direct relation between the *Libro de Alexandre* and the Ebstorf map, and the main obstacle may not be that Ebstorf was destroyed in an aerial attack on Hannover in the Second World War, but the loss of so many materials in between that could have laid out a material bridge for the transmission of this type of map into Iberia or, conversely, evidence that the Alexander-poet had travelled to northern Italy or Paris where contact with such materials would support cartography as direct source for this verbal elaboration. As interpretation, however, and in the rich cartographic cultural context I have been documenting, the simultaneous presence of Alexander's fame and the emphasis on the sin of pride in the poem is rendered visible through these *mappaemundi*. The description of the world in the *Libro de Alexandre* is not only similar to this type of map but is evidence that this particular source for the *Alexandre*-poet was indeed a visual map, one that that poet is looking at or rememorating or *re-membering* as he writes his poem. He uses it not only as a recollecting device, nor only as a locational device, but also as a hermeneutic, didactic, and compositional tool, shifting between the historical, the symbolic, the spiritual, and the eschatological, the way medieval cartography can.

Tent: Sites of Self

The Christianized map that is both Alexander's vision and the image of his blindness gives way, at the end of the poem, to yet another example of *mappamundi*, that painted in Alexander's tent and which can be put together with the mural or monumental map. There is some historical medieval evidence in royal contexts of mural maps, if not a surviving example, except for the didactic and probably apostolic map that can still be traced on the walls of the monastery of San Pedro de Rocas in Galicia, referred to above.[78]

The description of Alexander's tent begins in stanza 2576. It starts with the exterior and moves to the interior: the ceiling of the tent is described as containing a "divine" or heavenly history, spatially distributing the angels' heaven, hell, the Tower of Babel and the giants, the flood. Going down to one of the walls, we have the description of paintings of the months, a calendar,[79] followed by natural history and then by the history of mankind, ciphered through Hercules, Paris, and a siege of Troy barely sketched out. Between this and the third wall, which contains the *mappamundi*, a stanza anticipates or prescribes the interpretation of the passage as a *speculum principum*,[80] integrating the map as part of necessary knowledge, clerical and proper for a king. The passage is long, but it merits complete citation.

> ... era la mapamundi   escripta e notada.
> Bien tenié qui la fizo   la tierra decorada,
> como si la oviesse   con sus piedes andada.
>   Tenié la mar en medio   a la tierra çercada:
> contra la mar, la tierra   non semejava nada.
> Era éssa en ésssa   más yerma que poblada,
> della yazié pasturas,   della yazié lavrada.
>   Las tres partes del mundo   yazién bien devisadas:
> Asïa a las otras   avielas engañadas;
> Ëuropa e África   yacién muy renconadas,
> deviendo seer fijas,   semejavan annadas.
>   Assí fue el maestro   sotil e acordado,
> non olvidó çibdat   nin castiello ortado;
> non olvidó emperio   nin ningunt buen condado.
> nin río nin otero   nin yermo nin lavrado.
>   Tajo, Duero e Ebro,   tres aguas son cabdales,
> Cogolla e Moncayo,   enfiestos dos poyales,
> en España ave   estos çinco señales,
> con mucho buen castiello   e villas naturales.
>   ¿Qué mejores querades   que Burgos e Pamplona,
> Sorïa e Toledo,   León, Lixbona?
> Por Gascoña corrié   el río de Garona;
> en ésta yaz Bordel,   vecina de Bayona.
>   La çibdat de París   yazié en media Françia,
> de toda clerezía   avié grant abundançia;
> Tors yazié sobre Leire,   villa de grant ganançia;
> más delante corrié Ruédano,   río de abundançia.

Yazién en Lombardía   Pavía e Milana,
– pero detrás dexamos   Bergoña e Vïana,
Boloña sobre todas   pareçe palaçiana,
de leÿs e decretos   éssa es la fontana.

   En cabo de Toscana,   Lombardía passada,
en ribera de Tibre   yazié Roma poblada;
yazié el que la ovo   primero çimentada,
de su hermano mismo   la cabeça cortada.

   Si quisiéssemos todas   las tierras ementar,
otro tamaño livro   podríe y entrar;
mas quiero en la cosa   a destajo andar,
ca só yo ya cansado,   querríame folgar.

   Los castiellos de Asia,   con las sus heredades,
ya nós fablamos de'llos,   si bien vos acordades,
las tribus, los linajes,   los tiempos, las edades,
todos yazién en ella   con sus propïedades.

   Alexandre en ella   lo podié perçebir
quánto avié conquisto,   quánto por conquerir;
non se le podié tierra   alçar ni encobrir
que él non la supiesse   buscar e combatir.

(… the mappamundi was written and annotated./He who had drawn it had the earth well memorized,/as if he had walked it with his own feet.//The sea had surrounded the earth in the middle,/against the sea, the earth seemed nothing./It was there more barren than inhabited,/some had pastures, some was sowed.//The three parts of the world laid well descried:[81]/Asia had tricked the others;/Europe and Africa laid cornered,/they should be daughters but seemed step-daughters.//Such was the master, subtle and harmonious,/did not forget city nor gardened castle,/did not forget empire or any good county,/nor river nor lookout nor wasteland nor land.//Tajo, Duero and Ebro, three major rivers,/Cogolla and Moncayo, two strong hills,/there are these five signs in Spain,/with many a good castle and natural villages.//What better do you want than Burgos and Pamplona,//Soria and Toledo, Leon, Lisbon?/Through Gascony runs the Garona river,/here lies Bordel, neighbour to Bayona.// The city of Paris lies in the midst of France,/greatly abundant in all cleresy;/Tours lies over Leire, a wealthy town;/ahead runs the Rodans, a rich river./In Lombardy lie Pavía and Milan,/but behind we leave Bergoña and Viana,/Bologna above all seems palatial,/of laws and decrees this is the fountain.//At the end of Toscana, passing Lombardy,/on the shores of the Tiber lies populous Rome;/there lies he who had its foundations cemented,/by cutting his own brother's head.//If we wanted to mention all the lands,/another such book could be here entered;/but I would like to skip over a few things,/for I am tired, I would like to rest.//The castles of Asia with their estates,/we have spoken of them, if you remember,/the tribes, the lineages, the times, the ages,/they all lie in it with its properties.//Alexandre in it could all perceive,/how much he had conquered, how much he could still achieve;/there was no land that could rise against him or hide from him/that he would not know how to find and fight.)

The *mappamundi* – written, annotated, and "known by heart" or "rote," *decorada* – is described in eleven stanzas that have their initial thrust in the description of the tent in the *Roman d'Alexandre* (Willis 1935, 44). Willis, however, points out that while the first four stanzas follow the French text more or less closely, from stanza 2580, and for the next seven stanzas, the *Alexandre* once again deviates from any known source. The poet praises the detail of the map and invokes a first-hand experiential knowledge of the land as explanation for its precision ("como si la oviesse con sus piedes andada"). It is a T/O map, where the ostensibly small lands in comparison with the ocean are depicted, some deserted, some populated, some with pastures and some devoted to agriculture.[82] It is oriented to the east and decorated with cities and castles, rivers and outlook points, villages and barren places, empires and counties. From this point on the poet elaborates on his own, beginning of course with Spain's rivers, some (surprisingly secondary) mountains, castles, and villages, followed by mentions of Burgos and Pamplona, Seville, Toledo, and so on, to be followed by cities and rivers in Portugal, France, and Italy, noting the types of knowledge produced in each place. Asia is swiftly described, and the reader is referred to a previous description, as the digression ends with Alexander gazing at the map, taking in the vision of his empire and the possibilities for further expansion.[83]

The fourth wall closes the description of the tent with a summary of Alexander's feats, with the hero's personal history. Alexander's tent map is similar in more than one respect to the map that Theodosius II, Emperor of the East from 408 to 450, ordered to be made for him in 435. The map did not survive, but we know of its existence by the poem written in Latin hexameters that it accompanied, by the narrative map that complemented or supplemented the visual artefact. The

Latin hexameters read: "This famous work – including all the world,/ seas, mountains, rivers, harbours, straits and towns,/uncharted areas – so that all might know,/our famous, noble, pious Theodosius/most venerably ordered when the year was opened by his fifteenth consulship,/we servants of the emperor (as one wrote,/the other painted), following the work/of ancient mappers, in not many months/revised and bettered theirs, within short space/embracing all the world. Your wisdom, sire,/it was that taught us to achieve this task."[84] Not only does the *Alexandre* offer the illusion of a material complement to the poem's verbal map, but as Theodosius's, Alexander's map is vision of empire and knowledge, and artefact where power and learning merge and sustain each other.

What I want to insist on is that we can either assume that the description in the *Libro de Alexandre* is evidence for the existence of a painted *mappamundi* that the author uses as source, one that is now probably lost and will forever remain unknown to us, or that it is an imagined digression. We can go further and say that the coexistence of painted and narrative maps next to each other, both in history as with Theodosius II and within our very own *Libro,* suggests that perhaps not only competition, but especially supplementation between artistic forms is being thematized within the poem. That is, that the foreignness of the visual is made explicit within the poem to make us reflect on the roles of the spectator and the artist, on the power of representations, on the complementariness of languages. Perhaps this obsessive reference to the visual is but a reminder not only of the foreign sources that compose our poem, but also of the sources that remain unknown because they may be in a different format than that of the word. To consider the role of the visual is important not only as a reformulation of the clerical archive, or as an operation of rhetoric, but for its structural role in the composition of history, of fiction, as a tool for the cleric.

Maps in the margins, as gloss to the scientific or literary text they accompany, are closer to silent maps than to their elaborate thirteenth-century counterparts by dint of their size: they are there to fit in a margin, they are given half a folio or a folio at best: this must be enough to convey all different discourses in minimal fashion, perhaps with only an individual preference – for cities, for regions – highlighted on the map. The ability of such a map to rehearse all possible discourses does not, however, remain within the text: it is the cleric, the master, the teacher, whose performance of the map's discourses will actualize these possibilities, adapting them to different occasions.

The task of the cleric, then, crossed by the study of rhetoric and geography, the power of contemporary history as a discourse that would be invented just then, the role of the past and its relation to sacred history, is one that also mediates between the oral performance and the written archive.[85] If, as Jacob says, "a map is not a mimetic image, but an analogical image, the product of an abstraction that interprets the landscape and makes it intelligible by translating the profusion of what can be observed into a dynamic order of contiguities and relationships … [it] requires choices, exclusions, movements, and equivalences inside classes of permutable objects,"[86] wouldn't the cleric, used to analogies and parallels, contradiction and simultaneity, to subjecting any and all to the rigours of rhetoric, see in these operations of the map the very operations of fiction? And would not this cleric use these operations, this rhetoric of the map to turn fiction into an *aide-mémoire*, to invent fiction in those interstices between performance and archive, between actualization and fixity? What I believe is that the familiarity, the readiness to use these contraptions, the nimbleness in manipulating the functions of the map on the margin would lead not only in intradisciplinary fashion to the thirteenth-century monumental *mappaemundi*, but horizontally, rhizomatically even, to the composition of learned vernacular fiction, such as the *Libro de Alexandre,* in which the cleric is, but is not only, a student, a master, a translator. Intrinsic to these roles is the dexterous use of this mastery to activate knowledge, making of the cleric not only the archive *but also* its voice.

Alexander materials are explained in their variety and dissemination in this actualization made possible by the performance of multiple discourses, containing by contiguity or similitude the role of ancient history, the practice of translation, the location of the sacred past, the placing of humanity, the teaching of salvation, the learning of sin and treachery by example. As source, not only for content, and not only as reminder but also as repository and machine of techniques in the construction of this new language forged in translation, was the map. Expandable, immediately apprehensible and reproducible, the map, from the schematic T/O diagram to the elaborate works of later days, is the most eloquent of memorable sites, in the search for worldly knowledge, in the mystical contemplation of eternal time, and in the production of clerical fiction.

2 Bricks and Mortar

The phrase *mester de clerecía* has come to group a series of texts variously bound together by reasons of context of production, style, date, and the like, at times opposed to *juglaría*, based on the first stanzas of the *Libro de Alexandre*:[1]

> Señores, si quisiéredes   mio serviçio prender,
> querríavos de grado   servir de mio mester:
> deve, de lo que sabe,   omne largo seer;
> si non, podrié en culpa   e en riepto caer.
>   Mester traigo fermoso: non es de joglaría;
> mester es sin pecado,   ca es de clerezía
> fablar curso rimado   por la quaderna vía,
> a sílavas contadas,   que es grant maestría.
>   Qui írlo quisier',   a todo mio creer
> avrá de mí solaz,   en cabo grant plazer;
> aprendrá buenas gestas   que sepa retraer;
> averlo han por ello   muchos a coñoçer.
>   Non vos quiero grant prólogo   nin grandes nuevas fer:
> luego a la materia   me vos quiero coger.
> El Crïador nos dexe   bien apresos seer:
> ¡si en algo pecáremos,   Él nos deñe valer!
>   Quiero leer un livro   de un rëy pagano,
> que fue de grant esfuerço,   de coraçón loçano;
> conquiso tod'el mundo: metiolo so su mano.
> Ternem', si lo cumpliere,   por non mal escrivano.   (st. 1–5)

(Sirs, if you were to take my service,/I would be pleased to serve you with my craft:/man must be generous with what he knows/if not he could fall in sin and error./A work I bring beautiful: it is not of jonglerie,/a work is without sin as it is of cleresy/to speak a rhymed course in the fourfold way/counting syllables, which is great mastery./Whomever wishes to hear it, is my belief/will have from me entertainment and in the end great pleasure;/will learn good feats to be able to tell again/and so many will get to know it./I do not want to make a great prologue or news,/but take to the matter soon./May the Creator let us become learned,/and if we were to sin He should help us./I want to read a book of a pagan king,/who was of great worth, of a gallant heart;/conquered all the world, put it under his hand./I will take myself to be, if I deliver, to be not so bad a writer.)

Raymond S. Willis defined the *mester* of *mester de clerecía* as the "obligation laid upon every man, in his station, to make himself master of his 'sciences' and put it to service, to make it his lifework, or ministry," that is, he defined *mester* as *menester* or *ministerio*, thus tying the craft both to administration and caregiving.[2] Fernando Gómez Redondo has emphasized the oral, performative aspect of the mastery implied in this mode of composition, pointing to phrases such as "to speak a rhymed course" that illuminate the *clerecía* element of the phrase. This scholar's analysis suggests an overlap between performativity and composition, especially through the idea of *cursus* and the emphasis on rhyme, which points to the complex negotiation of notions of mastery, reception, audience, and so on that have busied scholars studying the poem.[3] The mastery to which the poet refers, then, would be one obtained, as has been argued many times, in the *studium*. Many have argued, convincingly though there is still a need for concrete evidence, that the school in question would be the *studium generale* of Palencia, which, founded around 1212 under the protection of Alfonso VIII himself, would lose ground to greater universities like that of Salamanca by 1246. In any case, study at the monastic and cathedral schools of the region and perhaps scholarly travel to France or Italy have been suggested to explain how the *Alexandre*-poet might have been educated and where the training evident in his work might have originated.

If in the prologue stanzas 1–6 are mostly the work of the Spanish poet, the last two begin to draw from Gautier de Châtillon's *Alexandreis*, the poet's main source, and emphasize again this very particular form of production that has nothing to do with originality, proto-nationalism, or a native tradition, but with a pedagogical environment: the poet wants to *read* a book of a pagan king. To read, in this context, means not only the performative reading aloud or reciting of the text, but interpretation as a form of literary creation and commentary as hermeneutic practice for composition.[4] Translation is both the pretext and the process through which this reading is achieved in *mester de clerecía*, a translation that will be the focus of this chapter, investigated from a variety of angles.

Surprisingly, when Isabel Uría Maqua analyses these much-commented-on first stanzas as a poetics of *mester de clerecía* within the context of university curriculum and the study of Latin grammar in the Iberian Peninsula, she does not consider *translation* – not even in terms of *translatio studii et imperii* – as integral to an overview of dialectal vernacular variants, known as Iberoromance in the peninsula. In tension with or as supplement to Latin, Iberoromance is, for a variety of reasons, different in its communicative/affective/political power within an active program of appropriation or reconfiguration of Latin forms to formulate literary romance languages from its models.

Uría considers Latinisms, figures, forced syntax, even the knowledge itself of a grammar in romance as a marginal effect, almost as a coincidental development of the study of Latin grammar. Not to consider the *Alexandre* as a translation results in the hypothesis that the language of *mester de clerecía* in general is but a (perhaps desirable) consequence of the study of Latin in Palencia.[5] Uría's careful analysis is not to be dismissed, to be fair, but it should be revised within Rita Copeland's historical appraisal of disciplinary disputes for hegemony. Latin grammar, in the clerical context of *mester*, refers not only to syllabic count but also to the disciplinary appropriation on the part of grammar in the Middle Ages of the functions of rhetoric, especially through hermeneutics. If the mastery to which the Spanish poet refers is a grammatical knowledge, we do not need to limit such knowledge to syllables and pronunciation, but can open this mastery up to articulate both a hermeneutics and a rhetoric, in their most public and civil sense, understanding *mester* not only as a common pedagogical culture but as a new form of persuasion coined in this language and brought forth by clerical translations. For, following Copeland again, it is within vernacular translation that the space and possibility for the recuperation of the political and ethical dimensions of rhetoric opened up, dimensions associated no longer with rhetoric but with grammar.[6]

I view translation in this chapter not only as *thematic* or *cultural* displacement, or as *political* transfer of meaning, but as reconfiguring operations from other disciplines or modes of thought into rhetorical practices made new in this emerging learned Iberoromance. In some sense this would be a verbal version of the practice of *spoliation* in architecture for instance, or a recycling of sorts. Translation allows the cleric to reinterpret what goes on outside of literature, to make use of those other tools that appear on his desk, to integrate them in his compositional process. This chapter will reflect on how the poem thematizes the particular novelty of composing by translating into a learned vernacular that as of yet had no set rules or limits or figures, a learned language that was open to a certain freedom of structure, of elaboration. The reflections on language and translation in this chapter also mean to suggest lines of thought on how this process responds to or works for the reconfiguration of the figure of the composing and performing cleric – the mediating cleric, as Julian Weiss would have it – in the sphere of influence of a new political figure in Castile, incarnated in the later figure of Alfonso the Learned, of course, but before in those of Fernando III and especially Alfonso VIII, whose reign is both conjured up and restrained within this poem.[7] The *Alexandre* poet, I will argue in these pages, consistently and consciously manipulates his sources to buttress this presentation of language as central to his version of the hero's biography. After some notes on what the language arts curriculum offered in the period, to aid in assessing the *Alexandre's* rhetorical arsenal from an informed perspective, I will read three separate moments that showcase language in a specific relation to translation and its limits. I then use these moments to reflect upon the task of the cleric as harnessing the potential of translation.

Courts and Clerics

Alfonso VIII was only three years old in 1158 when his father, Sancho III, died and he assumed the crown of Castile. Towards the end of his life, two mirroring events frame the shift of power on the peninsula from the Muslim south to the Christian north: Alfonso's defeat at Alarcos in 1197 and his victory at Las Navas de Tolosa in 1212. Iconic, to be sure, these events are but markers of long and contrasting processes begun and finished at different times, with cross purposes and with myriad different velocities and effects. At Alfonso's death only two years later, his daughter Berenguela would rule next to her brother Enrique I until 1217, following the unfortunate death of the infante Fernando who should have inherited the throne. Berenguela's son, resulting from her marriage to Alfonso IX of León, would reunite the crowns of Castile and León as Fernando III, ruling from 1217 to 1230.

It seems a trick of fortune that this period, so rich in events and long-reaching effects, would have produced such little documentation. To the frustration of historians, the period seems not to have been as intensely interested in historiographical projects as other periods, with notable exceptions in texts such as the *Chronica Naierensis* (ca. 1190), the genealogical *Liber regum* (original composed ca. 1200, with the Toledan version ca. 1220), and the later *Chronica regum Castellae* (ca. 1230).[8] Between these accounts and the emergence of *mester de clerecía*, Amaia Arizaleta locates in the work of chancelleries, in fragments of documents that she pieces together as a sort of microhistory, a discourse for the Castilian monarchy that moves between the historical, the literary, and the rhetorical. Among the different texts produced by chancelleries in the period, Arizaleta considers not only works such as the *Fuero de Cuenca*, the *Vita Didaci*, or the *Liber regum toletanus*, but also such works as Diego García de Campos's *Planeta* and the *Libro de Alexandre* as part of a universe of practices that also included donations, processes, ordinances, royal letters, and the like, produced in both cathedral and court in the service of the monarchy.

Arizaleta's goal is "to compile a repertoire and to compare some of the resources conceived from the end of the twelfth century by the chancellery of Alfonso VIII, which displayed rhetorical images of this monarch destined to be kept in the archives and in the memory of those who attended the public reading of the king's documents," focusing on how the chancelleries specialized in a historiography recorded in the king's own documents. The corpus she focuses on is a series of diplomas of Alfonso VIII's chancellery, especially the fragments devoted to dates and how these fragments are expanded upon to portray the king and his personal and monarchical history. These fragments, which Arizaleta calls "microfictions," are

> built from the narrative of filiation and the narration of the king's actions. The first of these narratives seeks to ensure the stability of the dynasty and proclaims the axiology of the monarch's descendence; the second narrative defends the preeminence of the Castilian monarchy over the other Hispanic monarchies, its best arguments lie with the heroic representation of the sovereign.[9]

The period considered here, 1170–1214, is crucial to my study of the *Libro de Alexandre* as a context of production, where the parallels between *Alexandre's* representational models for the composition of fiction and Arizaleta's analyses of the chancelleries's models for the composition of history bear out qualities and concerns that point to interdisciplinary solutions to common problems. Most remarkably, Arizaleta ties these historiographical models together by way of writerly, literary, rhetorical operations:

> We find ourselves, then, facing a displacement of the writerly mode of juridical memory to the represented historical memory, in which the literary codes begin to be visible. It is the lettered scribes of the palatine circle who, at the end of the twelfth century, begin to abandon the monotone and formulaic register of the everyday exercise of kingly power and who move from the "zero degree" of juridical writing to one that is increasingly artistic.[10]

The effects of such rhetorical operations are such that in them not only is the figure of the monarch built up in close relation to the cleric, but the cleric himself is transformed by the process. In a close reading of these passages, Arizaleta identifies a move from the representation of Alfonso VIII as promoter of the writing of his own power, as character of his own history, to author and authority of such writing. Tying up kingship with the power of writing, Arizaleta concludes, these clerics "projected onto the royal figure virtues peculiar to their state and office."[11]

Lineage, competing sovereigns and models of kingship, the virtues of the clerical office, and the writing of history through the biography of monarchs is the matter itself of the *Libro de Alexandre*. In many ways it is also that of the *Libro de Apolonio* and the *Libro de Fernán González*, if with different resources, intentions, and elaborations. The basic framework, however, is there to sustain the argument of a shared representational impulse in the sphere of sovereignty between historiography and fiction, *studium* and court. A particularly striking feature of these "microfictions" is the changes they exhibit over time, especially after the battle of Las Navas, as Arizaleta notes. Not as conscious exercises but as a collective and discursive development of the figure of the sovereign, from the neutral third person, the narrative changes to the first person, in the voice and the authority of the king himself, *ego preictus Alfonso*: "The narration is from now on subjected to the clear voice of the sovereign, not to that of his scribe. There is an explicit inscription of the royal word in the documents of the king."[12] This *ego* is both oral and written, it is both king and scribe, an individual and a collective "I" in which the task and figure of the cleric himself are projected onto the figure of the king.

Grammar of the Court

In a detailed study of Castilian and Leonese documentation in nine cathedral archives of the region (with consideration of monastic libraries
as well), Susana Guijarro González notes that the curriculum in northern Iberia, after the Muslim conquests in the south, was strongly influenced by the Visigothic schools, benefiting from the exodus of scholars
with their libraries as they moved north, a movement we noted in the
previous chapter.[13] The pervasiveness of the works of Isidore (especially the *Etymologies* and the *De viris illustribus*, along with the *De natura
rerum*) as well as of Cassiodorus' *Institutiones* may be explained in this
way, joining the general European textbooks on grammar and rhetoric,
Donatus's *Ars grammaticae* and Priscian's *Institutio grammaticae*, Cicero's
De inventione and the *Rhetorica ad Herennium*, which merged with a
monasthic sphere influenced by a French culture filtered through the
Pyrenees.[14] Some Christian grammarians can also be found in these
cathedral inventories, such as the commentaries of Audax, Servius,
and Pompey, along with classical authors such as Juvenal and Virgil.
Monastic libraries such as that of Domingo de Silos and San Salvador
de Oña also kept classical authors, and even if the number of copies in
those libraries pales in comparison with those of other European repositories, these spaces of learning also relied on glossaries and *florilegia* to
supply their students with the poetry and classical knowledge central
to the liberal arts.[15] Díaz y Díaz has argued for the movement north
of manuscripts of a Visigothic imprint, as well as for a Toledan *cache*
of classical authors that would have also served as a canon, including works of Cicero, Pliny, Lucan, Palladius, Terence, and Seneca, found
to be in the possession of Toledan archbishops of the thirteenth century.[16] Of works related to Trojan materials, a copy of Dares Phrigius's
De excidio urbis Troiae is number 126 in the inventory of the Cathedral
of Burgo de Osma, for instance.[17] And finally, also of interest for our
purposes is the presence of a number of encyclopedias written in the
twelfth and thirteenth centuries, such as Vincent of Beauvais' *Speculum
naturale* and a *De natura creaturarum*, commentaries on *De propietatibus
animalium* and, of course, Brunetto Latini's *Libro del Tesoro*, in several
bishops' libraries.[18] Crucial to this summary of findings in inventories
is the conclusion that the scholarly curriculum of cathedrals in León
and Castile, until the end of the thirteenth century, does not seem to differ substantially from that of monastic culture, even as it points to the
basis from which universities like Palencia, Salamanca, and Valladolid

were to emerge.[19] What is significantly different in this milieu is the increasingly important role clerics play in the competing and overlapping spheres of court and church.

Cathedral councils, archbishop sees, and royal chancelleries worked closely together, imbricating royal and ecclesiastical power, as in the kingdoms of Alfonso VII and Fernando II, whose chancelleries were controlled by the archbishoprics of Santiago de Compostela and Toledo, and, in a slightly different move, Alfonso VIII's appointment of the Archbishop of Toledo as *ex officio* administrative head of his royal chancellery in 1206.[20] Confirming what Arizaleta maintains for the chancelleries of Alfonso VIII and Fernando III, Guijarro González also argues for itinerant clerics between school and chancellery, precursors of the professional notaries of the thirteenth century, based on the inventories of cathedral libraries that reflect the interests in law treatises, juridical literature, and manuals of *ars dictaminis*.[21] The continued intervention of monarchs in the promotion of clerics – and the resistance of archbishops – to positions in councils, or to chancelleries, further underlines the overlaps between discourses and figures that church and monarchy shared.

At the centre of scholarly developments in the period is the elevation of the school of Palencia to the rank of university by Alfonso VIII, an event remarked upon by Lucas de Tuy in his *Chronicon mundi* and by Rodrigo Jiménez de Rada in his *De rebus Hispaniae liber* as symbolic of Alfonso VIII's character and his kingdom.[22] Adeline Rucquoi seeks to deepen these relations by arguing that the *studium generale* of Palencia had no relation to the cathedral school but was really a prolongation or a sort of institutionalization of the palace school under the image of the king as *magister*.[23] At the level of vocabulary, the documentation of different words to refer to varied positions within the schools does point to a specialization necessary only to more developed programs of study; *magister scholarum* as different from *magistri* is registered already at the end of the eleventh century in Palencia, and would appear at the turn of the century in Compostela, Oviedo, Salamanca, Coimbra, León, and elsewhere, sometimes alternating with the romance term, *maestrescuela*, and other terms such as *caput scholae,* and *praeceptor*. "At the turn of the twelfth century," writes Guijarro González, "the tendency seemed to be for the *magister* to fulfill indistinctly the functions of scribe, notary, librarian and teacher, while the *cantor* organized the chorus and, in consequence, would be in charge of the children composing it ... When in the thirteenth century their functions were formally regulated, the schoolmaster had already become an administrator of the cathedral school."[24] Rucquoi identifies these terms in wills redacted in León and Castile, where payment or inheritances in money and kind to *magisters* from *alumpni* and *alumpnae* indicate that teaching was happening beyond or outside cathedral schools, teaching that was organized and welcomed in the community.[25]

The *Alexandre* was part of a complex net of works including both historiographic and literary fiction that served as a model for composition and also as an ideological tool for the construction of sovereignty and the image of the monarch in thirteenth-century Castile. Whether externally, as a sort of imperial model, or internally, as a *speculum principum*, related to either Alfonso VIII or Fernando III – as has been suggested repeatedly from a variety of perspectives, by Arizaleta and Sánchez Jiménez, but also earlier by Michael and Cacho Blecua – these analyses multiply the roles the Alexander legend played in medieval Europe.[26] These remarks may be extended to the *Libro de Apolonio* and the *Libro de Fernán González* in their general sense. The point here is not only to reiterate these ideas, but to emphasize the palace or the court as an *interdisciplinary* space providing subject matter, correlations, parallels to the *Alexandre* poet, to underline that the cleric's role here, as has been suggested by Weiss but also by García, is one of mediation, and to qualify such mediation as one related to *interpretation*, an interpretation that is figured in the poem specifically as a reflection on translation, intimately tied to language and the scholarly labour on words.[27] As the delimitation of a task that involves all these spheres, this chapter is also an attempt to sketch an image of the self-produced representation of the intellectual, if one may call it that, in the thirteenth century – calling it an intellectual because it is there that a modern figure in this role is actually put forth clearly for the first time.[28]

Rucquoi provides further evidence of the bonds between palace and cloister from the second half of the twelfth century through the figure of the monarch himself. *Curialitas*, a neologism coined by Rodrigo Jiménez de Rada to list among the virtues that characterize Alfonso VIII (*strenuitas, largitas, curialitas, sapiencia, et modestia*), names symptomatically a new quality that was to serve as model for kingship from this point onward, translated as *camaradería*, "witness to the birth of a new way of being and behaving at court," as synonym for courtliness. Such novelty was not, Rucquoi notes by way of Diego García de Campos's *Planeta*, a mere code of behaviour but one of government, a model for sovereignty articulated not only in personal talents or moral qualities but also in learned virtues. Numerous remarks in royal documents from

the courts of Pamplona to Castile from the eleventh century onward attest to a close, affective, familiar relation between masters and students
that extended to their spheres of activity: "It seems that the court was
the place of formation of a series of future prelates who thus maintained privileged connections, not only with the king/*magister*, but also
and above all with the future king, the sovereign's family and the children of nobles, themselves students at court."[29] If the documentation
brought forth by Arizaleta fashioned the king as author/scribe, what
Rucquoi proposes is in effect king as *magister*. Both constructions col-
laborate to credit the king not only with the material power of writing
but also with the symbolic value of *sapientia*, clerical traits projected
onto sovereignty itself.

Court and sovereign are thus impregnated, produced, fashioned,
and regulated through a clerical model of authority – writing, teaching
– and behaviour – *curialitas* – profoundly invested in spheres that serve
as scenarios in the *Alexandre* and other works of the period: a particular expression of *largesse*, intellectual curiosity, and the administration
of diversity. Jiménez de Rada hailed Alfonso VIII's patience and toler-
ance with the court, which he characterized as *tam diversa, tam varia,
tam extranea multitudo*.[30] The *curia*, in Jiménez de Rada, is "the place
of reunion of foreigners, attracted by its sheen and the possibilities it
offers. The royal image derived from here is that of universality, of a
king who reigns óver all peoples, and it is difficult to not evoke here
the ultimate royal model, Solomon." Where Rucquoi sees the evocation
of a king, one may also see the suggestion of a space, for it is also not
difficult to see the story of Babel as a warning model. Rucquoi gives
ample evidence of the number and range of foreign visitors in the court
and the entourage of Alfonso VIII, not only because of his marriage
to Eleanor, daughter of Henry II of England and Aliénor of Aquitaine.
A steady flow of foreigners from the twelfth century onward moves
through the peninsula, whether crusaders, the intellectually curious,
troubadours, students, translators, diplomats, sculptors, jurists, chan-
cellors, painters, or prelates from England, Italy, Provence, Aquitaine,
Languedoc, who establish themselves in Compostela, Burgos, Toledo.
However, as Rucquoi points out, the cosmopolitanism of the court, as
in the variety of languages and diversity of customs that were to be
found there, was due not only to arriving foreigners but also to the
members themselves of the *curia regis*, whose travels as diplomats, students, and envoys exerted an influence in the court at their return.[31]
This cosmopolitanism prompts García de Campos in his *Planeta* to list

virtues and vices according to nationality, in tune with the characteriza-
tions the *Alexandre* offers in st. 1798, for instance, an ethnographic interest that Aníbal Biglieri suggests is the undertone to much geographical
literature of the period.[32]

The variety of peoples, the multitude and diversity at court of languages and cultures, will be elaborated in the *Libro de Alexandre* through
the recurrent narration of the Babel episode. The construction of the
Tower and the multiplicity of people, if in a warning key, serve as re-
minders of the period's courtly interest in the sponsorship of architectural projects, from Santo Domingo de la Calzada to Las Huelgas, while
also realizing a clerical rhetorical commonplace, to which I will turn
below. I should note that the building trope in the *Libro de Apolonio* may
also be read within this web of references.[33] The curiosity of the court,
expressed in the sponsorship and cultivation by many of its members
of poetry, of course, but particularly of the natural sciences, is also a
parallel to Alexander's characterization in the *Libro*. So is his *largesse*,
as is that of Apolonio's, modified from its qualification in the sources
to fit a particular Iberian model, linked to *curialitas*, focused on a way
of relating to the king and to a general courtly amicality, in an intellectual curiosity bound up within a clerical model of *sapientia*. Thus, as
Rucquoi underlines, "Alfonso X appears not as the inventor of a 'cultural concept' characterized by the role of *rex magister*, the putting in
place of translations, the interest for history and university politics, but
as the heir of a long Hispanic tradition," set in motion by historiographic but also by literary fictions.[34]

Arizaleta presses the argument further within historiography, finding that the web of connections between texts and individuals points
to a courtly setting for not only the reception but also the consciously
political composition of a work such as the *Libro de Alexandre* in an
article that details parallels between a number of these historiographic
and literary fictions, but focuses largely on the *Libro de Alexandre* and
Juan de Osma's *Chronica regum Castellae*. The detailed analysis of thematic parallels in the representation of monarchy in these texts clusters
around the themes of legitimacy of the sovereign, the representation
(and rejection) of proud kings, and the putting forth of an imperial
discourse, a representation done in the service of the king.[35] That the
Alexandre puts forth a model for sovereignty that closely mirrors the
work of Jiménez de Rada or Juan de Osma, detailed by Rucquoi as
new and made particular by the notion of *curialitas* I have identified
above, is further supported by Arizaleta with close readings of the

texts and the finding of historical parallels. The most notable texts and parallels read *Alexandre* episodes as conscious projections of events within the Castilian court, as with the narration of Alfonso VIII's investiture at San Zoilo de Carrión (read along Alexandre's own investiture) or Fernando III's speech to the Muñó *curia* to support war against Muslims (read along Alexander's harangue to support the campaign in Asia). In any case, Arizaleta's focus on the monarchic figure is relevant for the role she grants the cleric in the production of this representation. Here, as in her reading of diplomas, the scholar holds this to be a conscious production, terming it a propagandistic program with the cleric at its centre.

The key figure here, linking the spaces of cathedral and court, of fiction, diploma, and historiography, is of course the cleric. Arizaleta herself has researched elsewhere the porosity between these spaces, and has documented how in this period the king's chancellery employed these lettered clerics.[36] Problems arise, however, when one attributes a particular level of expertise to this group, for Arizaleta claims "the writing practices of notaries and scribes corresponded to those habitual ones in the manuals of rhetorical art," and goes on to argue that since the royal chancellery employed clerics with access to written culture, they "were capable of shaping texts which were essentially political and administrative documents through their command of stylistic, structural and even fictional procedures."[37] The nuance I mean to introduce has to do not with who was in charge of writing these documents, nor the changes and parallels the documents exhibit in terms of rhetorical resources, but more with the depth or tradition of this knowledge and its conscious and goal-oriented use by clerics as an imagined homogeneous group.

In a detailed study of the rhetorical origins and use of school rhetoric in the *Libro de Alexandre*, Peter Such provides consistent evidence that a learned, bookish, profound knowledge of the arts of rhetoric in the period cannot be sustained by the poem. Coupled with Charles Faulhaber's determinations that there is no evidence of a rhetorical tradition linked to the *artes poetriae* in thirteenth and fourteenth century Castile, Such's rhetorical analysis concludes one not need presuppose a direct knowledge of the arts of rhetoric nor of the *artes poetriae*. A more general school rhetoric, or what Colin Smith called the "retórica común," a *common rhetoric* drawn from general manuals of grammar, and the reading of both Latin and vernacular works that used, consciously and not, many of the *topica* and figures used in works of fiction such as the

Alexandre and in the chancellery documents that Arizaleta cites, seems much more likely. This of course calls into question Arizaleta's idea of a propagandistic program by a particularly clever and educated group of clerics working in chancelleries, designed to include both history and literature in a project to build a Castilian monarchy. Setting aside the arguments of intentionality (especially at the political level and as a sense of sovereign destiny), and the image of an especially talented and trained group, I find the idea of a common speech, a vernacular rhetoric forged in the grammar of schools and the needs of both pedagogy and bureaucracy, a much more attractive possibility for the construction of the cleric in the sphere of this new sovereign model, grounded in a learnedness that moves in a more contained spectrum but with a wide reach. As Such argues, it is not that the *Alexandre* does not make use of elaborate turns of language that can be identified as learned, as rhetorical, but that the intentionality and especially a relation of *dependence* on arts of poetry is not only unlikely but unnecessary, for the basic model of classical grammar studies and the interpretation and imitation of poetic models is sufficient, as is the choice of subject matter, Alexander, whose universal appeal and lessons in morality are commonplace.

This common rhetoric is, in its collective – if learned – production, in its *communality*, especially eloquent as one reads key episodes in the *Alexandre* that focus on language. If it was within the chancellery, as Roger Wright has argued, that the vernacular would impose its authority, I argue that the *Alexandre*, making use of such royal authority of the vernacular, is trying to put learned fiction in relation with the documentation machines in romance of chancelleries in order to place a different register for clerical voices within the court, a task of the cleric more related to a craft or art of language, a labour and not only a service or duty, in the sphere of the sovereign.[38]

This work of the cleric is one of mediation, at the core of the description of the chancellor according to the king himself: "The chancellor is the second officer of the household of the king among those who hold employments demanding secrecy. For, as the chaplain is the mediator between God and the king, spiritually, with respect to his soul; so, on the other hand, the chancellor is the mediator between him and men, as far as temporal matters are concerned."[39] The chancellor then holds an official position among those dealing with secrecy, with the intimate matters of court and king, whose task is to mediate, literally, in temporal matters, between king and men, duplicating or mirroring the figure of the chaplain, who mediates the spiritual matters between king and

God. What then is the role of the cleric, composer of learned fiction? In what sort of relationship to secrecy and truth do his texts stand? If the chancellor mediates through the language of the law between king and men, couldn't we say that the cleric mediates through the language of fiction to address the same crucial questions of the relevance of the past in the present, of transcendence, salvation and fame, of preparing the worldly for the eternal?

To return, then, to the question of the mediation of the cleric in learned fiction such as the *Alexandre,* one must take a closer look at how the poet reflects on his own craft. I will argue that *interpretation* as the negotiation of meanings practised in translation is at the centre of the *Alexandre*'s proposed place for the cleric within this network of texts, between law and fiction, history and its writing. This is staged in several ways at different moments in the poem through reflections on language and poetic craft articulated by way of tropes common to the period's rhetoric and to the role of memory. If in the previous chapter we saw how cartography served both as memory and as device for the production of fictions, this chapter looks at how the poet stages language and his own intervention as cleric to portray himself in different and complementary ways.

Just as the cartographer draws his maps according to places, the poet invents rhetorically from *loci* in the ductile and movable reorganization of their relations and that of *sedes* or the seats of argumentation. As Douglas Kelly has argued, "The selection and rearrangement of *materia* may be usefully likened to the practice of medieval cartography. Benoît de Sainte-Maure himself once saw his work as a fragmentary *mappa mundi,*" and further on states that "medieval maps are thus a *figura.* Their principles of order and representation are analogous to those we have been describing for poetic invention," recalling Geoffroy of Vinsauf's evocation of the cartographer next to the architect or builder at the beginning of his *Poetria nova.*[40] Just as Geoffroy of Vinsauf describes a *mappamundi* as a basic scheme of inventional memory, he makes the image of the map equal to the image of building: "Let the mind's interior compass (*circinus interior mentis*) first circle the whole extent of the material. Let a definite order chart in advance at what point the pen will take up its course, or where it will fix its Cadiz. As a prudent workman, construct the whole fabric within the mind's citadel; let it exist in the mind before it is on the lips."[41] If Cadiz is the topographic marker for the "end" or "point of arrival" of an itinerary, it is also the rhetorical founding stone for poetic building. Whether in the shape of lists, as in the much-interpreted scholarly itinerary in cartographic key, or as lists of languages or peoples that the *Libro de Alexandre* puts forth, these schemes are to be read as *inventional* structures, meant not (only) to be repositories but above all to be generators, to produce in the way the verbs *to map* and *to build* make us think of. These might make one ask, with Carruthers:

> But what can be the value of such lists? They come without any qualifying comment, a bunch of names plunked down in memorable packaging. In neither of Chaucer's poems, nor in the Inferno, do the figures named play any particular role in the stories that follow. They can mean nothing unless the reader wishes to make something of them – perhaps, in remembering these stories and the matter of these famous works, to keep them reverberating as a potential set of comparisons and contrasts to the rest of the work. We might think of them as providing us with a foundational inventory,

Yet we might also conclude with her that these are devices that spur the reader/listener to *interpret* according to her own set of *loci*, to invent anew. The sense of inventory and of discovery associated with the architect trope through invention, built on Jewish meditative traditions and early Christian exegesis, can thus be linked not only to the idea of cartography as *figura* in the *Libro de Alexandre* but as a common rhetoric to be developed imaginatively by the *Alexandre*-poet.[42]

The common *inventional* role of maps seen in the previous chapter extends thus to the visual programs they are often a part of. Of course, one should not take the visual programs of these manuscripts as literal or natural renderings of the memory buildings of the twelfth and thirteenth century, but they are indeed recollections, particular renderings of a cleric's own edifice of memory adapted or actualized for a particular purpose in a given manuscript. That is why, I believe, we have different versions of these diagrams across the manuscripts, from archways to *rotae* to *mappamundi* or horseshoe arches. We saw how these horseshoe arches could be seen as spatial diagrams, as cartographic devices of sorts, spatializing knowledge on the page, triggering a locational memory intrinsic to the cleric, educated in the basic monastic curriculum. These arches, however, are also a direct link between the cartographic and the architectural that Geoffroy of Vinsauf equated in the quotation above. The meditational practices encouraged or supported by architecture, as Suger of St. Denis, Hugh of St. Victor, and Thierry of Chartres imagined for their glosses on the *Rhetorica ad Herennium* or their building programs, is to be paralleled in these manuscript visual programs as a confirmation of the commonality of these practices.[43]

Isidore, one of the few *auctores* whose presence is certain in both the *Alexandre*-text and the poet's library, takes the concept of the *architectus* to mean particularly one who builds walls, and provides one more link between poetic composition and building by naming three stages in the "making of a building": *disposition, constructio,* and *venustas,* the analogy being invention, disposition, or ornament (or clothing).[44] We have already addressed how invention, disposition, and ornament in close reading of specific passages, beyond Such's meticulous analysis, could be taken further by exploring, for instance, the map in Alexander's text as taking part in both disposition and ornament, in the organization of subject matter and in the clothing of the poem. What I want to contribute now to these analyses is a study of how within this inventional program where the trope of building is central, bridging monastic meditation and poetic invention, translation makes an appearance. For that, we must turn to the poem's specific treatment of this form of interpretation.

Gibberish

Alexander has really barely appeared in the poem in stanza 6, but already in stanza 20 he has killed his mentor, Nectanebus, called Netánamo in our text, on account of the rumours that Nectanebus has fathered him, calling into question his lineage and right to power. Rumour, that particular register of speech and especially political speech, hovering between open gossip, propaganda, and suspicion and counting among its relatives murmurings, whispers, confidences, and the telling of secrets, thus marks Alexander's first political act. This type of speech, "speaking between their teeth" (*fablavan entre dientes*), may be damning, but it also prophesies Alexander's conquests as the population speculates on what the numerous prodigies and signs that announce Alexander's birth might mean. Rumour, from *rumor-is,* which is how I translate our text's *roído,* from *rugitus,* which means litigiousness, disputation, brings about other verbal contexts next to words and writing; speech and recitation; dictation, harangue, mumbling, appeals, sermons, mutterings, pronouncements, all of which make an appearance in this text, nuancing, characterizing, but also constituting a theoretical – that is, a speculative – view of the roles of language in this poem.[45] For the *Libro de Alexandre* may generally be about the great Macedonian conqueror, the superhero of the Middle Ages, but from this point of view the star of the show is undoubtedly language.

At the other end of the poem an episode marks off a limit with respect to language: the encounter of Alexander's troops with wild men – a collage composed of fragments of different episodes in the *Historia de Preliis*, thus making for quite an original mosaic – stages an encounter with a human other with an eye to cultural difference portrayed in linguistic terms:

> Entre la muchedumbre   de los otros bestiones,
> falló omnes monteses,   mugieres e barones,
> los unos más de días,   los otros moçajones.
> Andavan con las bestias   paçiendo los gamones.
>   Non vistíe ninguno   ninguna vestidura;
> todos eran vellosos   en toda su fechura;
> de noche, como bestias,   yazién en tierra dura.
> ¡Qui los non entendiesse   avrié fiera pavura!
>   Ovieron con cavallos   d'ellos a alcançar,
> ca eran muy ligeros,   non los podién tomar.
> Maguer les preguntavan,   non les sabién fablar
> que non los entendién,   e avién a callar.   (st. 2472–4)

(Among the masses of other monsters,/he found mountain people, women and men,/some were older, others were young./They were with the beasts grazing the pastures.//None of them wore any clothing,/they had hair all over their bodies,/at night, like beasts, they lay on the hard ground./He who did not know of them would be terrified! //They had to catch them with horses,/for they were very light-footed and could not be trapped,/though they asked them questions, they did not know how to respond/for they did not understand them, and thus kept silent).

There are several elements in the description of the encounter with the wild men that enable the association with monstrosity and thus with the catalogue of marvels that the Alexander legend was known for. There is, of course, the duplicated mention of beasts as context for these mountainous people. Their wildness, shown by their feeding habits, is reiterated by the mention of the body hair that covers them completely, and the savage, uncultivated, or uncivilized is underlined by their lack of dress and their sleeping directly on the ground, with no bedding literally distancing the human from the animal. It is after this series of traits that the poet mentions the terror they would inflict on any human coming in contact with them, but the poet underlines that this terror would be felt only by those *not understanding them*, that is, those who do not know who or what they are. This suggests a lack of *cultural* translation or perhaps even intends a linguistic understanding, an emphasis that suggests a disjunction between a wild appearance and the possibility of a violent nature, which is always rendered ambiguous in the presentation of wild characters. The *Libro de Alexandre* then remarks on the fact that knights and savages do not *understand* each other, that is, the *Libro* stages here a problem of communication, and particularly a linguistic difference that *is* a cultural difference.[46] The interval opened up by this difference can be overcome, as the poem has been repeatedly suggesting up to this point, by translation.

Translation and its discontents can be viewed, as is often the case, as related to originals. But the emphasis in the *Libro de Alexandre* is not on sources or on the *auctores* (even if *don Galter* is referred to directly in the poem), but on masters and their teachings. It is Aristotle who brings up the young hero on the clerical curriculum, with a reliance on memory, and with an emphasis on the hard work that study – the cleric's task – implies. The first time Aristotle shows up in the poem is after having been working without rest on a syllogism for an entire day and night. His eyes are thus glassy and his countenance pale; his hair is a mess, for his hairband is loose, his cheeks are sunken and, the poet adds with a touch of comedy, anyone barely nudging him would be able to cause him to fall. The poet then remarks: "You see, he has been reading!" As a stand-in for the cleric – one of many in the poem – Aristotle's devotion to his craft is duly emphasized here, and his correct teaching of the liberal arts to his disciple Alexander is a predictable *translatio studii* in itself, for classical knowledge is here rendered as medieval knowledge, detailed in its appropriate branches of study by Alexander himself from stanzas 38 through 45, going through grammar, logic, physics, rhetoric, music, astronomy, and so on. What I want to underscore is that translation, as the task of the cleric, is presented as *labour* – a meaning underlined in its physical effects through Aristotle's description – as a craft that requires a certain knowledge and mastery over its materials, talent that is here underlined as theory for the composition of learned Castilian literature and ultimately as the task of the cleric himself.

The task of the cleric, weaving craft, talent, and labour, has been elaborated in the poem before this scene with the wild men, as the poet incorporates the act of translation itself, transcribing a Latin (*sic*) epitaph taken from a gloss in Gautier de Châtillon's margins, inscribed upon Darius's tomb:

> Fizo un petafio   escurament' dictado
> – de Daniel lo priso,   que era allí notado –.
> Cuemo era Apeles   clérigo bien letrado,
> todo su ministerio   tenié bien decorado.
>   "Hic situs est aries tipicus, duo cornua cuius
> fregit Alexander, totius malleus orbis"
> (duo cornua sunt duo regna,   Persarum et Medorum).
>   "Aquí yaz'el carnero,   los dos cuernos del qual
> crebantó Alexandre,   de Greçia natural.
> Narbozones e Bessus,   compaña desleal,
> estos dos los mataron   con traïçión mortal."   (st. 1800–2)

(He made an epitaph, obscurely written,/taken from Daniel, for there it was noted./As Apeles was a well-lettered cleric,/he had all his ministry well known by rote.//"Hic situs est aries tipicus, do cornua cuius/fregit Alexander, totius malleus orbis"/(duo cornua sunt duo regna, Persarum et Medorum).//"Here lies the ram, the two horns of which/Alexander broke, natural of Greece,/Narbozones and Bessus, unloyal company,/these two killed him with mortal treason.")

Apelles writes the epitaph that is here transcribed by the Spanish poet. The transcription of the Latin epitaph cuts the stanza short, for it is only three lines (and it is not clear if the third line in Latin is part of the epitaph, if it is Daniel's or Apelles's explanation, or if it is Gautier's or a scribe's) and is copied in Latin directly from Gautier de Châtillon's *Alexandreis* (7.423–4). It is immediately translated by our poet into Spanish, semi-rigorously in the first two verses, while the other half of the stanza is a free elaboration, illustrative of what happens in the rest of the poem, adding, elaborating, digressing from the source, and adding materials from other texts in order to develop and sustain themes specific to the Spanish version.[47]

Such a reflection addresses translation only in the first instance: from one language to another. As Casas Rigall, the *Alexandre's* editor, notes, following Bienvenido Morros, the Latin quotation is followed by a gloss, probably taken from the poet's own copy of the *Alexandreis*, translated and rewritten and, most interestingly, relocated to the body of the poem. This relocation or displacement of words from the margins to the centre of the page is directly linked to Apelles's craft and work, his *ministerio* or *métier*, his *mester*, which the *translated gloss* serves to highlight as one having to do with memory and visual mnemotechnics, a process we analysed in terms of cartography in the previous chapter. On the other hand, it is hard not to notice the *deictic* nature of the Latin epitaph: *Hic situs*, recalling cartographic rhetoric in two ways, by the spatial linking of the tomb and the epitaph (or the Latin and the poem itself as translated on the page), and by the rhetorical move of supplementation of the material, in this case with the material relocated there from the gloss. *Deixis* and *supplementation* with other texts as a form of *digressio* are here integral to the simultaneous process of translation and composition in the vernacular.

To elaborate the questions of the craft of translating further, I want to emphasize that in this ekphrastic moment, as in the many others that the Spanish poet weaves into his version of Alexander, it is possible to see the cleric in the artistic figure of Apelles, an association that Julian Weiss and Amaia Arizaleta have cleverly analysed. Through this figure, it is possible to read the verbal into the visual, to appreciate the (visual) descriptions as masterful verbal elaborations the poet consciously emphasizes as his own task. Even indirectly, such associations with visual content refer one to the translation of tasks, thematizing in object and practice the discipline and business of the cleric himself.

Matters of Language

As a third and the longest exploration of the staging of translation in the *Libro de Alexandre,* I now consider the varying roles of the Tower of Babel and the city of Babylon in the poem. Inspired, as so many other themes in the *Alexandre,* by Isidore's *Etymologies* (11.1), Babel is taken up in the poem as an emblem of linguistic diversity and a symbol of pride, as it had been in Diego de Campos's *Planeta* or Rodrigo Jiménez de Rada's *Historia de rebus Hispaniae,* both of which mention Babel in their opening passages. Jiménez de Rada was himself known for his gift with languages, and Diego de Campos compared the archbishop's gift with the number of Babelian languages themselves in his prologue, dedicated to Jiménez de Rada.[48]

Babel's most familiar image is that of the Tower's architecture, a symbol that already in the Bible articulated a parallel, both moral and physical, between buildings and the human figure in which feet corresponded to the foundations, the torso to the body of the tower, eyes to windows, and so on. The Tower of Babel accumulates over this initial correspondence many other layers of meaning, of which the first is size: a Tower of Babel must be gigantic. This monumentality is the central motif in representations of the Tower by the Flemish school of painting, from which Brueghel the Elder's is the most familiar to our eyes. There, the Tower exceeds the clouds, and its highest point, in ruins, can only suggest an even more vertiginous height that could have been. At its feet, to the right, is a port, and to the left lies the city. Gesturing to the Roman Coliseum, the Tower is ruled by the spiral that climbs it and that is interrupted at an arch we cannot see. As interpretation of the Tower, this one does not forestall ambiguity: one cannot decide if what is being represented is a monument to success or the result of a disaster. The building figures there as a cipher of a moment of human history, a history that perhaps should have chosen as its first image another one before Babel. There, tower, language, and human have remained inevitably sutured in the beginning of history. As historical origin, it was taken up by the thirteenth century in Iberia with a variety of effects.

The episode of Babel is narrated in verses one through nine of Genesis 11. The passage contains a series of motifs that have been the object of study of numerous disciplines, from archaeology to philosophy to semiotics. I cite here the version of the *Bibia medieval romanceada*, the vernacular Bible, from the Escorial manuscript (as proposed by Castro Millares Carlo y Battistesa), which has Hebraic prose and fifteenth-century script:[49]

(1) E fue toda la tierra vna fabla e vnas palabras.

Et fue quando movieron de oriente, e fallaron una vega en tierra de Bauilonia, e estouieron ay.

Et dixeron cada vno a su compannero: Labremos adobes e quememos quemadura. E fue a ellos el adobe por piedra, e la cal era a ellos por barro.

Et dixeron: Dad aca, fagamos a nos villa e torre que su cabo llegue a los çielos; e fagamos a nos nombradia, porque no nos derramemos sobre la faz de toda la tierra.

(5) Et decendio la virtud de Dios a ver la villa e la torre que fraguaron los fijos del omne.

Et dixo: Ahe, un pueblo e una lengua tienen todos; e esto es lo que començaron a fazer, e agora se prouara todo lo que pensaron fazer.

Dad aca, decindamos e reboluamos ay su fabla, que no entienda uno fabla de otro.

E derramolos Dios de ay por toda la tierra, et vedaronse de fraguar la
   çibdad.
(9) Por tanto llamo el su nombre Bauilonia, que ay boluio Dios habla de
   toda la tierra, et de ay
los derramo Dios por toda la tierra.   (12–13)

(And the earth was all one speech and one word./And when they moved
from the East, and found a place in the land of Babyon, they rested there./
And they said each to their companion: Let's make bricks and mortar.
And they used brick for stone, and plaster for clay./And they said: Let's
see, let us make ourselves a city and a tower whose extreme reaches the
heavens; and let us make ourselves a name, so that we do not spill over
the face of the earth./And the virtue of God descended to see the city and
the tower that the sons of man had made./And it said: Lo, a people and
a language they all have, and this is what they started to do, and now it
shall all be tested what they'thought of doing./Come on, let us descend
there and muddle their speech, so that no one understands speech from
one another./And God spilled them from there to all the earth, and they
were forbidden to make the city./And that is why it was called the name
of Babylon, for there God mixed speech of all the earth, and from there
God spilled them all over the earth.)

At the level of vocabulary we can distinguish three emphases: space,
construction, and language as community,[50] summed up in the fourth
verse. The sons of man decide to undertake, first, the construction of a
city and a tower and, thereafter, the formulation of a name – a proper
name – that shall keep them united, language as a bond or guarantor of
community. Once building has begun, God observes humanity's success and, perhaps surprised, imagines the possibilities, anticipating
that now humanity will be able to do anything it sets its mind to. It
seems then as if, confronted with the possibility of the independence
of humanity, God himself felt abandoned or unnecessary and felt thus
the need to descend and confound the language of men, spilling them
all over the earth. The bond of language broken, the community divided; dispersion results in the abandonment of the communal project.
Humanity's work remains thus unfinished. The passages close with an
etymological explanation, a false one, explained through the Hebrew
word and resulting thus in "confusion," when the name that archaeology has recovered corresponds to Accadian *bab-ilu* or *babili*, which
means "gate of the gods."[51]

The version that Genesis transmits was established between the twelfth and seventh centuries (BC), and we owe the narration of the passage of Babel to the Yahvist tradition.[52] The Vulgate clearly distinguishes what happens to men and what happens to language through the use of *divisio* and *confusio*, a *divisio populorum* and a *confusio linguarum*, separating in this way what in the Hebrew text seems a double consequence of a single cause.

That Babel would be referenced in the *Libro de Alexandre* is not especially surprising, given that it is mentioned in its main source, Châtillon's *Alexandreis*; it is also dwelled upon in Isidore's *Etymologies*, in Diego de Campos, and in Jiménez de Rada, as I mentioned above. As a symbol of arrogance and the fall of the proud it must have seemed especially appropriate as prefiguration of the protagonist's destiny and the lesson of the entire work. But in contrast with these other contemporary works, which mention the episode briefly, Babel appears a total of nine times in the poem, many more than in the source, all at crucial moments. The configuration of Babel in the *Libro de Alexandre* is mainly manifest in the form of a historical digression within the description of Babylon, in the middle of the poem, but, supplemented by allusion or clearly referenced, the story recurs another eight times in the poem.

The most extra-textual reason for this repeated mention of Babel points to the popularity surrounding the Tower from the eleventh century onward. Among the representations corresponding to the period ending in the twelfth century, the Minkowski catalogue mentions twelve images, which include the first known representation of the Tower in a manuscript – within the Cotton Bible (sixth century) – while for the period corresponding to the thirteenth through the fifteenth centuries there are 157 representations, among them two in Jewish manuscripts copied in Spain in the fourteenth century, along with representations in elaborate *mappaemundi*, such as Ebstorf or Hereford, which attest to the cartographic import of the Tower. Paul Zumthor has suggested that, among other circumstances, the interest in this episode might have been furnished by the intercultural conflicts in Iberia and the contacts within it to an intensely active Jewish tradition around Babel, for in the European imaginary the transmission of Babel stories responds more to distant echoes of the Talmud than to the biblical text itself.[53] The Hebraic filiation of the episode responds not only to the *Bereshit Rabba*, the oldest Talmudic compilation, which assembles texts referring to Genesis, especially to Babel, but also to Flavius Josephus and his *Antiquitates Judaicae*, whose relevance for the Spanish medieval Alexander has been documented by María Rosa Lida de Malkiel.[54] The transmission of the episode, especially within Iberia, should also include Benjamin of Tudela, who described the Tower twice in his travelogue (second half of the twelfth century), and the *Barlaam e Josafat* (translated into romance in the thirteenth century, but circulating earlier in Arabic[55]), which attributed the building of the Tower to the semi-godly, semi-human giants of Genesis – the Nephilim of 6:1–4.[56] The link between the Tower and the giants is an equivocal reference that continues a long tradition, begun by Flavius Josephus, followed by Pseudo-Philo, and authorized through the Haggada.[57] Saint Augustine himself implicitly anchors the Babel passage in the epic of primitive giants, citing "Nebroth."

The Babel episode in the Bible is commented upon from many perspectives as the ciphering of a historical truth: Isidore confirms in his *Etymologiae* the literal truthfulness of the story, relying on Augustine, while travellers and chroniclers confirm its historicity through a geographic facticity, from the 1100s to at least the sixteenth century, from Brunetto Latini to Benjamin of Tudela, as mentioned before.[58] Diego García de Campos put it at the centre of Iberia's linguistic diversity, and Rodrigo Jiménez de Rada places himself in the midst of a contemporary Babel as foreigners flood Toledo in preparation for Las Navas.[59] The last group of references that articulate the episode against history have important theoretical consequences that Umberto Eco suggested in *La ricerca della lingua perfetta nella cultura Europea*, writing that "only from this point onwards the episode of confusion will be looked at not only as an example of pride punished by divine justice, but as the beginning of a historic (or metahistoric) wound that must be healed in some way."[60] This last emphasis on history seems at first "external" to the Genesis verses devoted to the episode of Babel. Medieval discussion on the idea of history imprints in this way a mark on the interpretation of the episode that guarantees the relevance of the motif of Babel in biblical exegesis, and in later evocations of it, as a form of knowledge, and not limited to the popular conflated image of Babylon as a city of perdition.[61]

The *Libro de Alexandre* articulates the references to the Tower and its version of the Babel episode around three clusters of ideas: history, pride, and incompletion. The Babel episode itself in the text functions as narrative centre of the digression on Babylon. This digression is mainly a description of the entry of Alexander in the city and a detailed description of the city itself, while the Babel episode takes the place of Babylon's past, its "history/story." In this structure, within the narration of a personal (hi)story, Alexander the Great's, the motif of pride as individual sin hinges individual and collective history. There is thus a linking of collective and individual history through pride or, more generally, through excess, for pride is, like lust or greed, a sin of accumulation. To develop these themes, the poet of the *Alexandre* devotes many more than the nine verses of the Bible to the episode. The poet of the *Libro* assembles, as I mentioned before, a long series of references throughout the text that anticipate or recall the narration of Babel at the centre of the poem.

In almost all of the references, it is clear that the *Alexandre* has incorporated the theme of the giants within the story of Babel, though the poem maintains a sense of collectivity by not actually naming a protagonist. The primitive legends of Babel had in fact emphasized anonymity, underlining the collectivity of the episode with the absence of a hero, as in our poem. It was the commentators of the biblical text who mixed in the figure of a Nemrod, a hunting hero taken from Genesis 10 (8–12), with the motif of rebelliousness, which was the interpretation given to the arrogance of wanting to make the Tower "reach the heavens."[62] The figure of Nemrod, whose name means "rebel," grew in importance; alluded to later by Bede, or Peter Comestor, he was already for Isidore of Seville one of the historical symbols of the Devil. The *Alexandre*, structuring a protagonist through the interweaving of the giant theme into the Babel references, manages to mould itself better to the medieval structure of epic.[63] Alfonso the Learned, only a few decades after our poem was composed, devotes a chapter of his *General estoria* to Nemrod, this new antihero, calling him the first king of the world, furthering the political tones of the episode. The *Alexandre* is, however, more subtle, and underlines mainly the motifs of pride – physically represented in the excess of the goal, in the gigantism of Tower and progatonists – along with those of multiplicity and unfinishedness.

Among the general information to be gathered from the scattered references is the description of the giants as strong, brave warriors, as Darius's relatives, in sum, as Babylonians. As for their language, we know that it is Hebrew, "an important language," a natural language, and that humanity did not know how to speak anything else, nor how to "write on wax," as the poem points out. The second reference to Babel, found in the description of Darius's shield, cited in the previous chapter, follows a reflection of the poem in which, in stanza 987, the poet has introduced the theme of vanity. Darius's shield – much as Alexander's – functions within the plot as a premonition. We are, of course, looking again at an instance of ekphrasis, but beyond these links to the visual, what is important for my purposes here is to note that this mention of Babel introduces a brief historical digression, the narration of the antagonism between Nebuchadnezzar and the Jews. The third reference to Babel is also an instance of ekphrasis, this time a description of Apelles's work on the tomb of Estatira, Darius's wife. This reference is presented within a more complete biblical context, following the fall of the angels, Adam and Eve, Noah, the plagues, the dark angel. Almost all biblical episodes mentioned in this fragment of the *Alexandre* are divine punishments; the exceptions are the mention of Abraham and Isaac, which is a test and not properly a punishment, and the mentions of Noah's sons. The connection between the giants and the Tower and dispersion (or spatiality) is emphasized directly in the other references, but also in their contiguity with the recurrent mentions of Sem, Cam, and Japhet. Finally, the third long passage that refers to Babel is enveloped by the description of the city of Babylon. I have detailed in the previous chapter the relations between the city and the story, citing other references to the Tower of Babel that buttress the identification of tower and city. The elaboration of the story itself and of the figure of translation is what I will focus on next.

Within the description of the city of Babylon, both as its past and as cause of its present configuration, the *Libro de Alexandre* writes a seven-stanza historical digression that elaborates freely on Genesis's Babel episode:

> Creo que bien podiestes   alguna vez oír
> que quisieron al Çielo   los Gigantes sobir:
> fizieron una torre – non vos cuedo fallir –;
> ¡non fue quien la podiés'   mesurar nin medir!
>
> Vío el Crïador   que fazién grant locura;
> metió en ellos çisma   e grant malaventura:
> non conoçié ninguno   omne de su natura
> ¡Ovo assí a seer   por su malaventura!
>
> Fasta essa sazón   toda la gent' que era
> fablavan un lenguaje   e por una manera:
> en ebraico fablavan,   una lengua señera;
> non sabién ál fablar   nin escrivir en çera.
>
> Metió Dïos entr'ellos   tamaña confusión,
> que olvidaron todos   el natural sermón;
> fablavan cadaúno   lenguaje en su son:

¡non sabié uno a otro   qué'l dizié o qué non!
  Si'l uno pedié agua,   el otro dava cal;
el que pedié mortero,   dávanli el cordal.
Lo que dizié el uno,   el otro fazié ál:
¡ovo toda la obra   por ende ir a mal!
  Non se podién por guisa   ninguna acordar:
ovieron la lavor   qual era a dexar.
Ovieron por el mundo   todos a derramar:
cadauno por su comarca   ovieron a poblar.
  Assí está oy día   la torre empeçada,
pero de fiera guisa,   sobra mucho alçada.
Por la confusïón   que fue entr'ellos dada
es toda essa tierra   Babiloña clamada.   (st. 1505–11)

(I believe you might have heard/that the Giants wanted to reach Heaven:/they built a tower – I am not misguiding you –/there was none who could measure or calculate it! // The Creator saw they were committing madness,/and put among them division and misfortune;/ no one recognized each other./That's how it had to be for their misguided enterprise! // Until that moment every one who was/spoke one language and in one way:/in Hebrew they spoke, a distinguished tongue;/they did not know another language nor to write on wax. // God put among them such confusion,/that they all forgot natural sermon;/they spoke each a language in their own way:/did not know what each other said or didn't say! // If one asked for water, the other gave lime;/he who asked for mortar, was given rope./What one said another did something else:/the entire work in the end turned for the worse. // They could not in any way agree:/and thus had to leave the labour as it was./They had across the world then to spill over:/each to his country went to inhabit. // In this way is the tower today begun/in a great way, a large part still remains./Because of the confusion that took place among them/that entire land is called Babylon.)

The *Libro de Alexandre* presents a division that is first and foremost a division of labour, prefiguring the urban interpretation of the city. The poet first establishes Babel's well-known status, linked to the giants and alluding to the Tower's size. He then has God characterize the enterprise as madness, thus putting among them a division that seals their destiny – "metió en ellos çisma e grant malaventura." The builders of the tower lose not an *original language* – which was for our poet, as for the Church fathers, unmistakably Hebrew, kept after the punishment of Babel by the chosen people – but a sense of belonging or community (*non conoçié ninguno omne de su natura*), and a linguistic unity expressed in a speech and a "way" (*Fasta essa sazón (…) fablavan un lenguage e por una manera*). The separation is not one between language and things, that is, the *Alexandre* does not stage a crisis of meaning but a separation between men, a crisis of community, of politics. Here, the poet does not address division specifically again, but only uses the term "confusion." Departing from the Vulgate's distinction between what happens to men and what occurs with languages, a *divisio populorum* and *confusio linguarum*, here it is the community that is both severed from itself and confused. Confusion is first characterized as a forgetting that renders speech individual, and thus communication is lost. The people of Babel become aware of this confusion in their inability to exchange materials, where the vocabulary of one trade is now incompatible with that of the other. This inability to translate technical languages is what leads the men to realize they cannot build the Tower anymore, and to abandon it. The Tower is left unfinished as humanity disperses, but its dispersion is not a sort of exile imposed by God, it is not the direct result of a divine command, it is a dispersal that stems from an internal exile from community, the consequence of an absence of translation that impedes communal effort. Linguistic diversity is an effect of forgetting that results in the individualization of speech that expresses itself in the way of technical languages.[64]

The division of labour is a direct result of God's intervention, which institutes a forgetting that ultimately results in an unfinished project. The lack of communication, or lack of agreement, prompts dispersal and separation, which in turn account for the world's population (and division of labour, again), in a mirroring or reduplication of the separation of Noah's sons Sem, Cam, and Japhet, so often recalled in medieval T/O maps. The most eloquent figure here, through its absence, is that of the translator, and so the Tower remains unfinished: translation as an unfinished project is thus established.

The recurrent motif of Babel serves the general purpose of underpinning the narrative at different moments with a reminder of pride and its punishment. In their own particular contexts, the Babel references allude to complex systems of meaning that link up to other, less thematic, reflections of the poet. In this specific elaboration at the centre of the poem, the Babel-Babylon passages stage the craft or labour of translation in a specifically political context. Babel, from Augustine to Benjamin to Steiner to Derrida, is of course not only the figure of linguistic difference but also the figure of its counteraction, whether taken as a reflection on a lost, pure, or natural language, as an unfinished/unfinishable project, or as the restoration of a divided community. *Alexandre's* Babel is as well a reversible sign, but read in context, at the centre (or slightly on the margins) of one of the greatest translating cultures of the West, and in anticipation of one of the largest and most important translation projects ever sponsored by royalty, it takes on a particular weight.

As learned Latin ceased to be a familiar language and thus lost its universal hold on the linguistic imagination in the northern kingdoms, and accents flourished and regional differences became more prominent, and especially as the Carolingian reforms underlined such differences in a way that separated the written from the spoken, this Latin became a grammatical language to be taught and learned, that is, it became an artificial language in relation to a mother tongue, the *sermo maternus*. As the interval became greater between a written Latin whose orality had to be learned again, and the vernacular, whose writing had to be invented, nostalgia for what had been lost, the secrets or truths of a sacred language, increased. From Abulafia to Dante, from Ramon Lull to Nicolas of Cusa, the search for a pure language was to be part of the drive to restore the gap opened up by linguistic confusion, ciphered in Babel's destruction. This tragic overtone, this reading of Babel as failed enterprise or at least as unfinished one, has been one of the most re-enacted possibilities of the episode, still present in thought on translation in figures such as Jacques Derrida, or in Walter Benjamin's title of his much cited essay on poetic language, "The Task of the Translator," where *task* translates *aufghabe*, which also means "the one who has to give up" or "defeat," as Paul de Man points out. De Man asserts that the main reason translation is at the centre of Benjamin's text on poetic language is the idea itself of failure; in this sense, de Man reads Benjamin's use of the figure of the translator as an *exemplary* figure.[65]

Babel is the origin of translation, as multiplicity of languages is what allows for and requires translation. Even if de Man's reflections on translation's relation to literature and philosophy concern an explication of Benjamin, and are thus far removed from our context, his characterization of translation as something that is both its own object and a theory of its object is especially illuminating for the *Libro de Alexandre*, if we think of the *Libro* not only as containing and elaborating episodes on Babel but also, in light of its self-conscious presentation and its inaugural role in a movement or mode of clerical composition, as a sort of theory of its own practice, and in many ways *exemplary*.[66] De Man writes that "one of the things [translation] resembles would be philosophy, in that it is critical, in the same way that philosophy is critical, of a simple notion of imitation, of philosophical discourse as an *Abbild* (imitation, paraphrase, reproduction) or the real situation," and later, "Translation is also, says Benjamin, more like criticism or like the theory of literature, than like poetry itself."[67] These reflections parallel the context of production and the intended or unintended effects of *mester de clerecía*, especially the *Libro de Alexandre*, for the *Alexandre* is a student exercise in translation; it translates actively, consciously, and productively a number of sources in Latin and French, incorporating materials from popular culture and elaborating its own pedagogical and political agendas.

Cleric as Translator

In the Bible, the Babel episode is an anonymous challenge to God that results in a punishment shared by humanity. This initial division and confusion is the quotidian mark of misunderstanding and foreignness. The medieval introduction of an individualized protagonist served the purposes of narrative composition, but by the time of Alfonso X a properly political content had also been explicitly developed. Alfonso devotes a chapter of his *General estoria* (chapter 19 of book 2) just to this protagonist, Nembrot, characterizing him as the first king of the world, thus making of Babel also a reflection on sovereignty:[68]

> Et sobrel linnage deste Nemproth, de qual de los fijos de Noe uinie por la linna uerdadera, fallamos como desacuerdo entre los sabios que desta estoria fablan. Los unos dizen que fue delos de Sem, como Methodio que cuenta que fue Nemproth fuert omne, et malo, et forçador, et uenador, et apremiador delos omnes ante Dios, et que fue delos fijos de Yray, fija de Heber, que fue delos de Sem (…) yl diera Dios alli el saber dell astronomia, e sabie por y las cosas que auien de uenir e las dizie e las enssennaua.

> (And of the lineage of this Nemphrot, and of which true line from the sons of Noah he came, we find a disagreement among the wise men who speak of this story. Some say he came from Sem, such as Methodius who tells Nemphrot was a strong man, and mean, and violent, and a sinner, and an oppressor of men before God, and that he was of the sons of Yray,

daughter of Heber, who was of those of Sem (...) and God have him the knowledge of astronomy, and thus knew the things that were to come and he said them and taught them.)[69]

In the *General estoria*, it is on Nemrod's advice that the sons of man keep together and search for a vast land for all to settle in, and arrive in this way and with those intentions to Shinaar in chapter 21: they shall remain together, against the divine wish for their dispersal. Alfonso X brings in here another tradition linked to the Babel episode, in which the goal for building the Tower would be to have a refuge in case God decided to flood the earth once again. In this case, the sin punished by divinity in the Babel episode would be that of lack of trust, incredulity, insolence, or even faithlessness.[70] A lack of trust in God's promise not to punish humanity again with a flood, a promise made repeatedly in Genesis and recovered by the *Biblia romanceada* and Alfonso X, is thus an important motif in Iberia. The construction of a tower so high that it could offer refuge to humanity without the need for God's warning depicts a god that seems unpredictable and not particularly trustworthy. The *Libro de Alexandre*, if it does not seem to know this interpretive tradition present in later Iberian texts, anticipates this overtly political version, underlined through two major figures in the poem: Darius, king of the Persians, who claims his lineage from the giants, builders of the Tower, and through Semíramis, the Babylonian queen who plans a city that mirrors the division and confusion of languages and people. There as well, translation is absent and the city cannot make use of its wealth or its diversity.

Population dispersal is reinforced as the catalogue of languages and nations is introduced, where the poet writes that these languages, this gibberish, is especially prone to confuse *menestrales*, those who work with a craft, task, or technique: "Este girgonz' que traen, estos lenguajes tales,/sonse controbadiços entre los menestrales" (for this gibberish it brings, these such languages, are prone to be confused by the masters/ minstrels, st. 1512). Casas Rigall understands *menestrales* to mean just workers, without specifying their particular craft, making the confusion between construction workers and language workers even more interesting and bringing it directly in relation to our earlier discussion of composition as building. But Casas Rigall also notes, even if he dismisses the possibility, that *controbar* (<conturbare) has a homonym with a different origin (<contropare) that denotes *figural* language.[71] In the thematic context of confusion I have been detailing, a confusion

that deals in craft and with languages, I find it especially productive to think of both of these possibilities simultaneously, for the *Alexandre*-poet is articulating a craft of language that has to do *not only* with a specific, divided labour but with the work on language as *figural*, that is, language that is a technique in itself, to be mastered and deployed: a *technè*.

The splitting of the community is the result of an absent and lacking figure, of he who could make sense of the gibberish, make understandings possible. If one's *technè* is language itself, as the *Libro de Alexandre* self-consciously articulates its own project as one of translation from different sources and multiple languages, Babel, in a strict sense, calls for the liberties and possibilities of such a translation, and in a general sense, it is an argument for the relevant task of clerical craft in the construction of sovereignty. In historically specific terms, this technical reference may very well point to different scriptural practices in the thirteenth century, as well as a performative difference that distinguishes this type of composition, *mester de clerecía*, from that of *juglaría*, the task of the cleric from that of the jongleur.[72] It might even point to a historical reality, as Juan de Osma inattentively and Rodrigo Jiménez de Rada self-consciously note in their cosmopolitan Toledo, noisy with the language of foreigners: "Et quia diuersarum nationum uarietas diuersitate morum, linguarum et cultuum discrepabant, de uoluntate principis in eadem urbe eiusdem urbis pontifex morabatur, ut dissidencium uarietaś per eius industriam sedaretur," writes Jiménez de Rada. As historian – as inventor of Castille, as Georges Martin has argued – Jiménez de Rada suggests that he himself, master of languages, interpreter of cultures, may be the one to harmonize such variety.[73] While the *Alexandre*-poet portrays himself implicitly in this position, he does not name himself directly as such a translator; in fact, the Babel of the *Alexandre* prompts us to think of yet another absent figure, that whom for lack of a better name we will call *author*. The lack of elaboration of an authorial figure calls attention to the task of the cleric as a collective enterprise, as a craft or technique to master and learn, as a communal discourse trying to map itself onto the politics and practices of the vernacular in thirteenth-century Castile.

Based on the productivity of the term "estoria" in the poem, a remark on terminology brings us back to the first theme articulated in the Babel passages, that of history. The term functions in general in its common meaning as "history of humanity." In the Bible, the passage of Babel is located just before history begins with Abraham and the story of Israel.

The first verse of the passage in the romanced version of the Bible, cited earlier in this chapter, follows Hebrew and not Latin, translating as "fabla" (speech) the Hebrew *sâphâh*, which would find a more precise translation in "labio" (lip) (the Vulgate translates *labia*), but the word can also mean "border," or "limit"; while *dâbhâr*, translated as "words," designates also the "event" or "history." This word, Zumthor observes, absent in the first ten chapters of Genesis, makes its first appearance in this episode. The Babel episode is thus placed at the lips, or on the border, of history. The project of "making ourselves a name," "fagamos a nos nombradia, porque no nos derramemos sobre la faz de toda la tierra," seems to be formulated then as a project of insertion in history. Zumthor writes:

> Name is a word applied to a being or a thing and which from then onwards is theirs, constitutive of its essence, conferring on it a power, signifying internally a call for life. "Making themselves" a name, on the part of a people as on the part of a hero, is to reclaim a right to existence, to affirm the eternity of an active presence among human communities and in the eyes of gods: that which we would call to enter into History.[74]

Genesis 17 says that men shall not be able to name themselves. This name, this power of language, as Abraham's example teaches, must come from God. The Babelian verse on the name is not developed in the *Alexandre*, though that our poet knew the passage is beyond discussion. Perhaps one might think of direct quotation of it as unnecessary, a form of *abbreviatio*, since the parallels between Babel and Alexander have been explicitly established and a reflection on Alexander's fame is repeated throughout the poem. "To make a name for themselves" an expression that in the Babel episode refers to a collective entry into history, can very well mean in this case an exemplary *individual* entry: that of Alexander's. To make a name for oneself, for Alexander, contradicts once again what is supposed to be the Christian moral of the poem, modifying the teaching to convey that pride is a *necessary* sin if one wishes to enter history, another form of fame.[75]

There are other meanings that overlap that of history in the word "estoria" in the poem, those of painting/sculpture and the most familiar of anecdote, plot, or story. Of the three most important references to the Tower, two are cases of ekphrasis, while the third corresponds to a historical digression that could have been taken from an equally ekphrastic situation in the *Roman d'Alexandre*. The Tower, then, in maps or figured as a minimal story within the narration of Babylon, serves also as a reminder of different forms of history, of the worldly and the human in the perspective of salvation.

After sin comes punishment: the confusion of languages and the dispersion of humanity. Eco writes that from the medieval period onward, "babelian iconography has been oriented to the exhibition at the foreground or background of human labor, construction workers, pulleys, freight elevators, plummets, rulers, mortar techniques, etcetera," and wonders if Dante's idea in *De vulgari eloquentia*, where the poet gives a particular version of the linguistic confusion in which the result of Babel is more a proliferation of technical languages than the birth of linguistic diversity, "a concept of the division of labor accompanied by a division of linguistic labor," might not come from a contact of the poet with iconography of his time.[76] The interpretation of the passage through the centuries would in some cases result, as it did for Luther, in the identification between people and language, an idea repeated in Hegel. Eco points out that in Hegel, however, this sort of foundation of the link that articulates the state is presented also as an "almost sacred celebration of human labor,"[77] making way for the *particular* idea of the state, that is, its peculiarity of *not* being universal in this sense since it allows for the existence of different nations, but which is universal in terms of social, political, scientific, and even ethical origins. Not only is there then a division between nations after Babel, but a scission within the interior of any community. From that limit or even onward, community would be forever marked by the division, and one might recall now the stanza in the long reference to Babel in the *Alexandre* in which "si uno pedía agua, el otro daba cal/el que pediá mortero, dávanle el cordal," and so on, to rethink it as a reflection on technical languages. History proper, according to this line of thought, commences with the confusion of language, the division of nations, and the scission of community. Many elements from the description of Babylon noted here hold up this interpretation beyond the iconographic influence that can be traced in the descriptions of port and city at the feet of the Tower. The recurrent use of ekphrasis and the use of "estoria" in reference to a "libro," probably a manuscript source, point us as well to visual stimuli from marginalia, which we have seen before being relocated from the margins to the body of the text.

Almost imperceptibly, there is a progression in an emphasis from *confusio* to *divisio*. There is already in Dante, as noted above, such an emphasis on the division of labour through technical languages. If one thinks of these technical languages as *mesteres*, types of mastery, the idea of "obligation laid upon every man, in his station, to make himself master of his 'sciences' and put it to service, to make it his lifework, or ministry," of *mester* as *menester*, then that leads us to the best known and most debated stanzas of the *Libro de Alexandre*, those at the beginning of the poem, in which the specificity of this new mastery or task is proclaimed.[78] There, *mester* should recall not only the final form of this task but the series of techniques implied, and most particularly, beyond syllable count and rhymed cursus, to the specific task of the translator/author of the *Alexandre*, in the compilation, collation, translation and rewriting of materials, in the infusing of properly rhetorical functions into the new language minted here, in the conjuring up of a world composed of pasts made present.

The definiton of mester as "ministry" evokes the ideas of pride and community, of individuality and collectivity in tension, combining ethics and justice common to classical thought and present in Christian thought, mentioned in the New Testament (Colosians 3:1–11, Luke 12:13–21),[79] but especially analysed in the expression of "exceeding oneself" in Plato's *Republic* (343A, 19), and in Aristotle's *Nicomachean Ethics*, which would only be translated towards the end of the thirteenth century but which circulated fragmentarily in Iberia before then. G.M.A. Grube, in the notes to his translation, writes that *pleonectein* is an important notion throughout Plato's *Republic* in its connections to pleonexia, which is that into which one falls when attempting to overcome everyone else, taking and receiving more each time. Pleonexia is in itself and at the same time the cause of injustice (359C, 35), for to attempt to surpass everyone makes the individual try to obtain that which belongs to others, what is not "one's own." This concept is contrasted with "doing or having one's own," which is, or is the cause of, justice (434A, 109; 441E, 117), in which relations between collectivity and individual, between labour and ethics, remain clear. The passages in the *Republic* point directly to the restriction to which every man should be subjected in terms of how his capacities, his *technè*, his "mastery," naturally show him these limits: "there are no two identical people by nature, but in all there are innate differences that make them apt for an occupation," Socrates tells Adimantus, "therefore, when one produces more, better and most easily is when each person does one job according to his aptitudes, at the right time, and without busying himself with anything else."[80] Any attempt at transposing, overcoming, surpassing the limits of individual specialization is the root of evil, it is injustice, error – sin, in clerical terms. Here, excess is linked not especially to pride, but to greed as the closest translation of "pleonexia," while the move in the *Libro de Alexandre* from an emphasis on pride to an emphasis on greed is directly related to the infraction of the duty of keeping to one's own mastery: the ban on breaking the limits of individual *technè*, which bears consequences not only for the debates over *clerecía* and *juglaría*, but for the task of translating itself.[81]

Pride and greed of humanity, divine punishment revealed as confusion, the Tower and linguistic unity belong thus to the series of events that precede history and anticipate it, history understood as the beginning of a great wound, as what exists *after Babel*. After Babel, this border of history in which we live under the principle of difference has become the figure of a new reflection on the (im)possibilities of unity. From George Steiner to Walter Benjamin or Jacques Derrida, as I mentioned, Babel is the name of translation, of the attempt to restore or celebrate the spilling of humanity, thinking less of the fabrication of a tower than of the formulation of a name.

Centuries ago, in northern Iberia, someone debated these possibilities while trying to imagine what place he as cleric, as master of a language, as mediator, would have in what he anticipated to be new, turbulent, cosmopolitan, wondrous times. He wrote himself, his present and future in a history of the greatest king of all, Alexander, bringing the past and the present together in the common process of *translatio studii et imperii*. There, the languages of Babylon speak of the possibilities of nation building through great, learned monarchs in spectacular and diverse urban settings. They speak of space and conquest, of military enterprises; they speculate on Castile's power through the many languages that cross it, of diversity as resource, of multiplicity as wealth. The builders of Babel whisper about self-naming and history making, they incite and warn of pride and fame, they cast the shadow of confusion and the splitting of community. Babel and Babylon conjure up a tower not of ivory but of words, words uttered in the vernacular, and the emphasis on rhetoric in both historiography and wisdom literature from this point onward, within a variety of other genres reflecting on monarchy and the court, on nobility and the preservation of power, inevitably points to a small giant, a humble Aristotle – a chancellor, a courtly scribe, a counsellor – a master of words wisely composed and properly said.

3 Coins on the Desk

The carefully composed and craftily recited stanzas of the thirteenth-century *mester de clerecía* are always mindful to provide readers with glimpses of Iberia in descriptions and comparisons but especially through curious formulations and eloquent rewritings.[1] These incite the reader to reflect upon the vernacular regime of literary composition by clerics that began to develop such a corpus in the thirteenth century, and on the tools and contexts that helped to shape it. The use of Iberoromance, for us modern readers – in contrast with the syntactical Latinisms – brings with it an unproblematized feeling of transparency of the context in which the works of *mester de clerecía* are imagined to have been produced, a genre of which the *Libro de Alexandre* is a key studious point of origin. The vernacular, however, one must be reminded, is here being "invented" through this genre as a language of culture, and therefore any irruption of the everyday world must be thought of as a creative intervention in the formulation of a learned Iberoromance. Next to an emphasis on this Latinate syntax and recitation techniques that underline the corpus' clerical production, the emergence of quotidian phrases, vocabulary, and figures of medievalization but especially of Iberization makes these texts a privileged site to study the articulation of the varied phenomena that from economics to the linguistic, from Aristotle to technology, come to revolutionize medieval culture from the twelfth century onward.

In this chapter I want to focus on the effects of a series of rapid economic transformations in the twelfth and thirteenth century that were made thinkable and workable through newly invented formulations and operations that find a way into literature. While I will not attempt a history of these economic changes in Iberia, I will make use of fragments of such a history as I see it being worked through these texts, at many points exercising an influence that I see turned into a novel rhetoric. One of the main arguments that this chapter will make is that the anxiety or ambiguity that many scholars have seen in *mester de clerecía* is a direct result of literature's engagement with economic changes, most visible in the story of coinage in Iberia and the particular events that take place in this particular field of economics in the same period as *mester de clerecía* will emerge. While of course these economic changes are the result of a myriad of processes, some of which are directly related to Iberia and some of which are not, it is the particular engagement with economic figuration within literature that I want to explore in this chapter.

In terms of coinage, for instance, Peter Spufford summarizes general problems in the Middle Ages, beginning with the abandonment of the Roman monetary system based on the gold *solidus* and *tremissis*, the silver *silique*, and the copper *nummus*. Of particular interest to our purposes in this chapter is not the story of the coins themselves, but Spufford's remarks on the disappearance of copper coins as directly related to the disappearance of urban life, where copper coins facilitated small transactions.[2] A series of demographic disasters, next to the lack of gold coins coming in through taxes or the shortage of gold to pay soldiers, was to result in payments in land on the one hand and a reduction in the demand for luxury goods on the other. By the end of the seventh century, no administration or army was paid regularly in gold, and one must assume payment was *in specie*. This loss of function of gold and silver coins as commercial tools is directly related to the practice of hoarding or treasuring gold coins, and the effects on the meaning of gold and silver, especially within literature, are here very evident. Such a panorama, generalized in Western Europe, was mirrored in the Iberian Peninsula with a negligible numismatic contribution from the Visigothic period. At the fall of the Caliphate in 1031, the Taifa kingdoms maintained a precarious monetary economy in the frontier zones through the payment of *parias*[3] to Castile, above all, while Galicia and León would benefit from the commerce brought by the pilgrimage route to Santiago, marking a difference in Iberia with respect to the rest of Western Europe. In León and Castile, Rodamilans points out, the *parias* would begin to flow in the second half of the eleventh century, and their influence would be palpable already in the second half of Fernando I's reign (1035–65).[4] The greatest changes would come about with the conquest of Toledo, and with the restructuring of state administration that Alfonso VI would implement.

In *mester de clerecía*, I will argue, there is a palpable anxiety provoked by the simultaneous presence of two exchange systems, a gift economy and a profit economy, with conflicting political and moral consequences that permeate the structure itself of the poems, a simultaneity brought about by the changes in economic flows. The inquiry into the language and the economic operations brought into play in *mester de clerecía* – *Libro de Alexandre*, *Libro de Apolonio,* and the *Libro de Fernán González* – set against other texts of the period, such as the *Poem of the Cid*, will allow us to see a much more abstract and pervasive intrusion of economics into the language of literature, as economics – and one should be able to say capitalism – can be seen to begin a slow but intense process of appropriation of the language of the epic, a pervasive process with such success that many of these expressions, concepts, operations of epic poetry seem today to be much more at home in the language of economics than that of fiction.

Short-Change, Loose Change

A reader of the *Libro de Alexandre* will be immediately struck by the frequency with which the vernacular, quotidian phrase "not worth an *x*" is used in this and other poems of *clerecía*, by a wide variety of characters and in multiple situations.[5] It is in this phrase that the context of exchange as such can be seen at its most basic level, in the possibility of substituting the ending words in this phrase, "no vale un," *not worth an*, with terms designating either coins, animals, vegetables, or fruits: *meaja, pepión, sueldo, dinero* (coins); *paja* (straw); *arveha* (bean); *gorrión* (swallow); *corteza* (bark); *figo* (fig); *langosta* (grasshopper); *puerro* (leek). The possibility of substitution in a lexicalized phrase such as this one, as measuring something or someone's worth, is symptomatic of that exchangeability of things that the measure of a coin has reintroduced, using itself as part of that list, illustrating what economic historians call *commodity money*, where coins are seen – and used – as commodities themselves.

As I anticipated above, in the Castilian and Leonese kingdoms of Iberia, the renewed payment of *parias* by Taifa kingdoms in the mid-twelfth century, next to the novel expansion campaigns that lasted through the reigns of Sancho III (1157–58), Alfonso VIII (1158–1214), and Ferdinand I of León (1157–88), would be able to sustain an economic revival that was materialized in the striking of the first gold coin known for Castile, the "áureo alfonsí" or "morabatino alfonsí."[6] Even though this coin would stop being minted by 1209, signalling a new depression, and was to be substituted by coins of lesser weight by 1214, the establishment of the wool industry in Castile, known as the *mesta* and crucial to the peninsula's economy well into the sixteenth century, assured the continued development of new economic figures of varied success, an economic growth artistically mirrored in the constructions of the cathedrals of Burgos (1221) and Toledo (1226), and in later thirteenth-century monumental enterprises as the Castilian economy burgeoned once more under Fernando el Santo and Alfonso X.[7]

But the story I want to tell here is not one of the luxury of gold spilling over the frontier zones hailing from Sudan to northern kingdoms, poured into monumental projects or royal treasuries, whether in fantasy or in reality. The most interesting economic story of *mester de clerecía* is not one trading in *maravedíes*, but one negotiating in small change. According to a study by Mercedes Rueda, the Tolleta coin, a billon piece, summarizes the history of the introduction of fractional currency in the Castilian-Leonese economy, emblematizing the history of coinage and economic revolution in late medieval Iberia. Coined at first by Alfonso I or Alfonso II, the Tolleta coin was probably also minted under Sancho III with the same type, and again under Alfonso VIII. Even if in the first third of the twelfth century its circulation – and that of its fraction, the *óbolo* – was relatively limited, it nevertheless allowed the majority of the population to participate in everyday transactions. In short, it was the small coin that revolutionized exchange, it was the fractionary coin that made commerce possible for everyone, and consequently, it was that coin which effected changes in the negotiation of meaning.

At the end of the twelfth century, the Tolleta *dinero* became a fraction of the Burgalese *dinero*, when *óbolos* disappear. By the first half of the thirteenth century, it was the only fractional coin circulating in Castile. During the reign of Alfonso VIII the Tolleta *dinero* was identified with *pepiones* as a fraction of the Burgalese *dinero*. It would once again be coined under Fernando III, and circulate at the beginning of Alfonso X's reign. Between 1214 and 1263 it would be the only billon *dinero* to circulate in Castile, old and new mintings circulating together. Following a distinct path from that of the coining of gold, this billon coin was indeed what the majority of the population would think of as money, a coin especially documented in areas that serve as context for the production of *mester de clerecía*: the Road to Santiago, what were the recently enlarged territories under Christian rule especially in their frontier zones, and somewhat surprisingly, the area of Soria.[8]

In the opinion of J. Gautier Dalché, the coining of this billon piece is the result of both a need for fractionary money for commercial use and the scarcity of silver Almoravid coin. There have been numerous interpretations of the role and relations between Arabic and Christian coinage circulating simultaneously throughout this period in Iberia. While some argue that the billon coins complement the panorama of Arabic coinage that was already circulating in the peninsula, others see in this billon coin a wink at a northern European alliance by way of image and economy in the hand of Alfonso VI. Within Toledo, especially in the years around 1085, the situation is particularly difficult to assess. Most scholars, however, agree on distinguishing two economic zones until the year 1130 when Toledo will serve as door between the areas. North of the Duero, dominated by agriculture and herding, the use of coinage is more restricted and the silver *sueldo* serves as money of account. South of the central mountain range, the gold Almoravid *dinar* circulates physically and is central to commercial activity in Toledo and for transactions with Islamic Spain. Through such transactions and by way of Toledo, "when Alfonso VIII (1158–1214) decides to coin the gold *maravedís* (1172), they had circulated already in Castile and León for some thirty years, even though these kingdoms had only coined billon since 1085." Alfonso's imitation of the Almoravid dinar in the *morabetino alfonsí*, both in weight and types, as Aben Saad of Murcia ceases to coin *dinars*, signifies the supplementation of a Carolingian silver system represented by the *dineros* with an Islamic system based on the gold *dinar*.[9]

Fernando Rodamilans Ramos interprets Alfonso VI's coining of *dirhams* in 1085 in the mint of Toledo as a clear political gesture, but sees in the change of this mint to that of billon *dineros*, following Carolingian models, a much more radical gesture. The Almoravid invasion temporarily blocked the flow of *dinars* into the Christian kingdoms, but soon after an Almoravid gold *dinar* or *morabetino* made its appearance, and two monetary regions were formed in the Castile-León kingdom, with the river Duero as border, as mentioned above. To the north, with Burgos as centre, a silver-based monetary economy used *billon* and a European money of account (alternatively, *sueldos*, *mencales*, and *morabetinos*), while in the south, centred first in Toledo and then in Seville, a gold-based monetary economy and the Andalusi system of account was maintained. In Castile, the measuring pattern was the *marco* or *media libra*, equivalent to 230 grams of silver (as was also the case in Portugal and England, but not in other places). In relation to this measure was the ratio of silver in each of the coins, a proportion named *talla*. Devaluation or debasement, a practice favoured by kings, would be mostly based on a modification of this relationship. The more pieces coined with a silver mark, the more devalued the coin would be even if its face, its image, was the same, because the law or quantity of silver in it would be reduced.[10] In medieval Castile, the purity or "good law" of a silver coin was measured in *dineros*, so that twenty-four *dineros* equaled pure silver. To complicate matters, this same term, *dinero*, would be used as a generic term for *billon* coin. As different economic practices surrounding coinage delved into the more delinquent, from devaluation to counterfeiting, the misrepresentation of the purity of a given coin would be exercised primarily on this, the most common of currencies – and the most plurivalent of terms.[11] The slipperiness of such a term, from a generic common coin to the measure of its "law" or "truth," is particularly interesting as the term is made to set the ambiguous equivalences of meaning in *mester de clerecía*, in particular in the *Libro de Alexandre*.[12]

I further suggest that this exchangeability in the market, this basic equivalence of everything to the abstract measure of *dinero* – increasingly abstract as coins, first, devalued by legal practices such as seigneurage or illegal ones such as counterfeiting or clipping, and then paper money, enter the market – is a process parallel to and intimately related to conceptual developments in literary composition.[13] Not only do fruits, animals, vegetables, and other things show up in the paradigmatic list of the phrase "not worth an *x*," but also coins, emphasizing a process that will end up establishing the equivalence of everything by the universal measure of money. Exchangeability at the level of vocabulary points to an aesthetic structure that is already governed by economic laws. As both the law and as subject to its law, these small coins – the *pepiones*, *meajas*, *dineros* that appear so often in the poems – are in terms of subversion and of articulation of ways of thinking productive in inverse proportion to their value as coins. Inside language, such an ambiguous reformulation of relations has vital consequences for literary composition. The exchange between words and coins is, in fact, wrapped up in the Greek word *seme*, which contains both of these meanings, a coincidence that provoked a long debate on the propriety of economic and intellectual exchange from Heraclitus's formulations to Plato's criticism of sophists as merchants of thought. The Greek association between types of politics, such as tyranny, or styles, such as the tragic, and coinage brought with it a political reflection and the suspicion, perhaps, of the coining of words as a politics in itself. The possibility or even the perception of a politics in the rhetorical use of economics within literary composition is what I would like to point at in these pages in the last instance, prompted by the expressions I referred to above, such as "non vale nuestro reino una vil cañavera" (our kingdom is not worth a stick), in which a sceptre is sarcastically alluded to and value is symbolically both rendered and debased.[14]

The process of exchangeability penetrates deep into the structure of literary composition as such throughout the pages of the *Libro de Alexandre*. This is not a question of themes, but one of structure, as Marc Shell noted in writing about the relations between these discourses: "This participation of economic form in literature and philosophy, even in the discourse about truth, is defined neither by what literature and philosophy talk about (sometimes money, sometimes not) nor by why they talk about it (sometimes for money, sometimes not) but rather by the figural, rhetorical interaction between economic and linguistic symbolization and production."[15] In the first verse of the *Alexandre*, a service is offered that, binding the listener/reader to a payment (or not), offers the mastery of a trade and forms that are different from those of *juglaría*, and that will give to whomever wishes to listen *gran placer*, great pleasure, beyond the utilitarian goal set in the background.

The relation between merchandise/trade and words, suggested by the offering of the poem as a service to be paid, is underlined in the body of the poem by the author of the *Alexandre*. This identification between the knowledge of the cleric-poet and the merchandise of any trader was split into contradicting associations in the Middle Ages. On the one hand, it meant praise of poets as philosophers with the title of *sophists* or *sophus* in the times of Charlemagne, but on the other hand it echoed Plato's accusations of sophists as being merchants of thought.[16] Medieval culture not only supported the identification between merchandise and words, market and knowledge, but also evaluated this identification in clashing ways. In between these basic ties between the market and the task of clerics, a whole series of correlating metaphors can be put to work. It is here that I want to locate the relation between economy and *superbia* or pride, established not only through a historical-economic context but more so as poetic causality that, within the narrative, ends up tying together the different themes woven in the *Libro de Alexandre*.[17] For if the identification between knowledge (or talent) and accumulated wealth in a sinful sense was already proposed by the Bible, as Ernst Robert Curtius noted,[18] hoarding – keeping from market circulation – either knowledge, talent, or money was qualified as a sort of greed, a sin that the poet of the *Alexandre* specifically distances himself from, even if in topical terms, at the beginning of the *Libro* when he states that it is his duty to disseminate knowledge, a knowledge here identified with the poem: "deve de lo que sabe omne largo seer/si non podrié en culpa e en riebto caer" (man should be generous with what he knows, for if he were not, he could fall into sin and error).[19]

The poet of the *Libro de Alexandre* is caught in the double bind of the conflicting evaluations of the identity between market and knowledge. His craft, self-defined, is a mastery over words, the negotiation of their meanings, their very enunciation as a source of pleasure and expression of the obligation to disseminate knowledge – that is, his task is that of preserving and transmitting a culture. To remain effective, productive, alive, this language must be *in* the world, and in the world, among other things, there is money, coming to inhabit language and its interstices, modifying relations, affecting signification. Mastery over money, but especially over its rhetorical possibilities, is thus also the task of the cleric. At a point when such mastery is just being claimed as a cleric's *doing*, this catch-22 is expressed as uneasiness, discomfort, and contradiction.

If Nietzsche (or a long host of modern readers) claims to reveal the morality of the language of capital, what a poem like the *Libro de Alexandre* shows is that morality is not added on later as a supplement of capitalism; it is not that capitalism is moralized, but that the language of capital itself is, at its inital core, a language of epic morality. There is no origin where morality and capitalism are separate entities whose languages are later to converge and which one would hope to disentangle in the modern world; capitalism is moral because its language is the language of epic. In the case of Spanish it is clear, as we will see from the *Poem of the Cid* to the *Libro de Fernán González*, that this coining of capitalism's language with the currency of epic built the moral dimension of capital in its very linguistic roots and imprinted it with the prestigious image of historic deeds. The contemporary gesture or need to "blast out" of this suture through absolute expenditure, anarchy, withdrawal, or silence can only remind us of capitalism's uncanny ability to restructure itself by appropriating emergent dimensions. If in these medieval texts the moral dimension of economics can still be isolated in processes separate from those of economics, as a profit or remnant that transcends it, it is because the mechanisms of transcendence, whether religious (as salvation) or secular (as fame), are still available and imaginable as separate. Our times, however, have seen the institutionalization of both these mechanisms through charity and celebrity, recapitalized dimensions of moral value, reinscribed into the vanity of the world, and it can be no coincidence that retirement, that delayed province of mortality, can now be invested with epic dimensions of new exploits, through variously coloured pills, adventures in the extreme, or other refashionings of self that amplify the world and blur the mortal horizon.

Though it might seem at first sight that the anthropologist Marcel Mauss, when formulating his theories on the gift based on the study of communal practices of southeast Asia, was not thinking of the Middle Ages, the example with which he opens *The Gift*, a Scandinavian *edda*, and the subject of the reflection with which he closes, Arthur and the Round Table, put together a medieval frame for his study. In recent years, medievalism has seen in Mauss's theory of the gift a useful approach to the representation and effects of practices on the construction of literary discourse. Thus, for instance, Marc Shell devotes one of his chapters in *Money, Language, and Thought* to the analysis of gift exchange in the work of Chrétien de Troyes.

The point of Mauss's theory is that the object exchanged in a society not only has an economic value, but more importantly, it establishes a deep psychic relation in which whoever gives a gift acquires a form of power over the receiver, who is then obliged, constrained not only to accept the gift but to return the "gesture." According to Mauss, it is contemporary capitalist society that insists on separating gifts from commerce, confusing gifts with charity or donations. As Judith Kellog has observed, with an eye to medieval texts, from the analysis of different forms of organizing the exchange of gifts and the articulation of this system with the economic organization specific to a society one can arrive at starkly different notions of community.[20] After Mauss, Georges Bataille took this analysis further, introducing the notion of expenditure and its role in the creation of hierarchies, relations, discourses. I want to contextualize the political economy of language in the *Libro de Alexandre* between these concepts by investigating what goes on in other texts produced in the same period .

At the turn of the thirteenth century medieval Iberia begins to see the economic effects of the military success of the Christian northern kingdoms, for the victories in 1144 suppose the reactivation of the payment of *parias*, which guarantees the flow of African gold – closed to the rest of Europe, which must keep following a silver standard – and the possibility of the first coin known to Castile is realized, as discussed above.[21] The representation of the effects of a new economy, visible in cathedrals, miniatures, stained glass, was also to be found in literature. Thirteenth-century literature, but perhaps most particularly fiction, offers a panorama of the distinct possibilities facing this new economy. As an effect, in part, of the economic changes affecting not only Iberia but all of Europe, with new techniques and instruments that can no longer be condemned or censored from the pulpit but that make their way into the ideology and the law, practices such as interest and profit, loans and currency exchange, exchange and use values, and other operations studied by economic history that enter into vocabulary and figuration. It is also the thirteenth century in which, through a language that finds expression in *mester de clerecía*, the courtly ideology studied around the Alfonsine "cultural concept," to barter with an idea of Francisco Márquez Villanueva, the most influential phenomenon in medieval Iberia until the end of the fifteenth century is articulated.[22] Economics, then, the invention of a literary language, and the discursive rehearsals of a politics are what I want to integrate in the following pages as a panoramic view on the gift, surveying two examples outside of *mester de clerecía*, the *Poem of the Cid* and the *Libro de Fernán González*, to focus on the *Libro de* Alexandre as the key text.

Coined Words

One of the most visible plots in the *Poem of the Cid* is that of gifts sent by the protagonist to Alfonso. Their value increases as the Cid ensures for himself an economic independence in exile regardless – or perhaps because – of the break of the vassal bond, brought about by royal ire instigated by rumours. To list the gifts: there are first thirty saddled horses and swords (vv. 813–18), called a gift (*don*) by the Cid and by Minaya and Alfonso a denigrating synonym, *presentaja*; the second embassy consists in a hundred horses, saddled and bridled (vv. 1270–4), once again called *presentaja* by Minaya for the king to take as *prenda*, a term that is also a synonym for gift, while Alfonso receives them as a true gift – *don* – from the Cid; the third embassy brings the tent of the Moroccan king, with two hundred horses (vv. 1789–94) as *presentajas* – this time clearly ironic, for the luxury of the gifts is dazzling – which Alfonso receives and sends his thanks for "que tal don me a enviado, aún vea ora que de mi sea *pagado*" (who has sent me such a gift, the time will come that will be payed/pleased by me). The translation undoes the double meaning of the original, in which the word *pagado* fuses the

meanings of payment and pleasure. When the Cid receives the messenger the double meaning is reprised, for the hero demands to know:
"¿cómmo son las saludes de Alfonso mio señor?, ¿si es pagado o reçibió
el don?"; vv. 1921–192 ("how is the health of my lord Alfonso? Is he
payed/pleased, has he received/accepted the gift?"). Within Mauss's
frame of obligation and power established by the gift exchange, the
Cid's presents are ambiguous at various levels. Perhaps – and this is
what I want to insist on – in an eloquent way they point to a transitional
moment in the economy of the gift. Even while gifts are a commonplace
of epic, the *Cid*'s unique engagement with money matters, as Joseph
Duggan noted, betrays a more insistent confrontation of a literary economy with a commercial rhetoric.

There are a number of complementary possibilities of analysis of the
Cid's gifts. If one considers Alfonso as the rightful lord of the Cid
– dismissing the possibility that exile has broken the links of vassalage – then the gift circulates in a direction opposite to the usual lord-
to-vassal, for what the Cid offers Alfonso is not a direct share of the
booty – which is what the Cid takes for himself after the battles, as lord
– but a gift offered from the hero's own possessions. From the point
of view of vassalage, it should be *largeza* or liberality, the seigneurial
generosity of Alfonso, being offered to the Cid, particularly in the form
of land, which the Cid does not need for he is obtaining it by his own
hand. Moreover, the Cid's gifts are neither symbols nor signs of something else but a pure spectacle of the Cid's newly acquired power, a
declaration of his status as potential lord in front of Alfonso and his
court. As such, one could read them as a declaration of equality, making them even more ambiguous. As the gifts increase in value and
spectacle, power over Alfonso is slowly aggregated; each time Alfonso
becomes more obligated to reciprocate, a gradation visible in the vocabulary itself used to refer to the gifts. This power indebts Alfonso to the
point that he must reconsider his decision to exile the hero, offering a
reversal as recompense, as returning the gesture, as payment. The gift is
thus forgiveness: that is where the exchange of gifts, started by the Cid,
ends its cycle, and where the moral and obligatory character of gift-
giving is evidenced, underlining the excess that guarantees Alfonso's
status and his hierarchical superiority over the Cid.

Following another line of interpretation, we can see the Cid's gifts as
key to the market economy in which profit is already exercising a fundamental and widely accepted role, that is, we should read the Cid's
gifts as a form of speculation, which is ultimately – if not continuously

– successful. This gift exchange, when one considers Alfonso's decision to exile the hero as unjust and as breaking the links of vassalage, is then a pure spectacle of power, akin to what Mauss calls potlach.

It must be remembered that the gift in itself, according to Mauss, does not have as a goal the creation of personal wealth, but that it is its mere circulation which is meant to sustain the seigneurial economy – the context of the *Poem* –, where what matters in the circulation of wealth is first the honour or prestige that wealth in itself provides, and in second degree the obligation of returning the gifts or even surpassing them under the penalty of losing prestige or authority. As Judith Kellog remarks, wealth in the epic thus evidences its symbolic value over its material value. It not only grants status within a community but binds, forces the individual to continue the cycle not as a direct payment but as reciprocal generosity.[23] In this way, gift exchange can regulate social relations through moral obligations, while the use of gifts as speculation, seeking something beyond reciprocity and sustainability of the community, breaks with this model.

The gifts in the *Poem of the Cid* underline the seigneurial bond as expected, even if by negation and in the opposite direction, but they also point to the possibility of creating this bond by different means. The gifts resemble Georges Bataille's notion of expenditure, where wealth proves its utility precisely when lost or spent, when publicly used to produce not more wealth but status, nobility, honour, and the like. In this line of argumentation, it is crucial to note that the Cid's first act as exile, when tricking the lenders into giving him money, is to invent a wealth he has spent ("espeso lo he"); indeed, he invents this spent wealth as barter to what he has lost, an expenditure that grants him enough credit to receive money from Rachel and Vidas. The Cid creates status by "spending" wealth, and this status thus produces more wealth for him. Thus, the Cid is a man who is self-made, but who subjects himself to a seigneurial bond as a gesture to the community that sustains this ideology. That is why he is not a rebel but a hero. If the Cid is to be read as subverting some code, it is not one of the nature of politics, or of hierarchy, but one of the process of creation of political bonds, deeply indebted to economic figuration.

Towards the second half of the twelfth century, the *Libro de Fernán González* shows marked differences in attitudes to economics. From the beginning, the link established from the fiction of the text to its material existence, that is, the relation between the protagonist count and the monastery of San Pedro de Arlanza where the book is written, the same monastery which is to receive the count in body and soul along with a generous donation, is one of direct, unambiguous economic relations: "Si Dios aquesta lid me dexa arrancar,/quiero todo el mio quinto a este lugar dar;/demas, quando muriere, aqui me soterrar,/que mejore por mi sienpre este lugar." (If God this battle allows me to win/I want to give this place my fifth;/moreover, when I die, I want to be buried here/so that forever this place benefits from me; st. 247), emphasizing how monasteries saw in poems such as the *Fernán González* a way to attract audiences and their pockets to their spheres of influence.

A reading of the *Fernán* along these lines can be extended beyond the opening lines not only from a vocabulary, abundant as it is, like its partners in *mester de clerecía*, in *preçios, mercados, dineros, valías*, and so on, but also from a main structure based on loss and recuperation, sack and booty, tribute and independence. A sample: the *Fernán* literally begins with the narration of the loss of Spain and its slow recuperation. Or take the protagonist's description by Nuño Laino, as he haranges the men to search for the hero by saying that "veamos que preçio damos a un cavero;/nos somos bien trezientos e él solo señero,/e sin el non fazemos valía d'un dinero:/pierde omne buen preçio en poco de mijero" (let's see what price we give for a knight,/we are three hundred and he is only one,/and without him we do not amount to a penny:/a man loses price in less than a mile; st. 666). Here, the hero's worth is first measured in number of men, and then this worth is repeated negatively, this time reducing the value of each of the men in the hero's absence to a similar formulation as that found in the *Libro de Alexandre*, in that it is a value less than that of a common coin. Finally, in the last verse of the stanza the value of a man assessed in coin is tested again, now by means of the territory in which this value holds its worth. The language and practice of currency is here crucial to the symbolic hermeneutics of the harangue. The speech is well received by the men, who seem to agree that their worth is predicated upon and guaranteed by the hero. However, what is most interesting in this episode is that they proceed to craft the stone image of the count as material substitute for his body, to then swear upon it and begin the quest for their lord. It is here that the symbolic value that real monetary culture must have (as opposed to the use of money as commodity in itself) is replicated in terms of epic worth, establishing the terms for a shared figuration. This figuration, to work, must not only bleed from economics into literature but must be shared by both clerics and audiences, conveying the signs of a culture that is all too familiar with these overlaps and rhetorical flourishes.

It is, nonetheless, the well-known episode in the *Libro de Fernán González* of the sale of the horse and the goshawk that holds the most potential for illustrating the radical changes that have taken place between economic and rhetoric from the beginning to the end of the thirteenth century.[24] Stanza 576 begins the episode, as King Sancho expresses his admiration of goshawk and horse and his wish to buy them from Count Fernán. The count, in an apparent gesture of courtesy, steps back from the transaction and instead proposes a gift, "mas quiero vos los dar" (but I want to give them to you). King Sancho immediately refuses the gift, attempting to subtract himself from the obligation of retribution and from the position of thankfulness and prestige that must be returned, a situation discussed above in relation to the *Poem of the Cid*. In the *Libro de Fernán González*, the king refuses to participate in the exchange system, establishing that (a) he considers himself of a different status with respect to the count and is therefore not in the same community of political bonds sustained by a gift economy; and (b) he will not consent to the count's attempt to subject him to a gift obligation. From there, the king will insist on buying, offering a thousand marks in payment. The count does not oppose the sale this time but instead speeds through the transaction, sets a date for its taking place, and in the last verse of st. 578 reveals why he has facilitated this option: his terms include a condition that if the payment does not come at the set date, it will double for each day of delay. This condition, as has been noted many times, is a highly usurous one.[25] The king's debt after three years becomes unimaginable, and lacking anyone to counsel him, he offers the only solution that comes to mind as substitute for payment: the independence of Castile from León.[26]

Beyond the strictly economical, what is striking about the ruse is that the count sets a trap for the king that fully relies on modes of perception of the acceptability of economic strategies within certain social circles. Thus, while the king believes he has averted a gift relation he finds unequal by refusing Fernán González's present, he strikes a deal, a market transaction (*un mercado*, the text calls it), in which he has no experience. The king cannot appraise his own wealth, that is, he has no concept of the credit he is able to guarantee, nor does he seem able to gauge the consequences of defaulting on his credit contract.

Within the seigneurial framework of the gift economy, the king's actions are wholly justified. What the text evidences is that the economic context in which this poem is composed is one in which a gift economy and a profit economy are in coexistence and frank competition;

moreover, the profit economy wins out. While the king represents the first of these, the count represents the second, with the added advantage of being familiar enough with the moral rules of the gift economy to manipulate the threat of obligation and the hierarchies implied in his favour, pushing the king to a different exchange in which he has no experience. The credit relation to which Fernán subjects the king is also an obligation. The increment of this obligation, and what the king fails to understand – interest – is such that it forces the king, it indebts him to the point that his hierarchy over the count is erased. Castile and the count become independent. The fiction of the usury is here a figure of politics.

In this temporal frame, it is the differences in approach through economic means to the relation between heroes and kings that is most revealing of the attempts of fiction to deal with how economy is changing relations by exercising different modes and figurations throughout the thirteenth century. Between the trajectories of the Cid and Fernán González, which seem to be at opposing ends of a process of capitalization of social relations, the literature of *mester de clerecía* offers ambiguities and contradictory attitudes towards this process.

The passage closing the episode of the sale of horse and goshawk highlights a specific reaction of the count faced with the benefit obtained from the ever-extending payment period: "al conde mucho plogo por que atanto tardava,/entendié que avría lo que el cobdiciava,/porque tanto tardava el conde y ganava, plaziel' de voluntad (the count was very pleased the king was taking so long,/he understood he would have what he coveted,/because if the king delayed and he earned, he was pleased). The count's reiterated pleasure is not only based on the defeat of his enemy, or on the subsequent independence of Castile, but seems to reside in the very production of interest, the awareness of the increase of capital in time, that period which was qualified for most of the Middle Ages as theft.[27] So, while the Cid insists on the system of gifts as a way of indebting the king, provoking forgiveness and regaining his status, playing with the limits of the gift economy in order to reaffirm the political bonds through the economic process, Fernán González's wit consists in the affective manipulation of the system of gifts to indebt the king through the credit system and splitting the seigneurial system and the gift economy. These were precisely the terms that would define the episode for the popular imagination. In the *Mocedades de Rodrigo*, the fourteenth-century poem telling of the Cid's exploits as a youngster, which gathers in it other episodes, among them the most important events of Fernán González's story, the episode of the sale is completed in this way:

> "Rrey, non verné a vuestras cortes   a menos de ser pagado
> del aver que me devedes   de mi azor e de mi cavallo."
> Quando contaron el aver,   el rrey non podía pagarlo:
> tanto creçió el gallarýn   que lo non pagaría al regnado.
> Venieron abenencia   el rrey e el conde lozano
> que quitasse a Castilla: el conde fue mucho pagado,
> plógol al conde   quando oyó este mandado.
> Assý sacó a Castilla   el buen conde don Ferrnando,
> aviendo guerra   con moros e con christianos,
> a toda parte,   de todo su condado.

("King, I will not come to your courts unless I am paid/for what you owe me for my goshawk and my horse."/When they counted the treasure, the king could not pay:/so much had the interest grown that the entire kingdom would not be enough./They came to an agreement, the king and the count/that he would leave Castile: the count was thus paid,/pleased was the count when he heard this decree./That is how he pulled out Castile, the good count don Fernando,/warring with Moors and Christians,/everywhere, in all his county.)

The count is, at the end, both paid and pleased with politics and economics tied up in his rhetorical abilities to negotiate, and so he continues, the *Mocedades* claims, to push Castile forward.

Speculation

In between the *Cid* and the *Fernán* lie the learned exercises of clerics to write fiction in Spanish, making use of a number of tools that lie beyond words and translation, tools that on the desk urge the cleric to move beyond and within the monastery and the court to reproduce stories in an Iberian context. Within the frame established by the contrasts between the acceptability of exchange systems in the *Cid* and the *Fernán*, the *Alexandre* and the *Apolonio* propose different figures, that is, different operations of economics made to work within thought and language to make sense of reality while serving the cleric's purposes. It is to these two poems that I turn now.

From the beginning of the poem, as I have anticipated, the poet of the *Alexandre* establishes his own role in the presentation of the text as one of economic exchange. Within the narrative, the plot itself is also structured in economic terms. Thus, the initial presentation of Alexander's main enemy, Darius, is situated in the context of debt:

> Füeron los de Greçia,   fasta essa sazón,
> vassallos tributarios   del rey de Babilón:
> avién a dar a Dario   sabida enfurçión:
> avienlo d'endurar;   que quisiessen o non.   (st. 22)

(The kings of Greece were up to this point/tributary vassals of the king of Babylon;/they had to give Darius the known forced sum,/they had to put up with it whether they wanted to or not.)

This debt becomes the original motivation and the initial strength (and worth, for *valer* means both) of Alexander.[28] Beyond the multiple linguistic registers that give away an economic meaning, from ambiguities and multiple meanings of words like *valor, precio, dar crédito,* and the like, I will focus here on a moment of speculation that in my eyes contains and anticipates the central theme of pride and the end, itself ambiguous, of the *Libro de Alexandre*.

In the episode following the antagonist's presentation, we are told of Aristotle's advice to the young Alexander as the latter questions the usefulness of knowledge to face the moral and tributary debt his people are subjected to. Aristotle proposes a long list, marked by different levels of exchangeability such as those I have mentioned before, with a particular emphasis on giving, on gift-giving as part of the liberality that should characterize the monarch. Towards the end, however, Aristotle details a rhetorical strategy for Alexander based on the linguistic counterfeiting of something's worth in order to obtain a conquest through the credit given to Alexander's words as true and just appraisal:

> Quando los enemigos   a ojo los ovieres,
> asma su cabtenença   cuanto mejor pudieres;
> mas atrás non te fagas   del logar que sovieres
> e diles a los tos   que semejan mugeres.
> Si ellos muchos fueren,   tú di que pocos son;
> di, si son treinta mill,   que son tres mill o non;

di que por todos ellos   non dariés un pepión.
¡Sepas que a los tos plazrá de coraçón!   (st. 67–8)

(When you can see the enemy,/judge their military strategy as best you can,/but do not step back from where you are/and tell your people they seem like women.//If there are many of them, say they are few;/if they are thirty thousand, say they are three thousand or not;/say that for all of them you would not give a coin;/know that yours will be truly pleased.)

This military counterfeiting, or speculative use of information to falsify or diminish an opponent's worth, produces pleasure in Alexander's men. One later witnesses that such pleasure, obtained through an economic rhetoric that places a higher value on them, results in the "esforçamiento de los corazones" – the *strengthening of hearts* – that is, in greater courage in battle that is inversely proportional to the devaluation of the enemy. This is a process that guarantees victory. The judgment, appraisal, or measuring that the word *asmar* conveys is here transformed by Alexander into a military strategy when he changes the enemy's worth through a word that, even if not equivalent to the truth, is nonetheless given full credit. The *Libro de Alexandre* works in fact as a ten thousand-verse narration of the speculative success of the conqueror.[29] Speculation, however, always carries with it the danger that such over- or under-appraising will not be taken to be true (i.e., that the credit system fails) or that the effect sought is not the one obtained (that the market changes).

Alexander's privileged ability to convey his power in a language suffused with economic markers and operations, that is, where language is itself a form of economics, is first established as the young boy returns home from his first knightly adventures and first victory in combat against Nicolao (st. 127–41), only to find Darius's messengers collecting the tribute. Alexander proclaims the census to be over from then onward and has the messengers bring these words to Darius:

Ide dezir a Dario   – esto sea aína –:
quand' non avié Filipo   fijo en la reína,
poniele huevos d'oro   siempre una gallina;
¡quando naçió el fijo,   morïó la gallina!   (st. 143)

(Go tell Darius – and this should be done soon –/that when Philip did not have a son in the queen/a hen always gave him golden eggs;/but that when the son was born, the hen died!)

Many different conquests ensue, first as chivalric exercises, then as armed knight and crowned king. The news reaches Darius, who is not used to wars anymore, as he has become accustomed to peace. In disbelief (or discredit), and not wanting his subjects to find him faint at the prospect of confronting Alexander, Darius threatens and swears to God that he will hang Alexander and his people. He then has letters written to send to Alexander.

The letter means to dissuade Alexander from engaging in battle. Calling him a foolish youngster, Darius warns the warrior that if he chooses to continue, he will apprehend him as a petty thief, in a variation of the theme of debt that characterized their relation before the rebellion. Darius has a series of gifts accompany his letter: *pitança*, food that is given as charity; *correuela*, a leash; *pello*, a ball; and a bag. Darius provides an explanation of the gifts in the letter: the food is because Alexander is deserving of it – meaning charity, debasing Alexander into a beggar; the leash is there for Alexander to subject himself – reducing him from a king to a tributary; the ball for him to play with – dismissing him as a little boy; and the bag to put away his *dineros*, coins of little value. Two stanzas later, Darius ends the letter with these words:

¡Non sé con qué enfuerço   buelves tú tal baraja,
ca más he yo de oro   que tú non aves paja!:
¡de armas e de gentes   he mayor avantaja,
que non es marco d'oro   en contra una meaja!   (st. 785)

(I do not know why you exert yourself in this matter/as I have more gold that you have straw,/of arms and people I have as great an advantage/as a golden mark has against a penny.)

Darius here conveys his confusion at Alexander's ambition faced with an evident imbalance of power, both economic and social, between himself and Alexander. He even coins this by weighing his own power as a gold mark and Alexander's as a *meaja*, a fraction of a small coin. The letter is read to Alexander and his troops, and they react with great fear. Alexander here resorts to Aristotle's advice: he proceeds to reinterpret Darius' words, from stanzas 787–92.[30] He tells his men to be happy about the great lands and riches that are Darius's, for they are to be theirs if they win. Instead of being intimidated by them, they should be stimulated to obtain them through battle. As for the great number of Darius's followers, Alexander says:

Muchas ave de gentes,   más de las que él diz',
mas todas son gallinas   e de flaca raíz:
¡tant'osarién alçar   contra nos la çerviz
quanto contra açor   podrié fer la perdiz!   (st. 791)

(Many people he has, more than he says,/but all of them are chickens and of a skinny root,/they would as much raise against us their necks/as the partridge would be able to against the hawk.)

The debasing comparison of Darius's men to chicken and partridges is continued in the next stanza with comparable invocations of flies (against hornets) and lambs (against wolves). These sets of comparisons are epic motifs that enter Iberian medieval literature from the French epic cycles, and that are present in some form or other in the *Historia de preliis,* but what is interesting is that they serve here not only as descriptors of the battle scene but as a linguistic devaluation that is set against the verifiable materiality of land and men. While Darius's worth is visible, concrete, verifiable in objects that can be counted or measured, Alexander's power, his linguistic ability, is effective not because of its relation to the real but because of the credit his troops grant his words. Thus, Alexander's men go back to Darius's letter and relabel it as a bluff:

"¡Señor" (Alexandre) – dixieron todos –, "en todo te creemos!;
¡des aquí adelant',   nunca más dubdaremos!;
¡Sólo que tú nos vivas,   por ricos nos tenemos!;
¡Por las bafas de Dario   un figo non daremos!"   (st. 793)

(Sir – they all said – in all we give you credit;/from here on we will never doubt/fear;/if you are alive, we will consider ourselves rich,/and for Darius's bluffs we will not give a fig.)

In response to Darius, Alexander has his own letter written up. In it, he addresses the gifts explicitly:

"Los donos que me diste   te quiero esponer,
– ¡maguer loco me fazes,   sélo bien entender! –:
la bolsa sinifica   todo el tu aver,
que todo en mi mano   es aún a caer;
    la pella que es redonda,   todo'l mundo figura

– ¡sepas que será mío,   esto es cosa segura! –;
¡faré de la correa   una açota dura
con que prendré derecho   de toda tu natura."   (st. 800–1)

("The gifts you gave me I want to explain to you/– even if you take me for
a lunatic, I can understand well –;/the bag signifies all your wealth,/that
is in my hands yet to fall.//The ball, which is round, figures all the world:/
know that it will be mine, that is for sure;/I will make of the leash a strong
whip/with which I will impose the law on all of you.")

With imperial overtones, the young hero showcases his flair for interpretation. These and other words, mentioned but not rendered by
the poem, are sent to Darius. In them, through them, Alexander has
managed to alter the value of things, both material – lands and arms
and men – and symbolic – the gifts given to him. His interpretation is
not merely different, but in fact has an effect on his men that makes
things and his men even more valuable.

An exchange of letters and gifts between Darius and Alexander occurs
once more (in st. 809–19), in a competition of symbolic gifts and speculative interpretations that once again increase the value of Alexander
and his men. Darius's and Alexander's exchanges are symptomatic of
the move from symbolic exchange, related to Darius, to a profit exchange, related to Alexander, as a speculative use of language where
interpretation and credit are strategic to the figure of authority, making of speculation a rhetorical figure that those who master language
well can benefit from. For exchange as such, as some scholars assume,
is *not* discredited in the *Libro de Alexandre*. It is in fact woven seamlessly
into the discourse of power relations. It is speculation as a new form of
exchange and its dangers that the poet of the *Alexandre* feels the need to
both appropriate as part of his task and to reject, on moral grounds, as
being against nature. Thus, what the author will link to the sin of pride,
the poem's major moral lesson, will be speculation *in excess* of credit or
in the wrong market conditions.

Alexander, as we all know, dies victim of his own blindness, betrayed
by one of his, punished through the complicity of Nature and Lucifer.
His is the sin of pride, we are told, and the poet inserts a *contemptus
mundi* at this appropriate moment. The poet proclaims mistrust in the
earthly, and conversely asserts his certainty in *mortality* as a limit and
as guarantor of *morality* in the political economy of salvation. The sud-
denness of this change of heart at the end of the poem in assessing

Alexander has often been interpreted as an ambiguity on the part of the poet and his time, an ambivalence whose causes have not been clearly determined. What is at stake, I suggest, is that the author on the one hand upholds the system that binds a community together morally and socially through gift-exchange as presented in epic, that is, he values it as a system for the constitution and sustainability of power among the nobility, but on the other hand he presents the new system of profit as one especially valuable in the hands (and on the lips) of those working or dealing with language, such as himself. This ambiguity is expressed from the beginning in the association between words and money, between merchants and clerics, as I argued here, folding back onto the poet himself, reflecting on the self-conscious presentation of the task of the cleric. One must go back, then, and reconsider the service of the *mester* he offers at the beginning, its interpellation of figures of power, but especially the foreseeable profit in the mastery of this new vernacular, craftily composed, and carefully pronounced.

Brokering Cleresy

While there is in both the *Libro de Alexandre* and the *Libro de Apolonio* a persistence of the economic as frame or trope, both texts also link the economic to virtue and virtuosity in divergent directions, proposing models for sovereignty that use the economic as a tool for the crafting of power in different ways. Both stories are bound to the East, to an Oriental Mediterranean that is as geographic as it is textual and bookish, mirroring other texts in circulation at the time, such as the *Fazienda de Ultramar* or the *Semejança del mundo,* suggesting travel and, especially, staging their plots – in the case of *Alexandre,* in part, in that of *Apolonio,* in its entirety – on the sea.

For Horace, there were forbidden journeys by sea, a prohibition marked by the sea's throwing itself against the ship, protecting an original division that the journey attempted to erase. It was also Horace who introduced the idea of the "ship of state" in political rhetoric, with the ensuing Quintilian interpretation of the "tempest" as civil war, associations that in the medieval poems considered here are added to an economic dimension. Horace compared the transgression of the limit of the ocean with that of Prometheus, who stole fire, and with that of Daedalus, who violated the forbidden space of air.[31] Land remains thus the only element appropriate to man. Within this elemental framework, stepping out of the boundaries of humanity is what explicitly structures the Alexander legend, and implicitly characterizes Apolonio from the beginning of his story. Extreme danger, risk, and the promise of profit of some kind link both stories on the socio-economic side of the trope. To propose that Alexander and Apolonio constitute models for princes as they control the ships of state is implicit in this blending of metaphors, but one should mention that the clerics who propose such an association would also be proposing their own role in that metaphor as that of pilot or helmsman: Cicero, Aristotle, and Seneca proposed metaphors of state and philosophy related to navigation, so that philosophy as helmsman for the navigation of life would be in tune with both Alexander's and Apolonio's clerical education, as well as with the model for royalty, advanced by Rodrigo Jiménez de Rada, who associated the role of king with that of master through the virtue of *sapientia*.[32]

The *Libro de Apolonio* begins, as we know, with the story of King Antioco's incestuous relationship with his daughter, which he succeeds in hiding behind a complex ruse that presents suitors with the challenge of solving a series of enigmas under the threat of death if they are unable to find an answer. Apolonio is characterized early on as having been trained in letters – the texts says he is *de letras profondado*, "steeped in books," for he has been schooled in solving riddles, "por solver argumentos era bien doctrinado" (st. 22) – allowing him to solve the enigma of Antioco's incest. This early characterization prepares the contrast between his clerical knowledge and his lack of worldly experience as he is confounded by Antioco's refusal to accept his answer. Thus is set up the opposition that has characterized interpretations of this romance, between knowledge understood as theoretical and bookish versus experience understood as life adventures. The failure of this clerical knowledge and the shame the protagonist feels prompt him to set sail, taking up adventures at sea (st. 34). Uría underlines that the shame at the failure of clerical knowledge to bring about the marriage is something not present in the Latin source but added by the Castilian poet, an addition that Uría reads as the initial mark of conversion from pagan to Christian king that will be further elaborated from the shipwreck to the final verses of the story, in a process of conversion that structures, in my opinion, the Iberian version of the story.[33] While the marks of hagiography are evident in the narration of Apolonio's life, it seems to me the poet would not want to characterize cleresy as failure. The failure – and ensuing humiliation, as I read it – is not one of incapability but of insufficiency, a clerical knowledge that must be supplemented with the experience of a life led virtuously, and notably, a virtue cast in economic terms.[34]

The first stanza announces a story of the good king Apolonio *and his courtesy*. This binary presentation highlights the protagonism of courtesy, as *curialitas*, as a supplement to Apolonio's sovereignty that will be detailed in the story itself. Immediately in st. 2, the logic of loss and recovery that structures the poem is introduced after using a general metaphor of *storm*, "temporal," to signify all of his troubles. The poet introduces the episode of Antioco, linking Apolonio to the plot in st. 18:

> El rey Apolonio, que en Tiro regnaua,
> oyó daquesta duenya qu'en grant preçio andaua;
> quería casar con ella, que mucho la amaua,
> la hora del pedir veyer non la cuydaua.

> (King Apollonius, who reigned in Tyre,/heard of this lady who was much coveted;/he wanted to marry her, for he much wanted her,/he couldn't wait to ask for her in marriage.)

The framing of Apolonio's initial embarkment is thus *cupiditas*, doubly understood as lust and as greed: it is implied he covets or wants ("amaua") Antioco's daughter because of the triangular desire that has increased her value ("preçio"). Apolonio's setting sail for Antioch's court is here not narrated, for he is next seen solving the riddle hiding Antioco's incest. In st. 23, *before* giving an answer to the king, the poet tells us that Apolonio understands the sin that the riddle hides and thus regrets having gone to Antioch, understanding he has fallen into a trap. Even then, so as not to be taken for a fool, he provides the truthful answer, publicizing Antioco's secret. Antioco does not receive the answer well and demands, on threat of death, that Apolonio find a different response to the riddle. Apolonio returns to Tyre and retires to his chambers to find a way out of this situation, an episode the poet uses to detail once again Apolonio's clerical background in st. 23. King Apolonio, however, finds no alternative answer in his books that can get him out of the trap. The stanzas that follow are particularly interesting:

> En cabo, otra cosa non pudo entender
> que al rey Antioco pudiese responder;
> cerró sus argumentos, dexóse de leyer,
> en laçerio sin fruto non quiso contender.

Pero mucho tenìa que era mal fallido,
en non ganar la duenya τ ssallir tan escarnido; /
quanto más comidìa qué l'auìa conteçido,
tanto más se tenìa por peyor confondido.
    Dixo que non podìa la vergüença durar,
mas querìa yr perdersse o la uentura mudar;
de pan τ de tresoro mandó mucho cargar,
metiòse en auenturas por las ondas del mar.   (st. 32–4)

(In the end, he could not find anything/to respond to king Antioco;/he
closed his books, stopped reading,/in suffering without fruit he did not
want to insist. // However he felt he had been wronged,/not winning the
lady τ being so scorned/the more he thought about what had happened
to him,/the more he took himself to be destroyed. // He said he could not
withstand the shame,/but would rather get lost or change his fortune;/
much bread τ treasure he ordered be loaded,/he went for adventures in
the sea waves.)

Apolonio does not search for a second *true*, new answer – for he knows
the answer he gave Antioco was the right one – but for a way out of
Antioco's trap. In this reading the only answer that clerical knowledge
can provide is truth, no alternative for that is possible, and therefore
his search in books – for lies – proves fruitless. Apolonio himself deems
such a search without results impractical, which one must read in terms
of politics. The conclusion that the hard work of a bookish search is not
worth it because no results will come of it anticipates the reflection in
the next stanza on profit. For as the poet remarks with a *but*, "pero,"
and this is crucial, Apolonio has not remained the same as he was when
he left for Antioch: his setting sail to get himself a coveted wife as profit
has left him wifeless and scorned. His journey not only did not bring
the reward he sought, but has discredited him. It is this loss of credit
that provokes shame and triggers his departure from his kingdom,
which he feels he has failed, linking thus the risk and profit model to his
sovereignty. This much is confirmed later on by the people of Tyre, who
retell the events to the traitor Taliarco, sent by Antioco to kill Apolonio.
Apolonio's failed journey and the ensuing shame and discredit frame a
new kind of sea travel, taken up in secret, in which abandonment of the
kingdom is both a self-exile (or a paradoxical search for homelessness)
and an abandonment of power, a journey without a clear goal and thus
much more dangerous. As a model for sovereignty, Apolonio seems to

lack that bond between *sapientia* and *fortitudo*, for to his bookish, cleri-cal knowledge there is no chivalric, battling self to correspond, as there is in Alexander and both historical and fictional kings of the twelfth and thirteenth centuries. If this model, which Martin Aurell relates to the matter of Rome, is absent here it is because, I argue, *fortitudo* is presented in another guise, substituted by another form of control of the environment or of the other: economic prowess.[35]

The story shifts back to Antioco, where the theme of *cupiditas* will be reasserted: Antioco's lust for his daughter will correspond to the greed he incites in men to kill or apprehend Apolonio, echoing Apolonio's own initial ambition. The duplicated vocabulary that is used here to express these nuances of *cupiditas* is telling of how much it structures the romance's moral dimension: "cobdiçia" and "adulterio," greed and adultery literally, but also in general "pecado" and "error," sin and er-ror, emphasizing their power to (re)produce more sin, to turn and trans-form men. Apolonio's journey, from here on, will sway between both poles of *cupiditas*, and his – and his family's – broaching of these situ-ations is the core of the simultaneously moral and economic lessons in the romance. Using Uría's conversion model as a first level, we can supplement the moral dimension with an economic one, where to the structure of generosity that undergirds sovereignty in other texts one can oppose a model of charity, subtly criticizing the excesses of liberal-ity and framing the economic within morality. Shell studies this as a moral-economic shift taking place in the twelfth and thirteenth centu-ries, where the model of *largesse* as the highest virtue in kings, using as examples Charlemagne and Alexander, undergoes a revision, shifting to a model of charity. *Largesse* or liberalness will be increasingly linked to *cupiditas* in relation to the reciprocity it demands. Shell eloquently calls this a change from an economy of desire to one of grace, where it is God who will be responsible for corresponding the gift, and terms it a *conversion*, this time a term profoundly steeped in economics. It is this layer of meaning that I suggest here is added to – not substituting for – a Christian morality as a model for sovereignty.[36]

Alexander's clerical education is not just assumed, as is Apolonio's, but in fact detailed in the first well-known stanzas of the *Libro de Alexandre*, as Aristotle's tutoring of the conqueror was one of the best-loved episodes of Alexander's biography. Ronald Surtz, in an article on Apolonio and Alexander as intellectual heroes, details how Alexander is presented in the *Libro de Alexandre* as warrior and equally as cleric, a trait copiously exemplified through the many erudite digressions in the poem. Set against the Cluniac and Cistercian spiritual reforms and their anti-intellectual programs, Surtz reads the characterization of both kings as a questioning and further legitimizing of clerical knowledge framed within a Christian perspective, one particularly linked to staying within the limits of one's role in the world: "The message of the *Libro de Alexandre* turns out to be the same as that of the *Libro de Apolonio*. The sage in his poem, the king in his governing, the warrior in his battles, he who exercises his task appropriately, will receive the prize or punishment he deserves."[37] I have mentioned above how the focus on the sea allows us to see how the limits Surtz suggests surround the tasks of kings and warriors are first set, then breached and broken. While Apolonio himself will *oppose* clerical knowledge to travelling, linking the sea to *cupiditas* and ultimately to economics, Alexander's clerical knowledge will be positively and intimately tied to his successful travelling across the seas to reach the lands he must conquer. In st. 115–19 Apolonio, as the sole survivor of the shipwreck that pushes him onto the Pentápolin coast, reflects on what it is that has forced him onto sea: it is sin, specifically his own greed, seeking marriage, and then others' greed seeking the reward offered by Antioco; it is also Antioco's sin seeking its revenge against the truth offered by Apolonio's knowlege; sins that have repeatedly conspired with the sea, resulting only in loss for Apolonio:

Dexé muy buen reyno do biuía onrrado,
fuy buscar contienda, casamiento famado;
gané enamiztat, sallí dende aontado,
et torné sin la duenya, de muerte enamiztado.
   Con toda essa pérdida, si en paz me xouiés'
(...)
   Mouióme el pecado, fízom' ende sallir,
por fer de mí escarnio, su maleza complir;
dióme en el mar salto, por más me desmentir,
ovo muchas ayudas por a mí destrouir.
   Fizo su atenençia con las ondas del mar,
viniéronle los vientos todos a ayudar ...

(I went to seek a challenge, a famous marriage,/I won enemies, left dishonoured,/and returned without the lady, on threat of death.//With all this loss, if I had stayed (...) Sin (the greed of others) displaced me, forced me to leave,/to scorn me, to fulfil its evil;/it ambushed me at sea, to further

discredit me,/it was aided by many in my destruction.//It (sin, greed) conspired with the waves of the sea,/all the winds came to help ...)

The king himself, telling his tale to a fisherman, explains that what
initially moved him out of Tyre was his own sense of worthlessness at
not having travelled: "teníame por torpe τ por menoscabado/porque
por muchas tierras non auía andado" (I took myself for clumsy and
of less worth/because I had not traveled widely).[38] Similarly, it will
be Alexander's excessive curiosity that moves him to break the limits
proper to humanity and seek to discover nature's secrets, in a spectacular fall from grace that condemns not knowledge, and particularly
not clerical knowledge, but the desire to exceed one's own capabilities,
recalling Surtz's argument, ciphered in the *Libro de Alexandre* by placing
the limit not at the meeting of sea and land but between the human and
nature. From the beginning, in fact, clerical knowledge for Alexander
is not marked as insufficient, as it is for Apolonio, but as inadequate
for his problems: "Grado a ti, maestro, assaz sé sapïençia;/non temo
de riqueza aver nunca fallençia./¡Mas vivré con rencura, morré con re-
pentençia,/si de premia de Dario non saco yo a Greçia!" (st. 46) (I
thank you, master, I have great knowledge/I fear not of ever lacking
any riches./But I will live with rancour, die with sorrow,/if from sub-
jection from Dario I don't relieve Greece!). Alexander's knowledge and
wealth are sufficient and great, but do not help him with his political
troubles, framed as were Apolonio's in terms of shame and dishonour
(st. 47). Thus, in many stanzas, Alexander prepares himself to move
politically. Once outfitted with advice and proper attire, he will first survey the lands and mountain passes, seeking adventure and later an-
nouncing his destiny under the provocation of Darius; knighted and
then crowned, he will challenge and subject the Armenians, Athenians,
and Thebans. In st. 245, after pacifying the lands, he will set sail as
a natural extension of his power, picking up the thread of the initial
provocation of Darius's request for tribute payments. The preparations
and the narration of this change of scenery do not betray any ambivalence towards the sea, there is no warning or premonition that clouds
the expedition, no moral digression on the part of the poet that tells
the reader this is a limit that must not be broken, no caution on water
as an element foreign to humanity, or beyond power. Here, the desire
to extend power across the seas is not coded negatively, but transitions
calmly onto the waters and into the ship. Moreover, clerical knowledge

will be instrumental for the articulation of a military strategy for the many conquests that follow, as in the multiple *mappamundi* that inhabit Alexander's strategic rooms, whether as he plans his extraordinary travels or as he recedes into his own habitations, or as rhetorical capability of transforming his resources into powerful weapons that will enable movement, displacements across land and sea.[39] How does the economic figure into the landscape? How does the maritime characterize the protagonist? How does the fluidity of the medium change the cleric's task, if the limits are untraceable?

Risk

Alexander's travels by sea are described twice, in very different terms. In st. 250–5, Alexander embarks in the direction of Asia.

> Mandó mover las naves   a los naveadores;
> desvolvieron las velas   de diversas colores;
> mandó cuémo guidassen   a los governadores;
> pora bogar aína,   dio muchos rimadores.
>   Andava por moverlas   el rey muy fazendado:
> dizié a los maestros   que livrassen privado.
> Dixo: "¡Quanto tardades,   prendo grant menoscabo,
> ca me está la vitoria   ya al puerto clamando!"
>   Ya ivan de la tierra   las naves despegando;
> ivan los rimadores   los rimos aguisando;
> ívanse a los griegos   los cueres demudando:
> ¡pocos avié ý d'ellos   que non fuessen plorando!
>   Ellos ploravan dentro;   las mugieres, al puerto,
> cuemo si cadaúna   su marido toviés muerto;
> El rëy Alexandre   dávales grant confuerto,
> diziéndoles: "¡Amigos,   tenédesme grant tuerto!
>   ¡Si nós daquí non imos,   en paz nunca vivremos!
> ¡De premia e de cueit   nunca escaparemos!
> ¡Por tres meses o quatro   que nós 'y lazraremos
> atamaña flaqueza   demostrar non devemos!
>   ¡Qui a sabor quisier'   de su tierra catar,
> nunca fará bernaje   nin fecho de prestar,
> mas es en una vez   todo a olvidar,
> si omne quisier' preçio   que aya a prestar!

(He ordered the sailors to move the ships/they unfolded the multico-
loured sails/he instructed the helmsmen on how to sail,/and to do it
fast he hired many rowers.//To get ready the king worked hard/and
told the pilots to hurry up.//He said: "The longer you take the more I
lose/for victory is calling me to port!//The ships are moving away from
shore/the rowers are setting a rhythm;/the Greek's hearts are changing:
/few of them were not crying.//The men cried inside; the women at
port/as if each had a dead husband;/king Alexander comforted them/
saying: "Friends, you do me harm!/If we do not leave we will never
live in peace!/Of subjugation and pain we will never escape!/For three
or four months we will toil there/we should not show such weakness!
// He who wants to see his lands/shall never achieve any greatness,/
but should forget everything at once,/if man wants to be appreciated
as admirable.)

Alexander's impatience for setting sail contrasts with the grief – and
fear of death – sailors and sailors' wives display by dragging their feet,
delaying departure, and general bawling. Alexander admonishes them,
saying that love of land makes cowards of many, and invokes a series
of heroes whose defiance of the ocean's limit brought them greatness:
Alcides (or Hercules) in Spain, Bacchus in India, Jason's victory and
prize in the search of the Golden Fleece, implicitly linking cleresy itself
– as knowledge – to the violation of limits.[40] Alexander does not look
back once, suggesting both courage and disaffection for his land, or
extreme ambition. As they travel farther from home, the tears subside
and Asia appears on the horizon, in a rhetorical turn of the gaze that
gives the impression that sailors do not ever lose sight of land, they
merely turn their heads. Alexander shoots an arrow to the coast, inaugurating the new limit set from the sea, the penetration of another land,
its domination, all of which frames the introduction of the *mappamundi*
digression that follows. Sailing the sea to Asia has proven to be swift,
safe, and eventless. Most importantly, Alexander is not condemned by
this horizontal displacement. Narration does not even hint at a threat
from the sea, it does not spend time on it, as the gaze from those left
behind is muddled by tears, the narrator seems to turn his head, blink,
and see Asia on the other side. They set up camp on shore and begin the
campaigns on land, forgetting the waters behind them.

Apolonio's first encounter with the sea is less glorious. At the beginning of the poem, he does not emphasize the risk of setting sail;

he seems almost unaware of possible danger at this early stage in the poem, which supports his bookish knowledge and further highlights his lack of experience. It is those on shore, similar to Alexander's story, who bemoan his departure, and the poet who caution against the sea's movable condition:

El mar, que nunqua touo leyaltat ni belmez,
cámiase priuado τ ensányase rafez;
suele dar mala çaga más negra que la pez ...   (st. 107)

(The sea, which never had any loyalty or offered protection, /changes secretly and becomes enraged easily;/it can make one's fate blacker than tar ...)

The moral connotations linked to the liquidity of the medium, that is, mutability and trickery, are mirrored positively in King Apolonio himself, whose loyalty and charity, fidelity and honesty will characterize him throughout. Without any complications other than sadness and tiredness from the trip, Apolonio and his crew arrive in Tarso. The tempest that will threaten him there will be one of economics: greedy men search for him seeking to win Antioco's reward, and meanwhile the city of Tarso, encumbered by hardship and high prices, may not be able to guarantee his safety. Apolonio here exercises another type of knowledge, his economic skills as merchant, and is able to guarantee a safe, if temporary, home for himself in Tarso by selling his cargo of food for a fair price to the town, then using the profit to build the walls around the city.

Both kings thus approach the sea as a metaphor for economics without fear, with no sense of the danger with which it threatens them. They both seem blind to the general knowledge of the sea's treachery of which their crews and, in Apolonio's case, the poet himself seem keenly aware. It is this blindness, and our foreknowledge of the treachery that both kings will be subjected to – Apolonio by Antioco at the beginning of the poem, Alexander by his own man at the end of his story – that is bound up with the kings' first navigation.

Holding on to a piece of wood, Apolonio will be thrown by the sea to its limit, a término, that is, to shore, losing men and riches, arriving in Pentápolin. Upon regaining consciousness the king will now lament that destiny has thrown him onto the ocean, which has sided with Antioco against him:

Nunqua deuía omne en las mares fiar,
traen lealtat poca, saben mal solazar;
saben, al reçebir, buena cara mostrar,
dan con omne aýna dentro en mal logar.   (st. 120)

(Never should man trust the seas,/they bring little loyalty, know not
how to comfort;/They know to show a good face when welcoming you,/
Only to trick you, once inside.)

It is with this shipwreck scene that the danger of sea travel is confirmed in the text for the protagonist and that an elaboration of the limit
between land and sea as *shore*, as a place for the negotiation of those
limits, of risk and profit, of loss and recovery, begins to be articulated
in the *Apolonio*. While the negotiations that allowed him to remain in
Tarso could have been taken for a stroke of luck, a sudden and interested trade of sorts, the encounter with the fisherman is one in which
Apolonio has nothing to trade but his own story. To the king's request
for counsel, the fisherman offers stories of experience, tales of change of
fortune and, at the end, is able to produce from less than nothing a gift
for Apolonio, emphasizing yet again in this extreme comparison the
increase in value that comes from complete loss.[41] The shipwreck, then,
is framed at this other end not with a negotiation based on liberalness
or generosity, as was the case with Tarso, but with one based on charity,
a shift to an economy of grace, following the pattern suggested by Shell
I recalled earlier in this chapter.

Courtesy will bring Apolonio back to his status as king, through
sport and song and cunning; he will marry Luciana to the delight of
Architrastes, her father, who has seen in Apolonio an equal. Strolling on
the beach, another shore character, a sailor from an anchored ship, will
beckon Apolonio to sail again, this time to reclaim both his own throne
and that of Antioch, now that the incestuous couple has been struck
by lightning as punishment for their sins. While the sea is agreeable
and calm for the most part of the trip, they are about to cross it when
fortune strikes again and Luciana, giving birth to Tarsiana, is afflicted
with a condition that makes everyone believe she is dead. Carefully
placed in a richly decorated coffin on the waves, body and treasure arrive
at the port city of Ephesus, where she is found by a doctor who happens to live by the sea, discovered to be still alive, and brought back to
health. Restored to life but lost to her family, she must remain there in
a monastery built on the shore next to Ephesus. Tarsiana, Apolonio's

and Luciana's daughter, is thirteen years later betrayed by her tutors and sold as a slave; she finds a home in a bordello in the port city of Mitalena on the island of Lesbos. While the numerous transactions involving women's bodies cannot be detailed here, I want to recall not only the emphasis on market, trade, ports, and shores that structures the stories of both Luciana and Tarsiana, but also the emphasis on language (as prayer or as storytelling and singing) that allows women to participate in this world of exchange. As with the male characters, Luciana and Tarsiana's effective use of language as a form of conversion brings them into the economy of grace the text seeks to emphasize: the poet remarks that all of the men who visit Tarsiana in the bordello are, as is Antinágora, *converted* by her words (st. 419).

Meanwhile, Apolonio will repeatedly lecture on fortune as logic of loss and recovery, set sail for Egypt and return ten years later to discover the betrayal of the tutors. Disconsolate, he sails for home, Tyre, but fortune intervenes: the sea takes away his power to govern the ship and God himself throws the pilgrims, *romeros*, to the shores of Mitalena. The episode of negotiation of identity between Apolonio and Tarsiana will take place in its entirety on the shore, on board the ship anchored at the port of the city. In st. 547, the sea itself, as God's instrument, will be credited with the recovery of his daughter. Now that the sea as instrument of God has been introduced, an angel will instruct Apolonio to go to Ephesus and find Luciana. By now, Apolonio has established that his life matters must be negotiated in the space between land and sea, and in st. 613 he enters Tyre, hoarding recoveries, reputation, and profit in his itinerary home.

Julian Weiss has paid close and eloquent attention to the mercantile characterization of Apolonio, and my reading is indebted to his work. Weiss begins by explaining *cortesía* as a concept that should be extended to include spaces and relations outside the court, and mentions the world of commerce, but resists the temptation to appeal to a rise of the middle class to justify confusion between courtesy and exchange. In my view, it is precisely in that confusion that the text gains actuality, making relevant the story of Apolonio in the context of thirteenth-century Castile, marking not only a distance from the Latin model but an alternative to the model of sovereignty in the *Libro de Alexandre*. According to Weiss, "*cortesía* functions as an ideological mechanism to remove individual identity from the realm of history and changing social relations: it negotiates the unstable process of acquiring, circulating and potentially losing material wealth, and confronts challenges posed by new forms of economic production."[42] Thus, *cortesía* would be the stable ground against which a commerce characterized by instability is staged. I read in this text, however, that travel as form of knowledge, travel by sea and even commerce itself are what characterize Apolonio not only as courtly king but *also* as successful and ethical merchant, capable of dispensing justice by distributing wealth and goods appropriately.

In order to support a tension or an opposition between courtesy and commerce, Weiss refers to Elánico's refusal to be paid a reward from Apolonio's treasure to compensate his honesty: "amiztat vender non es costumbre nuestra/Quien bondat da por preçio malamiente se denuesta" (st. 76) (it is not our custom to sell friendship/he who is kind for money offends himself). Weiss presses the point by saying that what has been traded in the name of friendship is not commerce, but a just price: "once again, though this time in relation to a specifically Christian identity, the poem denies that a contractual social relationship can be established on monetary terms."[43] However, what has actually happened is that Apolonio has traded in ethics – just price. By matching Antioco's bet on the greediness of men with generosity and gratefulness, Apolonio manages to transform the client bond between the men into one of friendship. It is in this twofold level where Apolonio, melding courtesy and merchantry, is king.

Weiss's analysis begins to suggest such a reading of the *Libro de Apolonio*:

> A commercial transaction is not openly repudiated, but silently assimilated into the hero's courtliness. The point is reinforced by having the commercial transaction immediately commuted into an act of courtly *magnanimitas*. This transformation of commerce into courtliness is effected by having the money reinvested in the construction of the town walls ... he transforms a commercial exchange into an act of *cortesía*, and in the process creates a space where *cortesía* (acts of the court) can take place.

But just one step further, and where Weiss stops, is the idea that this characterizes Apolonio with an identity that lies *beyond* that of cleric, king, or merchant, in a rhetorical combination that is capable of transforming the product of one of these identities into another by virtue of words. That is, it is within language where courtesy, sovereignty, and commerce coexist and may be traded for each other. When Tarsiana, in Weiss's words, "translates economic exchange into a moral and spiritual practice" and "her customers end up buying not her body but her life story, and with it their own moral redemption," it is precisely *in* language, as *translation*, where economics and spirituality trade in each other, overlap or merge in order to produce a new object of exchange that is again language, a story, produced by and within *curialitas*.[44] Thus, it is through language and virtue that Apolonio is able to curb the danger of greed, codified as the danger of sea travel and the breaking of limits, in order to make this risk work for him, to render it profitable. The violation of the sea is mollified through careful administration of morality and ethics, nevertheless obtaining the *preçio* for which the king has put himself in danger, in a medieval version of (moral) venture capitalism.

Alexander's engagement with the sea pushes us into thinking in terms of depth, and not of a horizon. The best-known maritime episode in the *Libro de Alexandre*, because it so appropriately illustrates how again and again the hero defies Natura, is Alexander's descent into the sea by having a sort of submarine built for him to go to the bottom of the ocean.[45] A few stanzas before, however, this journey – different from any other – is framed explicitly as the breaking of a boundary. Alexander's council mean to restrain their leader's urge to go further, calling it specifically greed, *cupiditas*, by addressing the king in this way: "La tu fiera cobdiçia non te dexa folgar;/señor eres del mundo: non te puedes fartar./¡Nin podemos saber nin podemos asmar/qué cosa es aquesta que quieres ensayar!" (st. 2274) (Your fierce greed does not let you rest;/you are lord of the world: but you are not satisfied./We cannot know and we cannot judge/what it is that you wish to attempt). The council warns that no reward can ever be great enough to make such risk-taking worthwhile: "Non es honra nin preçio pora omne honrado/meterse a ventura en lugar desguisado" (2270ab) (There is no honour or worth for honourable men/in venturing into uncharted places).[46] In st. 2289, as Alexander harangues his men to follow him further, he argues that of the seven worlds God made, only parts of a single one have been dominated. He refers here to the Earth as sphere as being conquered only in its landmass, most obviously by Alexander himself, suggesting that of the Earth itself both the seas and the skies remain to be explored. Alexander claims that God has sent him and his men to those parts precisely to discover the secrets of these realms, claiming that the risk entailed must be assumed in order to gain something, to profit, following Aristotle's advice.[47]

Alexander's men respond to his rhetoric, and they promise to follow him everywhere and set sail to a calm sea, with good winds, with no destiny or defined goal: "ivan e non sabién escontra quál lugar" (they did not know where they were going; 2297d). They swiftly sail into open seas, where they wander aimlessly, and where the poet remarks once again the unheard-of wilful navigation without having land in sight, through uncharted waters. The mutability of winds changes the waves, and the sea becomes enraged, while the king's material weapons– remarks the poet – cannot tame them. The danger increases as they go further into the sea and the storms multiply; but Alexander does not falter in his determination, to the admiration of his men. To this horizontal challenge of uncharted open sea, the poet now adds – if incredulously – the story of Alexander's submarine exploration:

> Dizen que por saber   qué fazen los pescados,
> cómo viven los chicos   entre los más granados,
> fizo arca de vidrio   con muzos bien çerrados;
> metiose él de dentro   con dos de sus crïados
> (…)
> Mandó que lo dexassen   quize días durar;
> las naves, con tod'esto,   pensassen de andar:
> assaz podrié en esto   saber e mesurar
> e meter en escripto   los secretos del mar.   (st. 2306, 2309)

(They say that to know what fish do,/how the little ones live among the grander ones,/he made a glass ark with all openings closed;/he went in it with two of his servants.//(…) He ordered to be left there fifteen days;/ after which the ships could prepare to leave:/with this he could know and measure/and write down the secrets of the sea.)

Even though he finds more trouble than Ulysses himself, with tempests and high winds alarming the sailors at high sea, where they know not how to pilot the ships, Alexander reaches the site and is lowered in his glass chamber into the waters. In the depths, the inhabitants fear and tremble in his presence, they kneel on their fins and pledge their scaly allegiance to the Conqueror. If Alexander's submersion exemplifies the excess in the hero that will be translated as *superbia*, this excess seems to be one that is considered in its verticality: the prohibition on entering the water seems to be codified negatively only in *submersion*. If greed was assimilated to the horizontal venture of sailing into open seas, it is not greed but vainglory, arrogance, and pride that codify this vertical crossing of limits. Alexander comes back successful from his challenge of the surface of the seas, he survives storms and enraged seas and fierce winds; but his quest to the sea depths with the explicit intent of discovering their secrets and putting them to writing is what triggers the digression, framed in terms of *superbia*, that will end with his betrayal and murder. It is as direct result of this episode that Natura, who suffers the affront of the crossing of (human) boundaries that Alexander undertakes, recruits the Devil with God's approval, and they send Antípater to punish Alexander's sin of pride in st. 2324–2457 (which includes the interpolated description of the kingdom of Hell).

The contrast in moral lessons – and the ensuing nuance as models for sovereignty – between the stories of Alexander and Apolonio, emblematized in the sins of *superbia* and *cupiditas* in terms of risk, are interesting in themselves but especially in their parallel use of an economic language and prowess that allows both kings to get what they want: superhuman knowledge, secrets, in the case of Alexander; profit, "ganançia" through managed risk in the logic of loss and recovery, in Apolonio's. The characterization of maritime space as one of risk, danger, and profit is similar, but the sins that threaten such endeavours are distributed differently: while for Alexander the horizontal, the surface economics of the sea is always profitable and it is only his readiness to accept the risks of depth that proves deadly, for Apolonio movement across water is always structured upon the careful negotiation at the start of every journey, his careful managerial attitude to arrival and departure at every port marking his fortune and salvation.

Several conclusions can be drawn from this difference in the presentation of the limits between sea and land, that is, Alexander's characterization of that limit as a coastline and only as inviolable limit in depth, versus Apolonio's elaboration of the limit as a space, as shore, where morality and economics are negotiated. First, a coastline reminds one of an aerial view of a bidimensional cartographic representation, supported by the many interventions of the cartographic in the romance that underpin a mappable, cultural view of the world, one particularly linked to power. This cartographic representation in turn works as imperial model, and as a reminder for the limit of the worldly as it points to the time and spacelessness of salvation, with which warning the poem ends.

Apolonio's shoreline is a perspective from land, a horizontal look from the ship or from the port town looking in to the market, a point of view that is underlined through the statues of Apolonio built in that precise space, mediating land and sea. As Apolonio sets sail for Egypt, leaving his daughter with Dionisia and Estrángilo, unable to overcome the death of his wife, the Latin source marks this new identity, a new voyage, not as father or husband nor as emperor of Antioch, for these identities have been taken from him or relinquished out of grief, but as merchant, *sed funga potius opera mercatus*, the Latin source remarks. The Iberian version characterizes this as a pilgrimage, but Tarsiana, Apolonio's daughter, will waver between the merchant and the pilgrim, "romero," making them alternatives to each other, similar and thus exchangeable: "Dios te salve, romero o merchante" (st. 489b). Alexander talks of his own craft in weapons and strategy in the beginning of the poem (st. 69) as his merchantry, his trade, "merchantería," bringing the parallels between kings even closer.

The *Libro de Alexandre* and the *Libro de Apolonio*, as has been pointed out many times before, propose models for kingship that should not be seen as contradictory but as evolving visions, modelled on the past, forged for the future, sustained by a moral framework. Alexander's is a continental, military project, while Apolonio's is a portuary, mercantile model. Alexander conquers and colonizes, Apolonio negotiates; Alexander's success is predicated upon his ambition and cautioned in its extreme version of pride; Apolonio's deferred deliverance is built on containment and careful calculation of risk and profit. These two models, built upon the sea, articulate different models of land: while Alexander merely sets camp on a coastline that he has set off as a starting limit for his military exploits through the arrow that marks Asia as his for the taking, Apolonio moves within a wider space than that of the ebbing waves. His is a shore, a port city; his fellow characters are kings as well, but also fishermen and merchants.

These two texts experiment with two possible models with underlying tones of imperialism and mercantilism that play out as alternatives only as long as the limits of (Christian) ethics are kept in check. A few decades later, Alfonso X will himself bring together the sea and the space of royalty, mixing once again the metaphors of sovereignty or governance and of sea travel, when quoting the ancient sages in the second *Partida* as saying that "the court of the king is like the sea," for as the sea, the court gives place to any and all, delivers judgment, counsel, and liberalness, and is subject to calmness and tempest.[48]

At the end of the Middle Ages, historically, blending imperialism and mercantilism, as Remo Bodei writes, the ocean's movements became normalized, depriving the sea of its specificity. Instability not only ceased to provoke fear or respect but, as it became normal or habitual, mutability itself came to be seen as something more durable and substantial. Whether we take the journey to be one of empire or of economics, when variations – rebellion, treason, and civil war as well as inflation, interest manipulation, or speculation – are seen as normal, they are in turn interiorized. Seen as the condition within, they do not provoke fear, they are not seen as abstractions but as substantial; they are not perceived as temporal but as the most permanent of conditions. This naturalization of space traceable through romance elaborations, first that of the forest, then that of the sea, as Ferdinand Braudel said, made of the literary Mediterranean facing the early modern world barely a puddle in the map of possible opportunities.

Afterword

The cleric read a word, a phrase, a sentence from the *Alexandreis*, said it out loud. Rolled it in his tongue, felt the echoes, the movement. Considered, probably out loud as well, options for translation. What common noises – yells, footsteps, rumours – might have interrupted this process, what worries, which everyday tasks might have detoured these possibilities into others? What other sources were there, on the desk, readily available to him? Were they physically there or made present by the vast archive of his memory? What other unrelated manuscripts might have been open in that room, then or on some other recent day? Is his offer of a service a cliché, or a radical metaphor for a student exercise, intended for a particularly intuitive student who is aware of the changing role of his community, moving every day between court and *studium*, between politics and the intellectual life?

I have taken these questions and considered their real possibilities, trying to discern how these tools and materials beyond the immediate limits of the texts might have been woven into the composition of these works. I believe that as this is a new discourse, a learned language that is being coined as these works are being put to writing, its permeability was higher, its openness greater, its capacity such that the borrowing from cartography or economics would have been more a tool than an irruption, more structural than ornamental. I have argued thus for an analysis of thirteenth-century texts such as the *Alexandre* and *Apolonio* in and of themselves, and for interpretation of their nuance and choice of materials as truly innovative, even when those particular episodes or details are traceable to a source: it is the assemblage itself that produces a unique text, which must be considered in its entirety, as a sum of its parts, and not only in its variations from the source, as a product of and for its time. Chapter 1 focuses on the use of cartography in the *Libro de Alexandre* as both a trope and a rhetorical structure. The numerous cartographic moments in the *Alexandre* are carefully studied to support the idea that the operations of a cartography considered as part of the cleric's habitual tools enable the cleric to use them rhetorically, appearing thus to structure the *Alexandre* as a particular and new form of translation. Such rhetoric would be supported by a long cartographic tradition in Iberia in which basic strategies such as *abbreviatio* and *digressio* become part of the cleric's tools for the workings of memory and invention. Furthermore, within cartography's history of its relation with text, appropriating and incorporating a wide variety of texts to activate their relations according to different needs is set against the *Alexandre's* strategy of translation.

Chapter 2 dwells on how translation itself is represented in the *Alexandre*, as it is portrayed numerous times through the figure and story of Babel. Working through careful readings of these passages, I argue that translation is there not only to present a story of origins, or as example of how the aggregation of texts recalls once again cartography as a tool for the cleric, but to present translation as labour, as a distinct craft or *technè* that calls for a particular set of skills and talent. As recuperating the properly political dimensions of rhetoric through translation, the emblematization of translation in the passages of Babel works as a sort of theory that is thus also a reflection on politics, and specifically on sovereignty and its relation to language. The *Alexandre* stops short of naming the translator, that is, the text does not explicitly name the cleric as the translator, but sets the stage for the cleric to articulate the task of translating as the task of the cleric, a service and a ministry at the centre of a new sovereignty.

Chapter 3 looks at how the idea of *mester* as ministry or labour of language is buttressed by the numerous interferences of the economic in the period's fiction. The comparison between different engagements between language and economics in the *Poem of the Cid, Libro de Alexandre, Libro de Apolonio,* and the *Libro de Fernán González* allow us to trace the rapidly changing attitudes towards economic operations in the thirteenth century. From an engagement with a gift economy in the *Poem of the Cid* to the unabashed embrace of the profit economy and brokering and speculation as linguistic tools in the *Libro de Fernán González*, these works show the cleric positioning himself within a changing society as someone who has the tools of economics on the tip of his tongue, tools that are presented as essential to the sovereign in a new political economy.

In the end, what I want to leave the reader with is the idea that the task of the cleric is not limited to working with literary language, when "literary" is understood at its most narrow, referring to negotiating declinations or scribal variations – I exaggerate to make a point. I want to open up the idea itself of the task of the cleric as one of reinventing language and its tools constantly, and permanently, with things outside language, discourses that lie beyond parchment, ink, desk, appropriating them, bringing them to inhabit within and structuring the language of fiction itself. Of course, once one looks up from the folio, there are many tools other than compasses or buildings or coins one might see; the ones I have studied may not even be the most important to others, or the most visible. But the crucial thing is to look up, to look around. As task, as labour, as ministry, the trade of the cleric is not ever finished, for it is also permanently reinventing itself. That is why "task" is so appropriate a word: speaking to something completed but also as something to be yet accomplished, it has a past and a permanent future, a sort of command or mission element to it. The cleric's task is then precisely that, making the new a thing of language, making language new.

Appendix: Working Corpus of Pre-1200 Maps in Iberian Libraries

These are my personal notes on the manuscripts, adding information on the maps or diagrams, especially those that note relations to arguments I make in chapter 1. Most catalogues give little or no information about the maps.

1. Escorial R.II.18, *Codex Ovetensis* (Geographico-historical Miscellany): Three Maps

7th c.: f. 24v (this folio presents two maps; the oldest is on the left and has an oceanic ring that is lacking in the one on the right).
9th c.: f. 25 (shows ocean ring and duplicates lines for the *T*; adds the names of Noah's sons to those of the continents outside the ocean ring).
Numerous other diagrams.

2. Biblioteca Nacional, Madrid, Vit. 14-3: One Map

8th–9th c.
f. 117v Bilingual map, provenance is the Archivo del Sagrario in Toledo; main legends in Arabic noting measurements, division of the earth among sons of Noah in narrativized way; legends in Latin are subordinated to Arabic ones; see Menéndez Pidal 169–72.
Other musical and geometrical diagrams.

3. Escorial &.I.14 (Miscellany): One Map (Missing) + Genealogical Diagrams

8th–9th c.

f. 74v Vandalized manuscript, rubricated cardinal points can still be read; last two folios with extensive Arabic writing that may be in Alvarus of Cordoba's hand.
Consanguinity chart and genealogical diagram.

4. Escorial T.II.24 (Computus Manuscript): One Map

late 9th c.
f. 175r Y/O map, provenance church of Salamanca; names of continents, ocean, *mare magnum, Tanais, Nilus, Palus Meotis*, cardinal points and a cross on the ocean ring; names of Noah's sons in Arabic; more Arabic writing on the zodiac drawn in f. 42v; abundant marginal notes in Latin and Arabic; see Menéndez Pidal 177–8.

5. Escorial P.I.7: One Map

late 9th c.
f. 222v Includes names like those of above, but in Latin; Y/O map, manuscript codes the name of Alfonso III in a labyrinth as owner of the codex; map's waters are turquoise, double ocean border, cardinal points, continents, Noah's sons.

6. Escorial P.I.8: One Map

9th c.
f. 187 A cross marks the Orient on the ocean ring; shows Paradise as the origin of the four rivers; with book 14 of *Etymologies*; provenance Pyrenees?; small map, very simple.

7. Real Academia de la Historia, cód. 25 (Composite Manuscript): One Map + Genealogical Diagrams + *Rotae*

10th c. (946)
f. 204v Copied by Jimeno (*Eximinione*); provenance San Millán de la Cogolla, map in front of *Etym.* 14.2 *De Asia* – some rivers and legends, Paradise, Noah's sons, a number of provinces, among then Spania, Asturias, Gallecia – its function is to situate the Iberian Peninsula in the *orbis terrarum*.
Numerous other diagrams; astrological, musical – similar to BNM, mss. vit. 14-3. Notable are the *rotae* and the genealogical diagrams on 145v and 146r.

8. Real Academia de la Historia, cód. 76 (Composite Manuscript): One Map

10th c. (954)
f. 108r Includes Isidore's *Etymologies* and two versions of a *De celo uel quinque circulis eius atque subterraneo meato;* provenance Cardeña; codex is closely related to RAH, cód. 25; map shows Paradise and the *fons paradisi*, sons of Noah and provinces, cities, a cross on the ocean ring.

9. Archivo Histórico Nacional, Madrid, cód. 1240, *Beato de Tábara*: One Map + Genealogical Diagrams + *Rotae* + Horshoe Arches

10th c. (970)
fol. 1v? Continents, Africa substituted by Libia, related to genealogical tables on the descendants of Noah, notes Noah's sons and qualifies the lands allotted to them by their "zone": – *temperatam, calidam, frigidam* – in a confusing way, cardinal points are also made to correspond to continents(?).

10. Escorial D.I.2, *Codex Vigilanus* or *Albeldense* (*Codex Conciliorum Albeldensis seu Vigilanus*) (Miscellany): One Map + Genealogical Diagram + Horseshoe Arches

10th c. (976)
fol. 17v Y/O map to the right of illustration showing Noah assigning to his sons, Sem, Cam, and Japhet, the three continents, symbolized by small mounts on which they stand; below it the folio shows an illustration of Paradise; an extensive gloss standing to the left of the image corresponds to chap. 3 of book 14 of *Etymologies*.
Numerous, luxurious illustrations. Genealogical diagram on 15r fuses the genealogical table with the antropomorhic/Christomorphic world, compare to &.I.14 and RAH, cód. 25.

11. Escorial D.I.1, *Codex Emilianensis* or *Códice de los Concilios:* One Map

10th c. (992 or 994)
f. 14 v Related to Escorial d.I.2, provenance San Millán o Albelda; on this folio illumination was not completed, only the outline has been traced and some goldleaf applied.

12. Escorial M.III.3: One Map

late 10th, beginning of 11th c.
f. 81 Excerpts of *Etymologies* bound with an Apocalypse and other materials;
map with book 14 of *Etymologies*.

**13. Real Academia de la Historia, cód. 78, *Códice de Roda* (Composite Ms):
One Map**

10th–11th c.
fol. 200v Vol. with two great blocks, the first with the work of Orosius,
Historia aduersum paganos libri VII, f. 1r–155r, and the second with fragments
of diverse texts by Isidore, chronicles, Saint Augustine, Smaragdus; related to
the scriptorium of San Millán de la Cogolla for its materials, for its content it
has been related to Nájera; three different inks, sons of Noah, climatic zones.
Other interesting illustrations in the volume are a city of Babylon and the
silhouette of Ninive and Toledo, for in their sinechdocal representation of
the cities they make use of cartographic techniques.

14. Archivo de la Corona de Aragón, Ripoll 106: One Map + *Rotae*

11th c.
fol. 82v In religious-scientific miscellany; the map is a very schematic drawing
that has been described as an "inverted pentagon"; it resembles an open
tryptich in which the central panel has been inscribed with *rotae* or circles
that contain Iberian names of cities: Narbona, Vrigancia civitas, Impurias,
Bracaram, Ierunda, Gadis, Barchinona, Terrachona, and Cartago, in brown
and red inks. The frame or ouside panel is inscribed with fish, while on the
superior "triangles" one can read Wasconia and Mare Terreno.

15. Biblioteca Nacional, Madrid, ms. 10008: One Map

11th c.
fol. 166v Copy of *Etymologies*; provenance is Toledo Cathedral; Y/O in
two inks; double border for the ocean ring; cross marks the east.

16. Escorial &.I.3: One Map + *Rotae* + Horseshoe Arches

11th c. (1047)
fol. 177v Luxury codex for Queen Sancha, wife to Ferdinand I and mother
to Sancho; copies the maps present in Real Academia de la Historia cód. 25

and 76; this Y/O map occupies an entire page, chronologically signalling a transition in the relation between map and text; Paradisus and *fons paradisi*, rivers, notable are the number of provinces detailed; interesting details, for example: *Libia qui tenet provincias xii. Africa. Terra de pedes latos.*

Uses *rotae* for titles, but especially interesting is an inhabited initial O that has a portrait that can be related to a Christomorphic T/O. In the rest of the volume there are other examples of decorated initial O's, related to rondels in textiles.

17. Biblioteca Nacional de Madrid, vit. 14-2, *Beato de Fernando I y Doña Sancha*: Two Maps + *Rotae* + Horseshoe Arches

11th c. (1047)

fol. 12v Square map; drawn/written by the scribe Facundo for King Fernando I and Queen Sancha of Castile and León; floating in a sea of linked *rotae*; Noah's sons, continents, climates.

fol. 63v and 64r The usual Beatus *mappamundi*; oval shaped; ocean decorated with fish and square islands; Adam and Eve in paradise are same figures copied in the genealogy on fol. 10v.

Numerous genealogical diagrams in the form of linked rotae that resemble rosaries or hanging jewelry.

18. Biblioteca Apostolica Vaticana, Ms. Reg. Lat 123: One Map

ca. 1050

f. 143v–144r. "Mappae mundi von Ripoll," T/O map oriented east, with zonal information. M.A. Vidier linked this map to Théodulf, bishop of Orléans, who writes in a poem that *Totius orbis adest breviter depicta figura* ("La mappemonde de Théodulfe").

19. Escorial S.III.5: Four Maps

12th c.

fol. 40v (climatic)

fol. 56v (climatic)

fol. 110v (climatic)

fol. 115r (climatic, oriented west)

Codex binds Macrobius – f. 1–72 – and Calchidius – f. 73–141; probably copied in France.

Interesting diagrams, on 134r, within a circle, a classification of animals glossing Plato; on 141v medicine recipes on a 13th c. Guidonian hand.

20. Escorial L.III.10, *De coniuratione Catilinae:* One Map

12th c.

f. 21v Map with Sallust's *De bellum Jugurtinum,* which is the second of three texts bound in this volume; names of continents and three toponyms, map has been erased and scraped on continental parts.

21. Escorial E.IV.13: One Map

12th c.

fol. 48v Delicately decorated, simple; cardinal points inside ocean ring; continents; notes on the distribution to Noah's sons; zones; one of the legends is for Hispania.

22. Escorial E.IV.24: Two Maps

12th c.

fol. 71r A copy of Macrobius's *In somnium Scipionis* with *Introductiones dialecticae*; climatic map noting inaccessible zones; heavily annotated mss. in at least two hands, numerous and diverse diagrams. Interesting, because of the student context it provides, is a tree of philosophy on 46v.

Notes

Introduction

1 I group together the *Libro de Alexandre*, *Libro de Apolonio*, and *Libro de Fernán González* not only because they are among the earliest examples of *mester de clerecía*, but because they are characterized by a *secondary* involvement with religious topics. See Isabel Uría Maqua, "II. La unidad del mester de clerecía," in *Panorama crítico del mester de clerecía*, especially 55–6, with arguments based on the previous chapter, which provides a historical overview of the discussion of the corpus. Weiss, in pp. 1–25 of his *The Mester de Clerecía*, presents a wider view of the definition of *mester,* and therefore his corpus includes more examples. For hypotheses on lost works pertaining to the genre, see Walsh, "Obras perdidas del mester de clerecía." I will use the editions of Juan Casas Rigall, Dolores Corbella, and Itziar López Guil, correspondingly; all translations are mine unless otherwise noted.

2 The process of writing – and not that of merely copying – is constantly referred to in these works, and the reference to books makes Pablo Ancos think that the awareness of the writerly nature of these poems would be shared by both cleric and audience when, even if the texts' main form of transmission was oral, the written text was present in such reading, whether out loud or as performance (*Transmisión y recepción,* 198, 204–5). Ancos's erudite study offers insightful remarks on the process of composition throughout, but see especially pp. 197–207.

3 See Gómez Redondo, "El fermoso fablar," Grande Quejigo, "Quiero leer un livro," and Ancos, *Transmisión y recepción*, who speak to the coincidence in works of *mester* of the figures of the copyist and the author in the same person, supporting the coincidence of process and project. The narrator-author of the *Libro de Alexandre*, Ancos concludes, "is an *escrivano* (scribe)

(a name that he also gives himself in verse 5d), and his narration is contained in a book, which is vocally disseminated" (205).

4 Ancos, *Transmisión y recepción*, 200. See also Bailey, *The Poetics of Speech*, especially the introduction, for a slightly different perspective that highlights the oral in the process of composition itself. Writing, *escribir*, is explicitly tied to the mode of composition in the *Libro de Alexandre*, and the task of the cleric in this process is in stanza 653, within the Trojan digression, transferred to Alexander himself (Ancos, *Transmisión y recepción*, 204n224; on the many references to writing and modes of composition related to writing see the list on p. 205).

5 García Fitz, "Was Las Navas a Decisive Battle?," 9.

6 That was before Juan Casas Rigall's extraordinary edition, however. The work of Amaia Arizaleta specifically on the *Alexandre* throughout the past decade has altered the place of the poem in medieval Iberian studies, and for specific passages or instances there are many more names to mention, and that will appear throughout this book.

7 Arizaleta's *La Translation d'Alexandre* and Michael's *The Treatment of Classical Material* are the most notable exceptions, in that they attempt a comprehensive account of the *Alexandre* from specific perspectives.

8 For general reflections on *mester* see Rico, "La clerecía del mester," and Uría Maqua, "I. El concepto de mester de clerecía," in *Panorama crítico del mester de clerecía*, esp. 36–51; for courtly and legal contexts see Gómez Redondo, "El fermoso fablar," and Rodríguez Velasco, "Theorizing the Language of the Law."

9 Copeland's *Rhetoric, Hermeneutics, and Translation in the Middle Ages* provides the general theoretical backdrop for this development. Uría Maqua, "I. El concepto de mester de clerecía," in *Panorama crítico del mester de clerecía*, and Rico, "La clerecía del mester," study the specific development in Iberia of a grammatical and rhetorical curriculum.

10 Raymond Willis devoted most of his work on the *Alexandre* to the question of sources and translation between languages. The crucial findings of this endeavour are duly noted even when I want to redirect the question of translation to a less obvious emphasis, that of space/place.

11 This is suggested by Arizaleta, *La Translation d'Alexandre*.

Chapter 1

1 The Otranto mosaic in the cathedral of L'Annunziata (1163–65) depicts an Alexander apparently mounted on the griffins that elevate him. An eleventh- or twelfth-century relief in the Basilica of San Marco in the Piazza San

Marco shows two baited griffins tied to a sort of platform in which
Alexander sits, while another object from the same period, a diadem in the
Museum of Historical Jewels of Ukraine in Kiev, shows the hero's upper
body as if emerging from a sort of pot or basket to which two griffins are
attached. A century later, in Santa Maria Della Strada, a thirteenth-century
tympanum above the south entrance shows Alexander on a more substantial aircraft made of unknown materials. Paris, Bibliothèque Nationale
ms. Fr. 786, f. 60v. (Tournai, middle or third quarter of 13th c.) shows four
griffins lifting a small house while Alexander peeks from a window, while
both London, British Library, ms. Royal 15 E VI, f. 20v. (Rouen, 1443–45)
and a woodcut from *Alixandre le Grant*, Paris, Le Noir 1506, elevate
Alexander in a cage. In Quintus Curtius (*Historia Alexandri Magni*, 15th c.,
Biblioteca Nacional de España, Vit. 22–9.2) Alexander is painted in a large
medallion set in the margin, and he seems to be sitting or standing on a
piece of earth as if detached from the surface itself of the world, carried by
four griffins, lowering his gaze upon the lower medallion, which depicts
the world as a large island crossed by rivers and populated by cities.

2 This is one way, if not the only one, in which cartographic representation
also distances itself from arguments on medieval visual culture in general
as put forth, for instance, in Jean-Claude Schmitt's insightful *Le Corps des
images*. In many of these collected studies Schmitt argues for a study of images that does not impose the methodologies for the reading of literature,
nor subordinates image to language but considers images unto themselves,
especially for medieval images. Cartographic representation, however,
establishes an explicit relationship with text, whether scientific or literary,
meditative, narrative or denotative. It is in this interplay that I see a sharing or borrowing of tropes and operations between the two discourses,
while trying to maintain the independence of each.

3 Edson, *Mapping Time and Space*, 4–5.

4 Carlos Benjamín Pereira Mira's *El "Codex Miscellaneus Ovetensis"* and *Éxodo
librario en la biblioteca capitular de Oviedo: El Codex Miscellaneus Ovetensis*
provide complete descriptions and a history of the volume.

5 See the detailed discussion of the representation of Paradise in medieval
cartography in Scafi, *Mapping Paradise*, esp. 84–124.

6 According to Agustín Millares Carlo, this manuscript could even be dated
to the end of the eighth century (*Nuevos estudios de paleografía española*, 41),
that is, right before the martyrdoms in Córdoba prompted the flight of
Mozarabs to Christian Spain. Thomas Glick accounts for different elements
of social, agricultural, and cultural life – including religious and dietary
questions – that can be attributed to these movements and settlements;

see his *Islamic and Christian Spain in The Early Middle Ages*, esp. 79–91, 169, 197–9, 219, 348–65, and bibliography.

7 Edson, *Mapping Time and Space*, 100, 116. The expression "geographical framework" is taken from David Woodward, "Medieval *Mappamundi*," 326. James S. Romm makes a similar argument for ancient thought through the notions of limit and origin in *The Edges of The Earth*, 20–6.

8 See Edson, *The World Map*, chap. 1, for the context of the Ebstorf within the elaborate *mappamundi* from the thirteenth century onward.

9 The best account of sources for the maps in the over twenty copies of Beatus's *Commentary* is John Williams, "Isidore, Orosius and the Beatus Map." Fourteen of the copies (or fragments) have maps, dating from the tenth to thirteenth centuries. Williams lists the manuscripts with maps on p. 10. See also volume 1 of his *The Illustrated Beatus* and Sáenz López-Pérez, *Los mapas de los Beatos*.

10 Gautier Dalché in fact counsels prudence in drawing conclusions based on the maps that appear in six of the *Nuzhat* manuscripts, since they were all copied at a considerably later period and especially because the text itself makes no reference to them ("Géographie arabe et géographie latine"). Another striking fact is that however astounding the information and impressive the scientific method employed in compiling that information and rendering it visually, Idrīsī's *Book of Roger* was only published in Arabic in 1592 and in Latin translation in 1619, and was published without the author's name and, more importantly, without maps. The map only appeared in print in the late eighteenth century.

11 See, among others, Tibbets, "The Beginnings of a Cartographic Tradition" and "The Balkhī School of Geographers"; Maqbul, "Cartography of al-Sharīf Al-Idrīsī" and *A History of Arab-Islamic Geography*.

12 Passages in the *Kitab al-masalik wa-l-mamalik* of al-Bakri, as well as glosses in three of its manuscripts, along with glosses in Arabic in Latin manuscripts of the *Etymologies* suggest a translation and confirm the circulation of Isidore across cultures. Gautier Dalché further mentions Ahman al-Razi's use of Isidore, and of the chronicles of Albelda and of 754 in the *Crónica del moro Rasis* ("Géographie arabe et géographie latine," see esp. notes 61, 62, and 64). The triangle formed by Orosius, the *Crónica del moro Rasis*, and the *Crónica Pseudo-Isidoriana* testify to historiographical influences in the Latin-Arabic direction; however, these cannot, based on evidence, be extended – or applied in reverse – to descriptive geography or cartography.

13 See Foer, "Secrets of A Mind-Gamer."

14 Jacob, *The Sovereign Map*, 179.

15 See Hazbun's interesting study on the arts of memory as social context and as part of the semantic field of *mester* in the *Alexandre* and the *Apolonio*, "Memory as 'Mester.'"

16 Menéndez Pidal, "Mozárabes y asturianos,"148.

17 Grant, *History of Natural Philosophy*, 100.

18 Grant, *History of Natural Philosophy*, 100–2.

19 Chenu, "L'Homme et la nature," quoted in *Didascalicon*, 164n36.

20 Julian Weiss's clarification of the concept and practice of didacticism for the *mester de clerecía* corpus, via Eloísa Palafox's insights, is crucial here. I will be referring to different aspects of the arguments in his introduction throughout; see here particularly 5–8.

21 Gautier-Dalché, "De la glose," 697.

22 Gautier-Dalché, "De la glose," 698. While Destombes (*Mappemondes*) documented 283 mss with maps dated before 1200, Gautier Dalché finds more than 400, and the list is more than likely not an exhaustive one.

23 Kramer, "The Earliest Known Map of Spain," 115. Kramer points out that "the literary text on the papyrus has been identified as coming from the second book of the *Geography* of Artemidorus of Ephesus … His eleven books, written about 100 BC, were a major source not only for Strabo, who wrote his *Geography* in the last decade B.C., and Marcianus of Heracleia, who compiled an epitome of Artemidorus's *Geography* in two books in the fourth century, but also for Diodorus Siculus, Pliny, Stephanus of Byzantium and others … It has long been known that Artemidorus had described the whole world, beginning with the Iberian peninsula, continuing with the rest of Europe, Asia Minor, India, Arabia, North Africa, and finally returning to the *stelai*, or gates, of Hercules at Gibraltar. Artemidorus was the first geographer to make use of the discoveries made by the Romans during the Punic wars in the western part of the *Imperium Romanum,* that is, in the Iberian Peninsula" (115–16). The organization of the description of the world follows a *periploi* and graphically describes a circle; narratively it also follows that shape, for which Iberia is both beginning and end, symbolically marking Iberia and making it both a geographic and a narrative point of departure and arrival – which marks an initial link between geography and narrative related to Iberia. The fragment recovered belongs to book 2 of the *Geography,* on Spain, and the map shows only the southwestern part of Iberia, is probably incomplete, and has no names.

24 Kramer, "The Earliest Known Map of Spain," 117–18. The story of the papyrus is extraordinary: it served first as a sketchbook and as a sort of catalogue of drawings (including of giraffes, tigers, and griffins, but also portraits of people) and then as mummy wrappings, was recovered by

Egyptologists in the early twentieth century, and was sold many years late to a German collector. It is now housed in Turin's Egyptian Museum. There is an extensive bibliography on the papyrus, and Kramer has numerous books and articles in German, English, and Spanish specifically on the cartographic elements.

25 See also the two collections based on the colloquium at the Casa de Velázquez, edited by G. Cruz Andreotti, P. Le Roux, and P. Moret, *La invención de una geografía de la Península Ibérica*, (vol. 1, *La época republicana* and vol. 2, *La época imperial*), especially Kramer, "La Península Ibérica" (in vol. 1), and, because of its importance to the medieval curriculum and its focus on the chapter on Hispania, Counillon, "La Représentation de l'espace" (in vol. 2).

26 Menéndez Pidal, "Mozárabes y asturianos," 139. The three oldest *mappaemundi* are the 776 Beatus, now lost; the Albi map (Albi Municipal Library, ms. 29) – a graphic gloss to an Orosius; and the Isidorian at the Apostolic Vatican Library (Ms. Lat. 6.028), all pre-800. The Beatus Iberian connection is obvious and needs not to be detailed here, but it is less known that the Albi map was probably drawn in Hispania or in the French southeast, for it is a codex in Visigothic script in which a passage from Isidore and a geographic chapter from Orosius are copied. The shape of the *oikumène* is reminiscent of a horseshoe, which recalls the map of the Strait of Gibraltar I refer to later on and has to remind a viewer of the horsehoe arches that came to characterize Iberian architecture, from the Romans, to the Visigoths to Islamic and Christian architecture. The Albi map has some 50 names taken from book 14 of Isidore's *Etymologies*, 45, also occurring in the text from Orosius that is copied in the ms. The Vatican map is of unknown provenance, but scholars suggest the French midi. It bears some 130 names, and is the most detailed of early *mappaemundi*. See Edson, "The Oldest World Maps."

27 An example of a mural *mappaemundi* that has been lost is that at Chalivoi-Milon, studied by Marcia Kupfer. The map, lost in 1885 to structural alterations, was approximately 15.6 metres long and 6 in diameter. It is known from two written descriptions linking it to medieval cartographic traditions, has been dated by Kupfer to the twelfth century, and, she argues, can be an iconographic prototype for the thirteenth-century Hereford *mappamundi*: "The lost nave painting at Chalivoy appears to have shared certain features with the imaginary *mappamundi* visualized by Hugh of St. Victor in his *De arca Noe mystica* of 1128–1129. The ideological agenda of the Chalivoy map, which describes the world so as to reveal the divine plan for its salvation in Christ, has a celebrated monumental parallel in

France, the central tympanum and lintel of the narthex at Vézélay. Indeed, the Chalivoy painting and the Vézélay sculpture can be linked historically to the same intellectual and political milieu. The Chalivoy map provides significant new evidence about the use of cartographic imagery in the public religious art of twelfth-century France ... [and] allow[s] fresh insight into the multiple functions of other monumental *mappaemundi* now lost and of large works on parchment" (541). Woodward remarks on wall maps and unbound large maps that have been lost ("Medieval Mappaemundi," 292, 335n238).

28 Moralejo Álvarez, "El mapa de la diáspora apostólica en San Pedro de Rocas," 315–23. Juan Sureda associates this map to the *mappamundi* in th Osma Beatus; J. Manuel García Iglesias agrees and goes on to relate it to the Lorvao and Oña Beatus (both Sureda and García Iglesias cited in Williams, "Isidore," 30). Williams states there is the possibility that the *mappamundi* in the Real Academia de la Historia (cód. 25) was influenced by a Beatus map, "for the likelihood that Castilian scribes in the 10th century had seen one is high."

29 Book 3 begins with the division of the earth in three continents, and after introducing Europe in general terms, Pliny goes on to describe Hispania, first in general and then by province. The fragment mentioning the map on the Porticus Vipsania, in chapter 3, is on Baetica.

30 Kitzinger actually names *mappaemundi* as source for the composition of the late twelfth-century floor mosaic in Turin ("World Map and Fortune's Wheel," 358). The cartographic depiction of the world, which houses an image of Fortuna at its centre, draws information, predictably, from Isidore. Its spatiality – a viewer of this map also "walks" the world – further emphasizes the interpellation of the allegory at its centre, while not excluding the abstract idea of the worldly rise and fall of empires within the frame of mortality, surrounded by the eternal kingdom of God. For the interpretation, which links the floor mosaic to the imagined floor map of Baudri in an architectural transposition of cosmography, see Barral i Altet, "Poésie et iconographie." For a general account of the relations between these floor mosaic *mappaemundi* and other more diagrammatic sources see Donkin, "*Usque ad Ultimum Terrae*."

31 The imaginary status of Baudri's map, which other scholars have considered based on a real floor map, is underlined by Tilliette, "La chambre de la comtesse Adèle."

32 Gautier Dalché ("De la glose") looks at a wide number of early medieval maps in manuscripts, among them some examples from Iberia. He argues for a codicological interpretation of the role(s) of maps in relation to the

texts they are bound with, a role that shifts from being a gloss to being it-self glossed by the accompanying text. This is an extensive, insightful view into the role of cartography in twelfth-century culture. I rely on it to tease out ways in which this culture might have intersected with the composi-tion of fiction in Iberoromance, specifically with the articulation of the first works of what we know as the *mester de clerecía*. However, especially in terms of the dating of the maps in the Escorial mss., and in respect to con-clusions on the Beatus *mappaemundi*, I prefer Williams's readings ("Isidore").

33 See Appendix for a list of manuscripts containing maps considered in this study.

34 The connections between cartography and mirrors cannot be elaborated upon here, but I point out some of these at the end of the chapter through through the notions of double vision, knowledge, and vanity underlined in the *Libro de Alexandre*.

35 This is but a sampling. Chronological errors are not intended but possible – especially for the first two manuscripts, since they would present the earliest examples of an "Isidorian" T/O map, for which the dating is con-troversial. I have compiled this corpus using Destombes, Gautier Dalché, Menéndez Pidal, and my own research. Some of these manuscripts contain more than one map. The corpus obviously excludes the Beatus *mappae-mundi* tradition, which has been extensively studied, as noted above, except for those Beatus manuscripts that also bear small *mappamundi* in the first folios. The corpus utilized here is intended to illustrate a more generalized familiarity with cartography, running parallel to the specific Beatus tradition.

36 The Beatus manuscripts have a very particular tradition of copying, dis-semination, and dependence upon a text. Most recently, see the work by Sandra Sáenz López-Pérez. From this tradition, I will only include the square map in the genealogical part of the *Beato de doña Sancha*, which is a second map, very different from the apostollic maps that appear in the usual place in the Beatus text.

37 See Appendix for an (idiosyncratically) annotated list of this working corpus.

38 "Isidore," 13.

39 "Isidore," 13.

40 Antolín notes the presence of the maps, including that of the Strait of Gibraltar, in his description of the manuscript, and points out that the manuscript has many marginal notes, including some in Arabic (*Catálogo de los manuscritos latinos*). Besides the general emphasis on geography and history as backdrop for the presence of these maps, which speaks to car-tography's role in thematizing the place of Hispania in geography and

history (item 5, for example, is a compendium of chapter 4 of book 14 of the *Etymologies*, on Europe), there are a number of other texts – if not visual renderings – that underline the organizational, structural role of cartography by their presence within this codex (item 3, f. 44, is the complementary Maritime Antonine Itinerary, followed by the itinerary of islands in f. 45; item 5 is a division of the ecclesiastical provinces of Spain; item 17, f. 95, is an inventory of books).

41 The manuscript has been digitized, and is available for viewing on PARES (http://pares.mcu.es/), the very useful and immense portal for Spanish Archives.

42 Its strange border and spatial distribution has also called comparisons with an inverted pentagon, or a mirrored map.

43 I am not able to consult Emily Steiner and Lynn Ransom's collection of essays *Taxonomies of Knowledge: Information and Order in Medieval Manuscripts*, announced for publication in November 2015, which will address many of the interesting problematics at work here.

44 *Medieval Grammar and Rhetoric*, 5.

45 *Medieval Grammar and Rhetoric*, 9.

46 For the textual history of the *Libro de Alexandre*, see Casas Rigall's edition.

47 I will elaborate specifically on this in the next chapter. For a catalogue and sources for the *Libro de Alexandre* see Such, "The Origins and Use of School Rhetoric," especially 76ff. On abbreviation in the *Alexandre*, see Casas Rigall, "La abbreviatio y sus funciones poéticas."

48 As Alexander's men disembark on the shores of Asia *as if they owned it*, the poet brackets his own geographical digression, *desputaçión*, arguing that it is a question of how the matter, the subject demands it, *la materia nos manda* (st. 276). This is, as Casas Rigall notes in his edition, the first long digression in the *Libro de Alexandre*. The first information we get about this *mappamundi* is the tripartite division, the information of the dividing seas as arms, the larger size of one part or continent, and its warmer temperature in comparison with the smaller two. After division, size and temperature, the poet notes orientation and only in the next stanza, 279 are the names of the continents noted, linking Europe to Christianity, Asia and Africa to Islam. It is notable that the names of Noah's sons are not invoked; also notable are the links to religion. In any case, it is clear that the source map has included zonal information in a T/O distribution. In 280, the poet notes the symbolic interpretation as the cross of the graphic disposition of the waters that divide the continents. The repetition in Casas Rigall's notes that these images and that T/O maps represent "discs" is unfortunate (see notes to 276–294 and 280bc in pages 203–205). The description of Asia up

to 287 does not seem to correspond to information provided by a map, for it is general in nature. The mention of Paradise and the *fons paradisi* in 287 seems to respond to cartographic information, followed by information on mountains, provinces and cities and due to the language employed: *yaz'en un rincón*, it lies in a corner; *Septentrión*; *En Asia yaz'Asiria*; *allí son*; *ý son*; and the mention of a series of place names with some historical elaboration the poet draws from memory, linking history and place. The description of the map in detail does not continue with the other continents, for it is Asia that is pertinent to the subject matter, where the hero and his men have disembarked and where the stage of the ensuing battles will be.

49 Casas Rigall annotates this beginning of the digression in his edition as being an image presented as a flat disk: this is misleading and supports one of the most pervasive clichés about medieval scientific knowledge, the idea that a "flat earth" had some currency. The fact that maps must be drawn on a bidimensional medium, such as parchment, is not evidence of an idea of a flat earth. All of the texts refer to the world as a sphere, and often the diagrams of eclipses or other cosmographic information that share a codex with maps confirm such spherical conception of the world. Today's world maps are also printed on bidimensional media, often framed within a rectangle, and no one argues that the contemporary *imago mundi* is a flat rectangular shape.

50 This last verse has been much discussed, but its meaning remains unclear. I am loosely following Willis's interpretation (*The Relationship*). See Casas Rigall's note to the verse on page 204.

51 "Ancora sulle ekphrasis," Marta Materni's article on ekphrasis in the *Libro de Alexandre* in the context of the *roman antique*, highlights patterns in description across languages and also the originality of the *Alexandre*. While it does not mention cartography, it goes over many of the same stanzas and provides useful comparative texts.

52 In Ian Michael's division the stanzas are found in the investiture passage from 89–126, with the *Roman d'Alexandre* as source (B or Venice recension, verses 84–410 (*The Treatment of Classical Material*, appendix, 287). Raymond Willis, in *The Debt of the Spanish Libro de Alexandre to the French Roman d'Alexandre*, notes that the passages devoted to sword and shield are taken from two different places in the *Roman d'Alexandre* (b 345–82 y b 713–57): "Both passages agree that the shield was made of the skin of a fish, but the first concentrates on its decoration and the second explains that the fish was a dolphin and that the shield had been made by necromancy. But disregarding for the moment the differences in the two accounts and regarding them as mutually supplementary, we note one fundamental difference

between the decasyllabic and the Spanish versions, namely, that the French poem presents the descriptive material as elements of a narrative, while the Spanish passage is pure description. In addition, minor differences are observable, but the points of similarity are numerous and significant" (15). He also remarks on the coincidence of the motif of the lion in the shield, but makes no mention of the *mappamundi* in the previous verses. Do these verses have a parallel, or are they some of those "negligible details only found in the Spanish"?

53 Rodríguez-Velasco reads the map of the shield in heraldic key in his *Ciudadanía, soberanía monárquica y caballería: Poética del orden de caballería,* and goes further to claim the the shield does not merely announce the future conquests, but is the "expression of the desire of geography and history," it is an emblem which constitutes a "discourse created by Alexander himself" as a result of a crisis of legitimacy, identity, and education. See especially pp. 230–5.

54 The Peutinger Table or Map has been dated to the twelfth or thirteenth century, but it derives from an archetype of the fourth century. This dating is possible by the suggestion of vignettes, in which a city, for example Rome, "is personified as an enthroned goddess holding a globe, a spear and a shield" (illustration caption, plate 5, in Harley and Woodward, *History of Cartography*, vol. 1).

55 Dilke, "Itineraries and Geographical Maps," 234–48.

56 Copeland and Sluitker make this argument of the road of reading as the other side of the coin in the basic study of grammar, with one side portraying linguistic logic and the other pointing at textual analysis and commentary (*Medieval Grammar and Rhetoric*, 18–19).

57 In stanzas 106–7 the poem goes back to the shield to relate that it was made of the skin of a fish, making it impenetrable, and that it had the magic power to bestow fatal consequences upon anything that struck it. Willis's conclusions on the relation of this specific passage to the French *Roman d'Alexandre* are that "certainly neither Alexandre de Paris nor L was the source … the *Alexandre* is, at best, a free reworking of the source material, and, consequently, one might be tempted to see in it the influence of other romances … the substitution of classical figures may well be due simply to an attempt on the part of the Spanish poet to tinge his work with a certain classical erudition in keeping with his main theme" (*The Debt*, 17–18).

58 See Arizaleta, *La Translation d'Alexandre*, 137–40.

59 See Casas Rigall, "Introducción," second section (18–30). In this description the mention of *Marruecos*, translating the Latin *magnae Kartaginis arces*, is particularly interesting in cartographic terms, for the first time that

Marruecos is mentioned in a geographic contexts is in Hugh of Saint Victor's textual description of a map in 1130 (Gautier Dalché, "Géographie arabe," 13). Aníbal Biglieri's notes on ethnography as related to geographical knowledge in medieval Spanish literature are thorough and the most interesting element of his *Las ideas geográficas y la imagen del mundo en la literatura española medieval.*

60 The best-known medieval itinerary map is of course Matthew Paris's route to the Holy Land, dated to the mid-thirteenth century, which marks staging points and distances. The manuscripts are available online on the British Library's website. The last stage in the itinerary is featured with a zoomable, interactive image on the online gallery as "Matthew Paris's Map of the Route to Jerusalem" (St Albans, c. 1250, British Library Royal MS 14 C vii, f. 5).

61 See an extended argument on ekphrases in Clara Pascual-Argente's insightful article "'El cabdal sepulcro': Word and Image in the *Libro de Alexandre*."

62 See Materni's comparison of the text of the *Alexandre* with the *Ilias Latina,* the *Roman de Thèbes,* Matthieu de Vendôme's *Ars,* and the *Semejança del mundo,* in pp. 34–5 of Appendice 2 of her "Ancora sulle *ekphrasis.*"

63 Especially interesting here and demanding further study is the common theme in both secular and sacred medieval art of depicting a sovereign or Christ himself with a diagrammatic, tripartite globe or orb. Frequently, as a reference to the end of the world or the Last Judgment, an orb is placed at Christ's feet. Perhaps also related to the link between cartography and power is the depiction of parts of the world or of cities on coins, as in the Ionian coin map (Harley and Woodward, *History of Cartography,* fig. 9.7), a connection that should be explored for medieval Iberia. Cf.: "A different medium for the dissemination of miniature map images is found in the Ionian coins probably struck by Memnon of Rhodes, who acted as a Persian general in Ephesus until the arrival of Alexander in 334 BC. In this series of Rhodian-weight tetradrachms, the obverse type is the figure of the Persian king, running or kneeling right. The reverse is a rectangular incuse with irregular raised areas, recognizable as a map depicting the physical relief of the hinterland of Ephesus ... the map images, of course, serve no practical purpose, but they have a symbolic or propaganda value" (*History of Cartography,* 158); also interesting are coins struck in Rome that represented the globe crossed by two bars as a symbol of empire (164).

64 See Arizaleta, "Del texto de Babel a la biblioteca de Babilonia. Algunas notas sobre el Libro de Alexandre," for the full account of sources for the passage.

65 On the *locus amoenus* in both the *Alexandre* and the *Alexandreis* see Pejenaute Rubio, "El locus amoenus."

66 Casas Rigall cites verses 435–348 of book 5 of the *Alexandreis*. I quote
    here David Townsend's translation of the passage: "Without delay, the
    Macedonian/from open hand doled Arbela's vast treasure/until the
    army felt the burden, and/their greed was sated by the recent plunder./
    Traversing Syria swifter than storms/borne on the South Wind, vanquish-
    ing its citizens/by force or friendship, now he burned to pierce/*the baked-
    brick walls* and gain the palaces/inside that city marked by praise of
    kings,/*which drew its lasting fame from tongues' confusion.*/From *Semiramis's
    town* he stood as far/as Saint-Denis lies from the Seine's broad waters,/
    when lo! that noble man Mazaeus and/his much loved son came forward
    as deserters,/surrendering themselves and *Babylon*/to Alexander's sway
    …" (lines 502–17 of Townsend's translation, p. 124, emphasis mine).
    As Townsend notes, this recalls the identification of Babel and Babylon
    in book 2, in the context of Darius's harangue: "If ancient monuments re-
    main, if memory/still serves our fathers' record, who knows not/that we
    trace back our lineage to the Giants?/Who has heard nothing of our strife
    with gods/the bricks baked by our forbears and the mortar/with which
    they built the Tower? Who forgets/the city whose eternal name derives/
    from tongue's confusion?" (lines 405–12, p. 63). The passage is narrated
    in greater detail in the *Roman d'Alexandre*, with the emphasis on biblical
    detail coming from the Spanish poet. See Bañeza Román, *Las fuentes bíbli-
    cas, patrísticas y judaicas*, 98–9.
67 Willis, *The Debt*, 24–31.
68 "El omne que crïado fuese en Babilonia/de duro entendrié la lengua de
    Iconia;/más son de otros tantos que cuenta la estoria,/*mas yo pora saberlos
    de seso non he copia*" (*Libro de Alexandre*, stanza 1517, my emphasis) (He who
    were raised in Babylon/would surely understand the language of Iconia;/
    there are so many more that the story tells/but to know them I have no
    sufficient brains).
69 Willis, *The Debt*, 31.
70 Beyond the long episode here studied, stanzas 88, 655, and 948 mention
    the Tower specifically; stanza 990 alludes to it through the giants and the
    confusion of languages; stanza 1241 mentions confused giants and a tall
    tower as absolutely original to the Spanish poet from a vague reference in
    the *Alexandreis* within Estatira's tomb ekphrasis; stanza 1369 mentions the
    Tower and the fight with the gods, in more classical overtones; stanza 2552
    mentions giants, Tower, and confusion. The latest editor of the *Alexandre*,
    Juan Casas Rigall, considers a mention of giants in stanza 2025 to be an al-
    lusion to the Tower, which I find improbable; conversely I consider stanza
    2586 as a mention of the episode, as Casas Rigall does not, where ending

with the geography and history of Asia in asyndetical *abbreviatio* with the allusion to the tribes and lineages of human history in the Babel episode seems the appropriate cap to the description of the third panel of Alexander's tent. The abbreviation alludes to the first *mappamundi* in the *Libro*, consonant with book 2 of Gautier's in which the detailed description of Asia includes the Tower.

71 Another instance of measuring, in this case *with his own feet*, in 2676d.

72 I have translated "logares convinientes" as "convenient places," since the sense of their being good or advisable mirrors the meaning in other texts, especially in the common phrase *tiempos y logares convinientes*. It is tempting, however, to hear also an echo of a spatial nature, where Marruecos and the Montes Claros are placed next to each other.

73 Casas Rigall explains 2461b *soyazientes* as *subjected to*, the lands that are subject to Morocco, in imperial key. I insist that the cartographic *spatial* connotation is more logical, also as a present participle of SUBIACERE, literally *lying below*, as in graphic depiction on a map oriented to the east.

74 Casas Rigall interprets this carpet as a "cape" that he labels a shroud, thus anticipating Alexander's death. There is, however, no reference to death in this particular episode and, as Casas Rigall himself notes, the poet, in contrast to his reaction to the submarine expedition, expresses no incredulity at the possibility of Alexander's flight (notes to page 684).

75 Rico underlines the structural role of this digression, this "pintura del mundo en forma humana," in the entire poem, *El pequeño mundo del hombre*, p. 59. See especially the beginning of the section "De la Edad Media al Siglo de Oro," 47–266.

76 Willis, *The Debt*, 40–1. Numerous scholars refer to this "world-as-man" vision, and some even call it an anthropomorphic map but they fail to note the Christic dimension.

77 See Suzanne Conklin Akbari and Jill Ross's rich introduction, "Limits and Teleology: The Many Ends of the Body," to their edited volume *The Ends of the Body* (3–21, esp. 6–9).

78 "Pope Zacharias (pope 741–752) was known to have had a world map painted on the wall of the Lateran palace, and Charlemagne possessed three silver tables described in the *Vita Karoli Magni:* one of Constantinople, one of Rome, and a third, a 'description of the whole world,' which has been reconstructed and interpreted by Estey and others as a celestial map" (Woodward "Medieval *Mappaemundi*," 303). For San Pedro de Rocas, see the beginning of this chapter.

79 Another interesting element to explore within cartography for the framing of the *mappamundi* is the representation of calendars as surrounding the

world, as in the Mappamundi of Giovanni Leardo, 1448 (Harley and Woodward, *History of Cartography*, vol. 1, plate 20). The *Catalan Atlas* itself contains, for example, a lunar calendar where the concentric rings also illustrate the elements, zodiac signs, astrological texts, and figures all framed by figural representations of the four seasons.

80 Already suggested by Arizaleta in "Alexandre en su *Libro*" and *La Translation d'Alexandre*; for the courtly context see also Gómez Redondo, "La materia caballeresca," and Carlos Alvar, "Consideraciones a propósito."

81 The original verb here, *devisar*, merges a general meaning of "division" with that of "being seen" or perceived, with a further specific meaning of "being distiguished pictorially," as in heraldics. Rodríguez-Velasco uses the term for his reading of the map on Alexander's shield as emblem. See note 53 above.

82 The strange precision on the part of the poet that Europe and Africa seem "adopted" ("annadas"), due to their significantly smaller size than Asia, while they should be "daughters," becomes absolutely understandable if read against the background of the allocation of the continents to Noah's sons. There is a gender change because of the *language*, feminizing the continents, but their metaphoric relationship remains a biblico-cartographic one.

83 H. Salvador Martínez has analysed the calendar in "La tienda de Amor, espejo de la vida humana."

84 Dilke, "Cartography in the Byzantine Empire," 258–9.

85 See Ancos, "El narrador como maestro en el mester de clerecía," *eHumanista* 12 (2009): 48–64, esp. 5off.

86 Jacob, *The Sovereign Map*, 23.

Chapter 2

1 On the traits of *cuaderna vía*, see Gómez Moreno, "Notas al prólogo del *Libro de Alexandre*."

2 Willis, "Mester," 212–14.

3 Gómez Redondo points out the different emphases provided by the variants: while *P* would emphasize composition, reading *fer*, *O* would underline the role of transmission in *leer* (*Poesía española 1*, note to page 274). Ancos offers an extensive discussion of this stanza in particular in its recitative and compositional aspects as part of the discipline of reading, but also in the context of Hugh of Saint Victor and John of Salisbury's typology of reading in the *Didascalicon* and the *Metalogicon* ("El narrador como maestro," esp. 53–7, and *Transmisión y recepción*).

4 The commentary of literary texts was an intrinsic part of learning a variety of disciplines, central to the language arts curriculum, which I will discuss below. See Gómez Redondo, "El fermoso fablar," and Grande Quejigo, "Quiero leer un livro," | 101–12. On oral and written diffusion of literary material as referenced in the *Libro de Alexandre*, see Grande Quejigo, and see also Ancos, "El narrador como maestro" and *Transmisión y recepción*. Ancos develops this notion in "El narrador como maestro," which I discuss later on in this chapter.

5 The scant evidence of the existence of a *studium generale* in Palencia, regardless of how many scholars insist there must have been a university, and the short period for which formal establishment of studies in theology and grammar can be said to have been offered here (1212–14), is just enough to characterize this as an interesting hypothesis until new information emerges. However, a cathedral school model and curriculum for the region are safer to consider, and it is in this general way that I will consider the intellectual and scholarly context of the *Alexander* poet. See Hastings, *The Universities of Europe*, 65–8, for the cautious approach that remains, to my mind, appropriate.

6 Copeland, *Rhetoric* (55n3 and elsewhere). For these reasons it is especially problematic that Such's "The Origins" has not been published.

7 As Amaia Arizaleta suggested in *La Translation d'Alexandre*.

8 On the *Liber regum*, see Francisco Bautista's overview regarding the *Chronica Regum Castellae*, "Escritura cronística e ideología histórica," 429, and his remarkable reconstruction in "Original, versiones e influencia del Liber regum." On the *Chronica Naierense* see Alberto Montaner Frutos, "El proyecto historiográfico del Archetypum Naiarense." The articles are part of two special issues coordinated by Georges Martin in *e-spania*; these particular ones highlight connections with politics and literature that are relevant to my argument here.

9 Arizaleta, "Topografías," 48, 49–50.

10 Arizaleta, "Topografías," 49.

11 Arizaleta, "Topografías," 50–1.

12 Arizaleta, "Topografías," 53. Arizaleta calls this mode of recording history a "fabrication," and attributes intention and conscious foresight of the results of such a propaganda (her words) to the chancelleries, attributing to these clerics a level of awareness and a consciousness of project that is not evident in their granting the king first the status of character and then the role of author. Insisting on terms such as "fabrication" or "propaganda machine" obscures the hybrid threads woven into such an enterprise, for these clerics had in fact the task, the obligation – *el ministerio* – and not

(only) an explicit and conscious goal, of producing text from and for the monarchy about events that were memorable not only for the king but for the general population. It seems at times that Arizaleta attributes the importance of battles such as Las Navas to a purely clerical "propaganda machine," as if they had not been memorable for a general population in different degrees and perspectives, and related to Alfonso VIII's figure, if not for these clerical snippets.

13 Documentation for both cathedral and monastic libraries is scarce for the period before the thirteenth century, in stark contrast with the ample number of inventories and catalogues for the period in the rest of Europe. The only exception in the inventory of the library of the monastery of Ripoll, which held, according to a 1047 document, some 250 works (Guijarro González, *Maestros, escuelas y libros*, 133). Guijarro González documents both books inventoried and books in circulation, finding that in the period covering the tenth to the twelfth century there are 135 mentions of books and in the thirteenth century 436. The distribution of these mentions is interesting, for the first two centuries are mostly references coming from the cathedrals in the kingdom of León (Astorga, León, Zamora), while the thirteenth-century references come mostly from Castile: Burgo de Osma and Burgos (122–7). The cathedral inventories of the thirteenth, however, do not explain the silence of previous centuries, which contradicts the evidence of production we have in manuscripts that we know to have been produced in the monasteries of San Pedro de Cardeña, Santo Domingo de Silos, Santa María de Albelda, and San Millán de la Cogolla (see Díaz y Díaz, *Libros y librerías* and *Códices visigóticos* and their extensive bibliographies, for a number of studies on this production).

14 The thirteenth century would see a change towards Aristotle's *Rhetoric*, whose absence before then from Iberian libraries has been noted by Faulhaber (see below). See also Martínez Casado, "Aristotelismo hispano en la primera mitad del siglo XIII" on Aristotle, Averroes, and natural philosophy in León. See Heusch, "Entre didactismo y heterodoxia" on the Iberian emphasis on an Oriental model of moral philosophy expressed in sapiential literature as reason for the lack of interest in the *Ethics* before the fifteenth century, nonwithstanding the introduction of concepts and elements through Boethius, Cicero, and other Aristotelian works. Precise documentation for the curriculum that clerics of the *mester* would have followed is further complicated by the lack of definitive evidence of place of composition for many of these works. Besides Berceo, other works have been alternately traced, due to dating, specific geographical markers, influence, linguistic evidence, and so on, from Palencia, as a Western limit,

all the way to the westernmost point of the medieval kingdom of Navarre. This area, generally known as the Rioja region, or even the High Rioja, was controlled at different times within the period I consider by both Navarre and Castile; therefore I consider studies focusing on both kingdoms. Guijarro Gozález notes that grammars popular in the eleventh, twelfth, and thirteenth centuries, such as Papias, Balbus, Villadei, and Peter of Blois, while not documented in cathedral inventories, were in the hands of clerics in León, for instance. For books and libraries in medieval Spain, see Faulhaber, *Libros y bibliotecas en la España medieval*.

15 Guijarro González, *Maestros, escuelas y libros*, 142. I mention only the "liberal arts" curriculum; Guijarro González also documents the important collection of theological and juridical works around which these cathedral schools and those dependent on them seem to have been built and that constituted the core of their holdings and interest, which also helps explain the development of a juridical discourse in the service of the royal chancelleries. See in the same work 143–60 for theology and 160–4 for law, and corresponding parts in each chapter. Scholastic theology of the twelfth century (Anselm, Peter Lombard, Peter Comestor, Peter of Poitiers) is especially well represented, and the *Opera omnia* of Hugh of Saint Victor was kept at the Burgo de Osma Cathedral. (152–3). Glossaries and florilegia as well as, curiously, works related to the new grammarians of the thirteenth century (Hugo of Pisa, Villadei, Peter of Blois) are more numerous in monastic libraries (285–6).

16 "La circulation des manuscripts," 11–61, and "La transmisión de los textos antiguos," 155. See also Guijarro González, *Maestros, escuelas y libros*, 145; Gonzálvez Ruiz, *Hombres y libros en Toledo*.

17 As I wrote above, I am only referencing books that seem to have informed the *mester* directly; however, there are many other interesting works that establish the preference for French and Hispanic authors, for instance, above English ones, or the striking absence of more Greek and Arabic scientific works, given the intense translating activity in Toledo, pointing to a specialized interest in those works that did not include cathedral libraries in the North.

18 Guijarro González, *Maestros, escuelas y libros*, 304–8.

19 Guijarro González, *Maestros, escuelas y libros*, 318.

20 See Reilly, "The Chancery of Alfonso VII," and Wright, "Bilingualism and Diglossia," 343. Wright reflects on the links between chancelleries, courts, and archbishophrics, though geared towards linguistic questions, for instance, in "Latin and Romance in the Castilian Chancery"; but see also

Linehan, "Don Rodrigo and the Government," for the enduring power struggles between bishops and kings over these appointments.

21 Guijarro González, *Maestros, escuelas y libros*, 261.

22 Lucas de Tuy's remarks (ca. 1236) come up in a list of achievements of the Castilian king, among them that he *evocavit magistros theologicos et aliarum arium liberalium* and that he *Palentiae scholas constituit*; Jiménez de Rada recalls among his virtues the building of the monastery of Las Huelgas and the Burgos hospital, as well as the institution of the *studium omnium facultatum* in Palencia (cited in Rucquoi, "La royauté," 216).

23 Rucquoi, "La royauté," 222; see also "La double vie du *studium* de Palencia."

24 Guijarro González, *Maestros, escuelas y libros*, 256.

25 Rucquoi, "La royauté," 219–20.

26 See, among others, Michael, *The Treatment*; Cacho Blecua, "El saber y el dominio"; Arizaleta, "La figure d'Alexandre le Grand" and *Les Clercs au palais*; and Sánchez Jiménez, *La literatura*.

27 García, "La médiation du clerc," and Weiss, *The mester de clerecía*. Ancos ("El narrador como maestro," note 20 to page 58) argues not against such mediation (or poets of *mester* as intermediaries, as Weiss puts it), but against the works themselves conceived as mediations, with this goal. I argue along the same lines, if with different intentions, below.

28 From a different set of readings, Weiss proposes this figure of the intellectual as well, using Gramsci eloquently; see his introduction to *The Mester de Clerecía*.

29 Adeline Rucquoi, "La royauté," 216, 221.

30 Cited in Rucquoi, "La royauté," 216.

31 Rucquoi, "La royauté," 223, 227–9.

32 Cited in Rucquoi, "La royauté," 230 (see 229–32 for examples); Biglieri, *Las ideas geográficas*. This ethnographic air has been noted by others for individual works, for instance Diego García de Campos (Rucquoi, 238); see Luis García Ballester, "Naturaleza y ciencia."

33 Related to this is Arizaleta's "Les vers sur la pierre" and Hazbun's "Memory as Mester."

34 Rucquoi, "La royauté," 240.

35 Arizaleta, "El *Libro de Alexandre*." The argument is constantly repeated throughout the article: for instance, "the lettered cleric which composed (the *Alexandre*) gave wings to the government program of a peninsular monarch –perhaps Alfonso VIII of Castile; more likely Fernando III – putting at his service his art of writing" (74); "we can affirm without a doubt that our anonymous author was a lettered cleric, among those who had

acquired the most knowledge in his time … its natural reception had to be courtly, the 'model' receptor of this text would have been the monarch, he for whom the poem was built" (79–80); "there abound in the *Alexandre* indications that the monarchic matter has been chosen, and perfectly accommodated for the exhibition of knowledge laid out by the arch-lettered poet" (80).

36 Arizaleta, *Les Clercs au palais*.
37 Arizaleta, "Topografías," 44–5.
38 Wright, *El Tratado de Cabreros*.
39 *Partida II*, title 9, law 4, 312–13.
40 Douglas Kelly, *The Art of Medieval French Romance*, 66.
41 Geoffroi of Vinsauf, *Poetry Nova of Geoffrey of Vinsauf*, 17.
42 Carruthers, "The Poet as Master-Builder," 887–91.
43 See Carruthers' remarks on this on p. 895.
44 Carruthers, "The Poet as Master-Builder," 896.
45 *Theory* is, of course, a medieval word, brought from Greek into Latin from a common root (*theastai*) that also gives us *theatre*, linked through shared meanings related to speculation, contemplation, and the like. In Antonio de Nebrija's *Vocabulario español-latino* of 1495, *theoria* is listed between "speculation" and "species" where it designates both the contemplative and the art of speculation, from theory to the perception of its quality.
46 See Pinet, "Walk on The Wild Side."
47 See Casas Rigall's notes to stanzas 1800–2, p. 545. See also Michael Agnew, "Como en libro abierto."
48 Arizaleta cites other sources on Jiménez de Rada and his linguistic ability in "El orden de Babel," 7. Arizaleta looks at these different uses of Babel as reflections on the division of nations based on language, underlining Jiménez de Rada's mention of frontiers and Diego de Campos's pondering of the resulting civil wars. In an observation not directly relevant to her reflection, I want to note how remarkable it is that Diego de Campos reflects on this division as an Iberian phenomenon, while Jiménez de Rada's mention not only of frontiers but of the division into nations and dispersal along climates and provinces recalls cartographic habits that also explain the inventories of peoples that follow, in a similar order to that of the *Alexandre*: "*Proh dolor, hispania suis intestinis preliis sepe sepius inconsolabiliter devastata: ab ignotis et advenis non nunquam legitur occupata. Hinc est quod diversarum linguarum vestigia. Velut reliquias et fracmenta hydiomatum adhuc hodie servat hyberia*" (Diego de Campos); "*loquele diversitas conuictos, mores et animos uariauit unilingues, aliam et ceterarum linguarum alias sortite sunt regiones, et prout unius lingue professio exigebat, diuersos populos effecerunt,*

et ab inuicem segregati climata prouincias et patrias diuiserunt" (Jiménez de Rada, *Historia de rebus Hispanae*), cited in Arizaleta, "El orden de Babel," 8, 9.

49 This is to serve as a contrasting text only, for these types of Bibles were probably produced only from the mid-thirteenth century onward and could therefore not have been a source for the *Libro de Alexandre,* or the *mester* in general in its beginnings. However, they do offer a roughly contemporary version of the story with interesting differences in emphases.

50 See Zumthor, *Babel,* 34ff.

51 The Hebrew reference and beyond, to Accadian, resolves the nomenclature problem in the *Libro de Alexandre* ("Babel" versus "Babilonia" and "Babilón"), which Arizaleta discusses in "Del texto de Babel," 59 and notes. For archaeological research and architectonic identifications of the work, including the superposition of a temple on the Tower of Babel that supports the interpretation of the episode as an act of idolatry followed by divine punishment, see Parrot, *La Tour de Babel,* and Contenau, "La tour de Babel."

52 The other tradition that serves as a source for Genesis 11 is the Priestly or Sacerdotal; it seems though that only for the last verses, and the Babel episode only corresponds to the first nine, none of them related to the Priestly tradition; the Elohist tradition is not a source for the first eleven chapters of Genesis.

53 Zumthor, *Babel,* 34.

54 See her "Notas para el texto del *Alexandre*" and, especially, "Datos para la leyenda de Alejandro." Flavius Josephus's text reads as follows:

113 Nebrodes, who was the son of Chamas, the son of Nochos, raised them to insolence and contempt of God. He was bold and physically brave. Now he persuaded them not to attribute their prosperity to God but to consider that their own virtue brought this to them.

114 And little by little he transformed the state of affairs into a tyranny, believing that only thus would men be free of fear of God if they would continue to use their own power; and he kept on threatening that he would take revenge on God if He wished to flood the earth again. For he would build a tower higher than the water could reach and he would execute vengeance also for the destruction of his forefathers.

115 The masses were eager to follow the views of Nebrodes, considering it slavery to submit to God. And they built a tower omitting nothing of zeal nor showing hesitancy in doing the work. And, owing to the great number of laborers, it reached a height more swiftly than anyone might have expected.

116 However, its thickness was so strong that its height appeared smaller to those who saw it. It was built of baked brick bound together

with bitumen, in order that it might not collapse. Seeing them thus out of their mind, God decided not to obliterate them utterly because they had not even been brought to their senses by those who had first perished,

117 but he cast them into factional strife by causing them to speak various languages and causing them not to understand themselves owing to the variety of languages. The place in that they built the tower is now called Babylon because of the confusion in the original clarity of language. For the Hebrews call confusion "Babel."

118 A Sibyl also mentions this tower and the difference of languages of men in the following words: "When all men spoke the same language, certain ones built a very lofty tower in order thereby to go up to heaven. But the gods sent winds and overthrew the tower and gave each one an individual speech. And for this reason it happened that the city was called Babylon."

119 And Hestiaios mentions the plain that is called Senaar in the land of Babylonia in these words: "Those of the priests who were saved took the consecrated objects of Zeus Enyalios and went to Senaar in Babylonia."

120 From that time on they were scattered owing to their diverse languages and they established colonies everywhere, and each group occupied the land that they came upon and to that God led them, so that every continent, both the interior and the coast, was filled with them. And there were some who crossed the sea in ships and took their residence on islands.

121 Some of the nations preserve the names given by their founders, but some changed them, in order to make them appear more intelligible to their neighbors. The Greeks are the ones who are responsible for this. For when in later times they came to power they made the glory of the past their own, adorning the peoples with names intelligible to themselves and imposing upon them a political constitution as if they were descended from themselves.

Some relevant paraphrasing from the copious notes to this resource:

Philo comments on Nimrod (*Quaestiones in Genesim* 2:82) that "the impious man is none other than the enemy and foe who stands against God. Wherefore it is proverbial that everyone who is a great sinner should be compared with him as the chief head and fount," and both the *Jerusalem Targum* on Gen. 10:9 and the *Midrash Gen. Rabbah* 37.2, *Pirqe de-Rabi Eliezer* 24, also refer to Nimrod as a sinner and insolent, contemptuous of God, and relate him to the Tower (n. 286 and 287). Note also that while Nimrod is referred to as a hunter in Gen. 10:9, the Palestinian Targumim "hunter" is here interpreted as "rebel," synonymous with "sinner," and the *Midrash*

Gen. Rabbah 37.2 takes it to be a metaphor, explaining "hunter" as "he snared the people by words" (n. 288), which brings this back to rhetorical ability, a craft of words. Insolence is the translation of *hubris* in Josephus. Josephus and the rabbinic tradition (cited in this source are *Erubin* 53a, *Ḥagigah* 13a, *Pesaḥim* 94b; *Ḥullin* 89a, *Abodah Zarah* 53b, *Midrash Gen. Rabbah* 23.7, 26.4, and 42.4, *Pirqe de-Rabbi Eliezer* 34, cited by Ginzberg [1925, 5, 201n88]) coincide in making Nimrod a protagonist, instigating both the rebellion against God and the construction of the tower. Note 297 also emphasizes how Josephus articulates this rebellion in political terms by calling it a strife, στ ἀσις, "discord," "dissension," "civil war," "revolution," "internal feud," a nuance not present in the biblical text but picked up by medieval writers such as Diego García de Campos (consulted in PACE: Project on Ancient Cultural Engagement, Flavius Josephus, *The Judean Antiquities*, Whiston, http://pace-ancient.mcmaster.ca/york/york/texts.htm).

55 A medieval legend associated with that of the young Buddha, in which the son of a king is prophesied to become a great religious leader, Josaphat, who in this version is converted into Christianity, staging another form of translation.

56 There is more on the Nephilim in the Bible in Num. 13:33 and Dt. 2:10–11. In his translation of Genesis, Robert Alter explains that "the idea of male gods coupling with mortal women whose beauty ignites their desire is a commonplace of Greek myth, and E.A. Speiser has proposed that both the Greek and the Semitic stories may have a common source in the Hittite traditions of Asia Minor. The entourage of celestial beings obscurely implied in God's use of the first person plural in the Garden story here produces, however fleetingly, active agents in the narrative. As with the prospect that man and woman might eat from the tree of life, God sees this intermingling of human and divine as the crossing of a necessary line of human limitation, and He responds by setting a new retracted limit" (*Genesis*, 26).

57 Josephus includes Nemrod in his story in relation to the biblical text, keeping from the Yahvist narration only the motif of the language confusion. The dispersal of humanity does not appear in this story, so the rupture seems to have more spiritual consequences than anything else.

58 Zumthor, *Babel*, 86–7.

59 Arizaleta, "El orden de Babel," 22.

60 Eco, *The Search for the Perfect Language*, 26–7.

61 Vincent Barletta's *Death in Babylon* focuses on fifteenth- and sixteenth-century uses of the Alexander legend as a trope for imperial expansion in the early modern period. His historical frame for the articulation of the

trope uses a detailed account of Plutarch and other classical authors but eschews analysis of the medieval Castilian Alexander, especially that of the *Libro de Alexandre*, which is treated very briefly at the end of chapter 2.

62 Zumthor, *Babel*, 41.

63 Zumthor, *Babel*, 88. In the *Commedia*, Dante devotes three passages to the pride of the builders and the language confusion: one in Hell, another in Purgatory, and a last one in Paradise. He does not, however, mention the name "Babel" nor speak of a Tower, though "Nembròt" is responsible for the loss of the first, original language (see Zumthor, *Babel*, 89).

64 I have elsewhere studied this episode in consonance with Umberto Eco's suggestion, briefly mentioned above, that the Babel episode in Dante's *De vulgari eloquentia* bears similar characteristics, perhaps betraying the influence of iconography, where the division of languages is also articulated as a division of labour, or tasks; see my "Babel historiada, traducida."

65 De Man, "Conclusions," 33.

66 It is Weiss who calls *mester de clerecía* a mode, in coincidence with Benjamin's characterization of translation as a mode of writing ("Introduction," in *The Mester*).

67 De Man, "Conclusions," 35 (see note 11).

68 For a development of the ideas of sovereignty especially in terms of empire, see Weiss's chapter "Dreaming of Empire in the *Libro de Alexandre*" in *The Mester*, 109–42; for a general argument concerning the relations between clerics and monarchy, see Arizaleta, "La alianza de clerecía" and the detailed *Les Clercs au palais*.

69 Alfonso el Sabio, *General estoria*, "De nemproth el primero Rey del mundo & de yonito fijo de Noe," *Libro segundo*, 19, fol, 17r. Added capitalizations. Consulted through Gago Jover's transcription, available online.

70 Chapters 11 and 20 of the *Libro primero*. The *General estoria* narrates a version of the episode that presents Nemrod as a *governor* rather than as constructor or incidental figure. This figure of the tyrant will be picked up within the hispanic tradition, for example, by Pedro Calderón de la Barca in *La torre de Babionia*, staged in Seville in 1657, which ciphers the episode as a reflection not on history but on politics.

71 Casas Rigall in his edition of *Libro de Alexandre*, notes to stanza 1512, p. 490.

72 See Gómez Redondo, "El fermoso fablar," for an emphasis on the performative aspect and its development into a poetics and politics of speech in later periods.

73 *Historia de rebus Hispaniae*, quoted in Arizaleta, "El orden de Babel," 22–3. See also Georges Martin, "La invención de Castilla."

74 Zumthor, *Babel*, 123, 51–2.

75 This reminds one of course again of Benjamin, especially his 1916 essay "On Language as Such and on the Language of Man," in which Benjamin argues for a contrasting role of language similar to what we have been presenting. Benjamin relates original sin to a fall into language as mediation. Jacques Derrida relates this essay to "Critique of Violence" by stating that sovereign violence would be this power to name, a statement here clearly presented in the Babel episode itself. The interesting difference is that while Derrida links this authority to a "signature" or a "seal," the *Biblia romanceada* links this power of naming to a speech and a "making" that is marked by *technè*, that is a *poiesis* that is impossible.

76 Eco, *The Search*, 287.

77 Eco, *The Search*, 285–6.

78 Willis, "Mester de clerecía," 212–14.

79 See William Barclay, *New Testament Words*, s.v. "pleonexia," where he summarizes that

> pleonexia is a sin which the NT again and again most unsparingly condemns. The work occurs in Mark 7.22; Luke 12.15; Rm, 1.29; II Cor. 9.5; Eph. 4.19; 5.3; Col. 3.5; I Thess. 2.5; and I Pet. 2.3, 14. Theregular AV translation is 'covetousness.' Once, in Eph. 4.19, the AV translates it 'greediness.' The RSV retains 'covetousness' in most passages but translates 'greed practice' in Ep. 4.5 and 'greed' in the II peer passages. Moffat varies more: He retains 'covetousness' in Luke 12.15, but his regular translation is 'lust,' which he uses in seven of the passages. Once, in I Thess. 2.5, he uses 'self-seeking.'
> ... In classical Greek it means 'an arrogant greediness,' the spirit that tries to take advantage of its fellow-men. The corresponding verb, *pleonektein*, means 'to defraud' or 'overreach.' Polybius, the Greek historian, has one suggestive use of the word. The Stoics had a phrase by which they described 'that which is fitting' – *ta kathekonta* – by which they meant that kind of conduct which a good man ought to produce. Polybius says that the man who is guilty of this covetous conduct uses methods that are not fitting for a man to use. Pleonexia was a word much in the vocabulary of the ordinary people and it is common in the papyri. There it is connected with conduct which is 'quite shameless,' with 'overreaching ambition,' with 'violence,' with 'injustice,' with the 'cupidity' for which a man in his better moments will be sorry, with the 'rapacity' of a dishonest official who is out to fleece the district of which he is in charge. By the Latin moralists it is defined as *amor sceleratus habendi*, 'the accursed love of possessing.'

Theodore, the early commentator, describes it as 'the aiming always at getting more, the snatching at things which it does not befit a man to have.' Cicero defined *avaritia*, which is the Latin equivalent, as *injuriosa appetitio alienorum*, 'the unlawful desire for things which belong to others.' In Rom. 1.29 *pleonexia* is the sin of the godless world. It is the sin of the world, of society, of the man who has turned his back upon the laws of God. It is the very opposite of the generosity of the love of God and of the charity of the Christian life (233–4).

80 Plato, *Republic*, 370B–C.

81 More elaboration on how the move from pride (*superbia*) to greed (*avaritia*) affects the text and its interpretation would be productive, but is impossible here. *Avaritia* is also a sin of excess, like lust and gluttony. While gluttony cannot be attributed to Alexander, in other versions (not the Spanish one) lust is certainly an attribute of the Macedonian king. Christianity associated greed especially to wealth, and it was seen as a sin against God (as in Aquinas). In Dante's *Inferno*, greedy sinners were bound and laid face down on the ground for having concentrated too much on earthly matters – very much in the spirit of the *Alexandre* and nicely visualized in the *mappaemundi* lesson of the limits of humankind in mortality, synonymous with the earthly.

Chapter 3

1 Other sources include the twelfth-century *Roman d'Alexandre*, the tenth-century *Historia de Proeliis*. the first-century *Ilias latina*, and to a lesser extent Isidore's *Etymologies*, Flavius Josephus, Quintus Curtius Rufus, Ovid, and Cato, among others. Raymond S. Willis and Ian Michael have devoted many careful pages to dissecting these sources and assessing other influences. See especially Michael's chapter "The Nature of The Sources and the Work of Earlier Critics" in *The Treatment*, 12–27.

2 Spufford, *Money and Its Use*, 23–5.

3 *Parias* were fees, taxes, or payments that the Taifa kingdoms paid the northern Iberian kingdoms for protection from attacks.

4 Rodamilans Ramos, "La moneda y el sistema monetario," 27.

5 See Nykl, "Old Spanish Terms of Small Value," and Sas, "No vale una paja," for approximations to this phrase.

6 Ubieto Arteta, *Ciclos económicos*, 130.

7 Ubieto Arteta, *Ciclos económicos*, 136–8.

8 Rueda, "Primeras acuñaciones," 95–7.

9 Rueda, "Primeras acuñaciones," 43, 45.

10 Rodamilans Ramos, "La moneda y el sistema monetario," 27–9.
11 See Sargent, *The Big Problem of Small Change,* especially chaps. 4 and 5 on medieval economic theory and the problem of small coins; the author refers to the experiments and problems with small coins in medieval Iberia and later in numerous other chapters.
12 See Rodamilans Ramos, "La moneda y el sistema monetario," 30. For a later use of this play or slippage in economics as poetics, see Round's insightful piece on the *Libro de buen amor*, "Juan Ruiz and Some Versions of 'Nummus.'"
13 Dorothy Severin studies a series of Hispanomedieval works with such expressions in "No vale un dinero."
14 See Rossi, "Los sustitutos nominales de 'nada,'" 19n27, who relates it to New Testament iconography.
15 Shell, *Money, Language, and Thought*, 4.
16 Curtius, *European Literature*, 296ff.
17 Weiss, "Apolonio's Mercantile Morality," has analysed how the *Libro de Apolonio*, another example of a *mester de clerecía* work of secular theme, "incorporates economic transactions within the vast spectrum of social exchanges which constitute Apollonius's courtly identity," following a variety of situations, among them the exchange of gifts as the anchoring of a hierarchy, especially in the gifts to cities by the king, as well as in the sexual economy guiding Tarsiana. My reading here of the *Alexandre* is indebted to Weiss's insightful conclusions on the articulation between economy, identity, and courtesy in the *Apolonio* according to the specific characteristics of the period and of what has been called the commercial revolution of the thirteenth century.
18 Curtius, *European Literature*, 133.
19 Avarice is a sin characteristic of kings and princes in the *Alexandre's* criticism of contemporary society, in an original passage inserted after the description of Darius's tomb composed of fifty-six stanzas (1774–1830). See Michael, *The Treatment*, 163–4.
20 Kellogg, *Medieval Artistry and Exchange*, 3.
21 Ubieto Arteta, *Ciclos económicos*, 120.
22 The phrase is used by Márquez Villanuea in his *El concepto cultural alfonsí*, often criticized for his crediting of Alfonso as unique herald of a wide number of changes; for a succint view of Alfonso's production relevant to this study, see Fernández-Ordóñez, "Alfonso X el Sabio."
23 Kellogg, *Medieval Artistry and Exchange*, 140–41.
24 The couple of goshawk and horse comes generally from the east and was widely disseminated as motif in medieval Iberia. On its iconography, see

Marcos Marín, "Una nota" and "Tejidos árabes," and Fernández Puertas, "Lápida del siglo XI." Among many examples, the embroidered linen cloth found in the Monastery of Oña has been related to this topic in two ways: either as a gift or as part of the booty taken from the Castilians by the Muslims at the battle of Alhandega, the so-called "vestes preciosas," or during the attack of Abd al-Rahman on the monastery in 934; the caliph's attire as booty would be a pleasant form of revenge, with a later political utility (Casamar and Zozaya, "Apuntes sobre la yuba funeraria de la Colegiata de Oña [Burgos]," 58), though these claims are still much debated. At first scholars argued for a date at the end of the eleventh century or the beginning of the twelfth, but other scholars have given an earlier date considering the luxury of the piece, as probably a gift to King Sancho Garcés at the beginning of the eleventh century. The relation of the church to the Fernán family, as abbey of San Salvador, where a grandson of Fernán González would erect in 1017 the family burial site, is another element to take into account. The kufic inscription has been studied by Fernández Puertas, who gives a caliphal date to the cloth due to its ornamental themes and based on the transcription of its epigraphic border" ("Lápida del siglo XI").

25 To offer a contemporary comparison: the Alfonsine workshop laid out several standards for the establishment of interest, going from an APR of 75 per cent to the more common 20 per cent APR, which the Vidal Mayor also records, and underlines that charging interest over interest is a form of usury and may not be demanded under any condition. The terms of the sale of horse and goshawk go much further than these forbidden terms and thus cannot be taken as revealing of contemporary practices but as poetic license to highlight the symbolic function of the usury.

26 Versions of the sale of the horse and the goshawk are plentiful, and include the following medieval ones: *Crónica rimada* (o *Mocedades de Rodrigo*); *Libro de Fernán González*; *Crónica general*; *Libro del caballero Çifar*; *Crónica de 1344*; *Romancero*; *Tah'rikh iftitah al-Andaus*, Ibn al-Qutiyya al-Qurtabien; *Kitab ak-iktifa fi akbar al-Khulafa*, Abu Marwan b. al-Kardabus at-Tawazarien; and *Kitab ar-Rawad al-mitar*, Ibn 'Abd al-Munim al-Himyari.

27 Le Goff, *Your Money or Your Life*; the concept is secularized in Marx as the theft of alien labour time.

28 In medieval French, *onor* can mean both honour and the fief, the land with which a lord honours his vassal; in Spain, especially in the kingdoms of the Pyrenees, the *honores* were "compensation in land given to certain public functionaries so that they would give a service which could only be

rewarded in this manner," a property figure central to the development of feudalism (Vicens Vives, *An Economic History of Spain*, 143).

29 Michele Leroux Gravall's dissertation on harangue, "The *Arenga* in the Literature of Medieval Spain," is essential for the comparison of some of Spanish medieval literature's most canonical texts, and is the only systematic study on medieval harangue. The analysis is thematic, for the most part, and typologizes harangues into battlefield and campaign ones. Pages 78–114 are devoted to the *Libro de Alexandre*. Of special interest is her analysis in 104–8, where she emphasizes failure in harangue, highlighting the failure of Alexander's *rhetoric* to lift the sadness out of the hearts of his men as they leave for Asia in st. 261, a failure that curiously does not reflect badly on the speaker (or his rhetoric) but rather increases the homesickness the men feel as they see their loved ones behind them. In the last instance, it is a failure of language in relation to the affect for home.

30 These stanzas were obviously understood to be one of the greatest lessons of the book, for they are one of the fragments of the *Libro de Alexandre* that Francisco de Bivar copied in his book, guaranteeing the *Alexandre*'s fame, but to us, more importantly, they serve as warranty for the transmission of specific passages.

31 Hans Blumenberg details these tropes in philosophy in the first part of his *Shipwreck with Spectator*; see especially 11–12.

32 The link between master and king through *sapientia* is one that is often used to explain Alfonso X's own project; its elaboration within *mester de clerecía* is thus part of a clerical program of insertion in political and courtly life. I here follow Adeline Rucquoi's analysis of images of sovereignty in the thirteenth century ("La royauté," 222); her study can be complemented by Arizaleta's work on clerics at court. See on this matter especially *Les Clercs au palais*.

33 Ronald Surtz's remarks on Apolonio's reliance on knowledge that comes from books, and not from God, as in the Latin source, reinforce this conversion model ("El héroe intelectual," 265); see also Uría Maqua, "El *Libro de Apolonio*."

34 Shortly after Apolonio sets sail, a storm shipwrecks the fleet and Apolonio is the only survivor. While Uría reads this as the event itself marking conversion (leaving the humiliation as a preparation for this event), Surtz reads in the shipwreck a punishment for the protagonists' desire to seek adventure in the sea. As an expected trope in sea travel, the shipwreck serves to characterize the sea as unstable, as a space inappropriate for humanity, as a space for trial from which one may emerge successful or fail

and die forever lost. The symbolic dimensions of the sea, widely elaborated in medieval literatures, were of course always present.

35 See Aurell, "Le *Libro de Alexandre*," especially 67–70.

36 Shell, *Money, Language, and Thought*, 35ff.

37 Surtz, "El héroe intelectual," 273.

38 Surtz reads this same stanza as a condemnation of clerical knowledge, where I see no signs of a condemnation of erudition but simply a statement of curiosity.

39 See chapter 1 for the connections with space and cartography.

40 Arizaleta ("El *Libro de Alexandre*," 90), following González Jiménez (*Fernando III el Santo*, 87–8), suggests a parallel between this harangue of Alexander over the Asian expedition and Fernando III's harangue in Muñó, recorded in the *Chronica regum castellae*, inciting the war against Muslims. See also note 29 to this chapter.

41 The fisherman's sharing of his poor dress is, as has been noted many times, one more link to hagiography, both to the episode in the life of Martin de Tours and to other works of *mester de clerecía*, such as Gonzalo de Berceo's *Vida de Santo Domingo*, in which the same scene is mentioned. Note that it is an episode of charity that is being presented here.

42 Weiss, *The Mester*, 504.

43 Weiss, *The Mester*, 508.

44 Weiss, *The Mester*, 509, 510.

45 See Juan Manuel Cacho Blecua's remarks on knowledge with regard to Nature in "El saber y el dominio de la Naturaleza."

46 Neither Jesús Cañas nor Casas Rigall provide insight into *desguisado* in their editions, so I extrapolate from the meaning of *guisa*: manner, care, will, form; and *aguisar*: to make, to prepare, to set up.

47 As Casas Rigall notes in his edition, the "seven worlds," probably a reference to Isidore's *Etymologies* but likely to have been brought into the body of the text from a marginal note, as happens elsewhere in the *Libro de Alexandre*, does not appear in Gautier (note to st. 2289, p. 639).

48 *Partida II*, tit. 9, law 28.

Bibliography

Agnew, Michael. "'Como en libro abierto': La construcción de un modelo exegético en el *Libro de Alexandre*." *La corónica* 29.2 (2001): 159–83.

Alter, Robert, trans. *Genesis*. New York: London, 1996.

Alvar, Carlos. "Consideraciones a propósito de una cronología temprana del *Libro de Alexandre*." In *Nunca fue pena mayor: Estudios de literatura española en homenaje a Brian Dutton*, ed. Ana Menéndez Collera and Victoriano Roncero-López, 35–44. Cuenca: Ediciones de la Universidad de Castilla-La Mancha, 1996.

Ancos, Pablo. "El narrador como maestro en el mester de clerecía." *eHumanista* 12 (2009): 48–64.

— *Transmisión y recepción primarias de la poesía del mester de clerecía*. Valencia: Universitat de València, 2012.

Antolín, Guillermo. *Catálogo de los códices latinos de la Real Biblioteca del Escorial*. 5 vols. Madrid: Imprenta Helénica, 1910–23.

Arizaleta, Amaia. "Alexandre en su *Libro*." *La corónica* 28.2 (2000): 3–20.

— "La alianza de clerecía y monarquía (Castilla 1157–1230)." In *Actas del Congreso Internacional de la Asociación Hispánica de Literatura Medieval, León, 20–24 de septiembre 2005*, ed. Luzdivina Cuesta Torres, 239–48. León: AHLM, 2007.

— *Les Clercs au palais: Chancellerie et écriture du pouvoir royal (Castille 1157–1230)*. Paris: SEMH/Sorbonne, 2010.

— "La figure d'Alexandre le Grand comme modèle d'écriture." In *Alexandre le Grand dans les littératures occidentales et proche-orientales: Actes du colloque du novembre 1997*, ed. Laurence Harf-Lancner, Claire Kappler, and François Suard, 173–86. Paris: Centre des Sciences de la Littérature, 1999.

— "El *Libro de Alexandre*: El clérigo al servicio del rey." *Troianalexandrina* 8 (2008): 73–114.

- "El orden de Babel: Algunas notas sobre la conciencia lingüística de la clerecía letrada castellana en la primera mitad del siglo XIII." *e-Spania*, 13 June 2012. http://e-spania.revues.org/20985.
- "Del texto de Babel a la biblioteca de Babilonia: Algunas notas sobre el *Libro de Alexandre*." In *La fermosa cobertura: Lecciones de Literatura Medieval*, no. 16, ed. F. Crosas, 35–69. Pamplona: Ediciones de la Universidad de Navarra/ Publicaciones de Literatura Española, 2000.
- "Topografías de la memoria palatina: Los discursos cancillerescos sobre la realeza (Castilla, siglos XII y XIII)." In *Memoria e Historia: Utilización política en la Corona de Castilla al final de la Edad Media*, ed. Jon Andoni Fernández de Larrea and José Ramón Díaz de Durana, 43–58. Madrid: Sílex, 2010.
- *La Translation d'Alexandre*. Paris: Klinscieck, 1999.
- "Les vers sur la pierre: Quelques notes sur le *Libro de Alexandre* et le *Libro de Apolonio*." *Troianalexandrina* 5 (2005): 153–84.
Aurell, Martin. "Le *Libro de Alexandre* dans son contexte: Clergé, royauté et chevalerie lettrée au XIIe siècle." *Troianalexandrina* 8 (2008): 59–71.
Bailey, Matthew. *The Poetics of Speech in the Medieval Spanish Epic*. Toronto: University of Toronto Press, 2010.
Bañeza Román, Celso. *Las fuentes bíblicas, patrísticas y judaicas del* Libro de Alexandre. Las Palmas de Gran Canaria: author's edition, 1994.
Barclay, William. *New Testament Words*. Philadelphia: Westminster John Knox, 2000.
Barletta, Vincent. *Death in Babylon: Alexander the Great and Iberian Empire in the Muslim Orient*. Chicago: University of Chicago Press, 2010.
Barral i Altet, Xavier. "Poésie et iconographie: Un pavement du XIIe siècle décrit par Baudri de Bourgueil." *Dumbarton Oaks Papers* 41 (1987): 41–54.
Bataille, Georges. *The Accursed Share: An Essay on General Economy*. New York: Zone, 1988–1993.
Bautista, Francisco. "Escritura cronística e ideología histórica." *e-Spania*, 2 December 2006. http://e-spania.revues.org/429.
- "Original, versiones e influencia del *Liber regum*: Estudio textual y propuesta de *stemma*." *e-Spania*, 9 June 2010. http://e-spania.revues.org/19884.
Biglieri, Aníbal. *Las ideas geográficas y la imagen del mundo en la literatura española medieval*. Madrid/Frankfurt: Iberoamericana-Vervuert, 2012.
Blumenberg, Hans. *Shipwreck with Spectator: Paradigm of a Metaphor for Existence*. Cambridge, MA: MIT Press, 1997.
Cacho Blecua, Juan Manuel. "El saber y el dominio de la Naturaleza en el *Libro de Alexandre*." In *Actas del III Congreso de la Asociación Hispánica de Literatura Medieval*, ed. Toro Pascua and María Isabel, 197–207. Salamanca, Spain:

Biblioteca Española del Siglo XV, Departamento de Literatura Española e Hispanoamericana. 1994.

Cantar de mio Cid. Ed. Alberto Montaner Frutos with an introduction by Francisco Rico. Barcelona: Galaxia Gutenberg/Círculo de lectores, 2007.

Carruthers, Mary. *The Book of Memory*. Cambridge: Cambridge University Press, 1990.

– *The Craft of Thought: Meditation, Rhetoric, and the Making of Images, 400–1200*. Cambridge: Cambridge University Press, 1998.

– "The Poet as Master-Builder: Composition and Locational Memory in the Middle Ages." *New Literary History* 24.4 (1993): 881–904.

Casamar, Manuel, and Juan Zozaya. "Apuntes sobre la yuba funeraria de la Colegiata de Oña (Burgos)." *Boletín de Arqueología Medieval* 5 (1992): 75–95.

Casas Rigall, Juan. "La *abbreviatio* y sus funciones poéticas en el *Libro de Alexandre*." *Troianalexandrina* 5 (2005): 63–96.

Cohen, Esther, and Mayke B. de Jong. *Medieval Transformations: Texts, Power, and Gifts in Context*. Leiden: Brill, 2001.

Conklin Akbari Suzanne, and Jill Ross, eds. *The Ends of the Body: Identity and Community in Medieval Culture*. Toronto: University of Toronto Press, 2013.

Contenau, G. "La tour de Babel." In *Le Déluge babylonien*, chap. 3. Paris: Payot, 1952.

Copeland, Rita. *Rhetoric, Hermeneutics, and Translation in the Middle Ages: Academic Traditions and Vernacular Texts*. Cambridge: Cambridge University Press, 1991.

Copeland, Rita, and I. Sluitker. *Medieval Grammar and Rhetoric: Language Arts and Literary Theory AD 300–1475*. Oxford: Oxford University Press, 2009.

Counillon, Patrick. "La représentation de l'espace et la description géographique dans le livre III de la *Géographie* de Strabon." In *La invención de una geografía de la Península Ibérica, 2: La época imperial*, ed. G. Cruz Andreotti, P. Le Roux, and P. Moret, 65–80. Málaga: Casa de Velázquez, 2006.

Curtius, E.R. *European Literature and the Latin Middle Ages*. Trans. Willard R. Trask. Princeton: Princeton University Press, 1967.

de Man, Paul. "Conclusions: Walter Benjamin's 'The Task of the Translator.'" Messenger Lecture, Cornell University, 4 March 1983. Published as "The Lesson of Paul de Man," *Yale French Studies* 69 (1985): 25–46.

Destombes, Marcel. "The Mappamundi of the Poem 'Alexandreidos' by Gautier de Châtillon (ca. A. D. 1180)." *Imago Mundi* 19 (1965): 10–12.

– *Mappemondes, A.D. 1200–1500: Catalogue*. Amsterdam: N. Israel, 1964.

Díaz y Díaz, Manuel C. *Códices visigóticos en la monarquía leonesa*. León, Spain: Centro de Estudios e Investigación San Isidoro, 1983.

- *Libros y liberías en la Rioja altomedieval*. Logroño, Spain: Servicio de Cultura de la Excelentísima Diputación Provincial, 1979.
- "La circulation des manuscrits dans la Péninsule Ibérique du VIIIe à XIe siècle." *Cahiers de Civilisation Médiévale* 12 (1969): 11–61.
- "La transmisión de los testos antiguos en la Península Ibérica en los siglos VII al XI." In *La cultura antica nell' Occidente latino dal VII all 'XI secolo*. Spoleto: Centro italiano di Studio Sull'Alto Medioevo, 1975.
Dilke, O.A.W. "Itineraries and Geographical Maps in the Early and Late Roman Empires." In Harley and Woodward, eds., *The History of Cartography*, vol. 1: *Cartography in Prehistoric, Ancient and Medieval Europe and the Mediterranean*, 234–57.
Donkin, Lucy E.G. "*Usque ad Ultimum Terrae*": Mapping the End of the Earth in Two Medieval Floor Mosaics." In *Cartography in Antiquity and the Middle Ages: Fresh Perspectives, New Methods*, ed. Richard J. A. Talbert and Richard Watson Unger, 189–218. Leiden: Brill, 2008.
Duggan, Joseph. *The Cantar de mio Cid: Poetic Creation in its Economic and Social Contexts*. Cambridge: Cambridge University Press, 1989.
Eco, Umberto. *The Search for the Perfect Language*. Oxford: Blackwell, 1995.
Edson, Evelyn. *Mapping Time and Space*. London: British Library, 1997.
- "The Oldest World Maps: Classical Sources of Three VIII Century Mappaemundi." *The Ancient World* 24.2 (1993): 169–84.
- *The World Map, 1300–1492: The Persistence of Tradition and Transformation*. Baltimore: Johns Hopkins University Press/Santa Fe: Center for American Places, 2007.
Faulhaber, Charles B. *Libros y bibliotecas en la España medieval: Una bibliografía de fuentes impresas*. London: Grant and Cutler, 1987.
Fernández Ordóñez, Inés. "Alfonso X el Sabio en la historia del español." Alicante, Spain: Biblioteca Virtual Miguel de Cervantes, 2009. Digital edition from the collection edited by Rafael Cano, *Historia de la lengua española*, Barcelona, Ariel, 2004, 381–422. http://www.cervantesvirtual.com/nd/ark:/59851/bmc5bok8.
Fernández Puertas, Antonio. "Lápida del siglo XI e inscripción del tejido del siglo X del monasterio de Oña." *Miscelánea de estudios árabes y hebraicos* 26 (1977): 119–27.
Foer, Joshua. "Secrets of a Mind-Gamer." *New York Times*, 15 February 2011.
Gago Jover, Francisco, ed. "General Estoria I." In *Prose Works of Alfonso X el sabio: Digital Library of Old Spanish Texts*. Hispanic Seminary of Medieval Studies. 2011. http://www.hispanicseminary.org/t&c/ac/index-en.htm.
García, Michel. "La médiation du clerc dans le *mester de clerecía*." In *Les Médiations culturelles, domaine ibérique et latino-américain: Acts du colloque*

organisé à la Sorbonne par le GRIMESREP, les 25, 26 et 27 janvier 1988, 47–54. Paris: Université de la Sorbonne Nouvelle-Paris III, 1991.

García Ballester, Luis. "Naturaleza y ciencia en la Castilla del siglo XIII: Los orígenes de una tradición: El *studium* franciscano de Santiago de Compostela (1222–1230)." In *Semana de Estudios Medievales de Nájera (1995),* 145–69. Nájera, Spain: Instituto de Estudios Riojanos, 1996.

García Fitz, Francisco. "Was Las Navas a Decisive Battle?" *Journal of Medieval Iberian Studies* 4.1 (2012): 5–9. doi:10.1080/17546559.2012.677160.

Gautier Dalché, Patrick. "De la glose à la contemplation: Place et fonction de la carte dans les manuscrits du Haut Moyen Age." In *Testo e Immagine nell'Alto Medioevo,* 693–771. Spoleto: Presso la Sede del Centro, 1994.

– "Géographie arabe et géographie latine." *Medieval Encounters* 19 (2013): 408–33.

Glick, Thomas. *Islamic and Christian Spain in the Early Middle Ages.* Leiden: Brill, 2005.

Gómez, Miguel. "Las Navas de Tolosa and the Culture of Crusade in the Kingdom of Castile." *Journal of Medieval Iberian Studies* 4.1 (2012): 53–57. doi:10.1080/17546559.2012.677174.

Gómez Moreno, Angel. "Notas al prólogo del *Libro de Alexandre.*" *Revista de Literatura* 46 (1984): 117–27.

Gómez Redondo, Fernando. "El fermoso fablar de la clerecía." In *Propuestas teórico-metodológicas para el estudio de la literatura hispánica medieval,* ed. Lillian von der Walde Moheno, 229–82. Mexico: Universidad Autónoma Nacional de México-Universidad Autónoma Metropolitana, 2003.

– "La materia caballeresca: Líneas de formación." *Voz y letra* 7.1 (1996): 45–80.

– ed. *Poesía española 1. Edad Media: Juglaría, clerecía y romancero.* Barcelona: Crítica, 1996.

González Jiménez, Manuel. *Fernando III el Santo.* Seville: Fundación José Manuel Lara, 2006.

Gonzálvez Ruiz, Ramón. *Hombres y libros en Toledo (1086–1300).* Madrid: Fundación Ramón Areces, 1997.

Grande Quejigo, Francisco Javier. "'Quiero leer un livro': Oralidad y escritura en el mester de clerecía." In *La memoria de los libros: Estudios sobre la historia del escrito y de la lectura en Europa y América,* vol. 2, ed. Pedro Cátedra, Ma. Isabel Páiz Hernández, and L. López Vidriero, 101–12. Salamanca: Instituto de Historia del Libro y de la Lectura, 2004.

Grant, Edward. *History of Natural Philosophy. From the Ancient World to the Nineteenth Century.* Cambridge: Cambridge University Press, 2007.

Guijarro González, Susana. *Maestros, escuelas y libros: El universo cultural de las catedrales en la Castilla medieval.* Madrid: Instituto Antonio de Nebrija de estudios sobre la universidad/Universidad Carlos III de Madrid, 2004.

Harley, J.B., and David Woodward, eds. *The History of Cartography.* 2 vols. Chicago: University of Chicago Press, 1992.

Harvey, L.P., and D. Hook. "The Affair of the Horse and the Hawk in the *Poema de Fernán González.*" *Modern Language Review* 77 (1982): 840–47.

Hazbun, Geraldine. "Memory as 'Mester' in the *Libro de Alexandre* and the *Libro de Apolonio.*" In *Medieval Hispanic Studies in Memory of Alan Deyermond*, ed. Andrew M. Beresford, Louise M. Haywood, and Julian Weiss, 91–120. London: Tamesis, 2013.

Heusch, Carlos. "Entre didactismo y heterodoxia: Vicisitudes del estudio de la ética aristotélica en la España escolástica (siglos XIII–XIV)." *La corónica* 19.2 (1991): 89–99.

Hugh of Saint Victor. *Didascalicon of Hugh of St. Victor: A Medieval Guide to the Arts.* Trans. Jerome Taylor. New York: Columbia University Press, 1961.

Jacob, Christian. *The Sovereign Map: Theoretical Aproaches in Cartography throughout History.* Chicago: University of Chicago Press, 2006.

Kelly, Douglas. *The Art of Medieval French Romance.* Madison: University of Wisconsin Press, 1992.

Kitzinger, Ernst. "World Map and Fortune's Wheel: A Medieval Mosaic Floor in Turin." *Proceedings of the American Philosophical Society* 117.5 (1973): 344–73.

Kramer, Bärbel. "The Earliest Known Map of Spain (?) and the Geography of Artemidorus of Ephesus on Papyrus." *Imago Mundi* 53 (2001): 115–20.

– "La Península Ibérica en la *Geografía* de Artemidoro de Efeso." In *La invención de una geografía de la Península Ibérica, 1: La época republicana*, ed. G. Cruz Andreotti, P. Le Roux, and P. Moret, 97–116. Málaga: Casa de Velázquez, 2006.

Kupfer, Marcia. "The Lost Mappamundi at Chalivoy-Milon." *Speculum* 66.3 (1991): 540–71.

Le Goff, Jacques. *Your Money or Your Life: Economy and Religion In the Middle Ages.* Cambridge: Zone/MIT Press, 1988.

Leroux Gravall, Michele. "The *Arenga* in the Literature of Medieval Spain." PhD diss., University of North Carolina at Chapel Hill, 2007.

Libro de Alexandre. Ed. and with an introduction by Jesús Cañas. Madrid: Cátedra, 2003.

Libro de Alexandre. Ed. and with an introduction by Juan Casas Rigall. Madrid: Castalia, 2007.

Libro de Apolonio. Ed. Dolores Corbella Díaz. Madrid: Cátedra, 1992.

Libro de Fernán González. Ed. and with an introduction by Itziar López Guil. Madrid: Consejo Superior de Investigaciones Científicas/Instituto de la Lengua Española, 2001.

Lida de Malkiel, María Rosa. "Datos para la leyenda de Alejandro en la Edad Media castellana." *Romance Philology* 15.4 (1962): 412–23.

– "Notas para el texto del *Alexandre* y para las fuentes del *Fernán González.*" *Revista de Filología Hispánica* 7 (1945): 47–51.

Linehan, Peter. "Don Rodrigo and the Government of the Kingdom." *Cahiers de linguistique hispanique médiévale* 26 (2003): 87–99.

Little, Lester K. *Religious Poverty and the Profit Economy in Medieval Europe.* Ithaca: Cornell University Press, 1978.

Maqbul, Ahmad S. "Cartography of al-Sharīf al-Idrīsī." In Harley and Woodward, eds., *The History of Cartography*, vol. 2, bk. 1: *Cartography in the Traditional Islamic and South Asian Societies*, 156–74.

– *A History of Arab-Islamic Geography (9th–16th Century A.D.).* Mafraq, Jordan: Al al-Bayt University, 1995.

Marcos Marín, Francisco. "Tejidos árabes e independencia de Castilla." *Bulletin of Hispanic Studies* 63 (1986): 355–61.

– "Una nota sobre épica e iconografía." *Revista de filología románica* 2 (1984): 233–7.

Márquez Villanueva, Francisco. *El concepto cultural alfonsí.* Madrid: MAPFRE, 1994.

Martin, Georges. "La invención de Castilla (Rodrigo Jiménez de Rada, *Historia de rebus Hispaniae*, V): Identidad patria y mentalidades políticas," https://halshs.archives-ouvertes.fr/halshs-00113284/document.

Martínez, H. Salvador. "La tienda de Amor, espejo de la vida humana, (LBA, estr. 1265–1301)." *Nueva Revista de Filología Hispánica* 26 (1977): 56–95.

Martínez Casado, Angel. "Aristotelismo hispano en la primera mitad del siglo XIII." *Estudios filosóficos* 33 (1984): 59–75.

Materni, Marta. "Ancora sulle *ekphrasis.*" In *Del peccato alessandrino*, Paris, CLEA (EA 4083) (*Les Livres d'e-Spania* "Études," 3), 2013. http://e-spanialivres.revues.org/606.

Mauss, Marcel. *The Gift: The Form and Reason for Exchange in Archaic Societies.* London: Routledge, 2002.

Menéndez Pidal, Gonzalo. "Mozárabes y asturianos en la cultura de la alta edad media: En relación especial con la historia de los conocimientos geográficos." *Boletín de la Real Academia de la Historia* 134.1 (1954): 137–48.

Michael, Ian. *The Treatment of Classical Material in the* Libro de Alexandre. Manchester: Manchester University Press, 1970.

Millares Carlo, Agustín. *Nuevos estudios de paleografía española.* Mexico: Fondo de Cultura Económica, 1941.

Montaner Frutos, Alberto. "El proyecto historiográfico del *Archetypum Naiarense.*" *e-Spania*, 7 June 2009. http://e-spania.revues.org/18075.

Moralejo Alvarez, Serafín. "El mapa de la diáspora apostólica en San Pedro de Rocas." *Compostellanum; Revista de la Archidiócesis de Santiago de Compostela* 31.3–4 (1986): 315–40.

Morros Mestres, Bienvenido. "Las glosas a la Alexandreis en el Libro de Alexandre." *Revista de Literatura Medieval* 14.1 (2002): 63–107.

Nykl, A.R. "Old Spanish Terms of Small Value." *Modern Language Notes* 42.5 (1927): 311–13; republished *Modern Language Notes* 46.3 (1931): 166–70.

PACE: Project on Ancient Cultural Engagement. Flavius Josephus, *The Judean Antiquities*, bk. 1, Whiston chap. 5, Whiston sec. 1. http://pace.cns.yorku .ca/York/york/texts.html.

Parrot, André. *La Tour de Babel*. Neuchâtel: Delachaux-Niestlé, 1970.

Pascual-Argente, Clara. "'El cabdal sepulcro': Word and Image in the *Libro de Alexandre*." *La corónica* 38.2 (2010): 69–98.

Pejenaute Rubio, Francisco. "El locus amoenus del *Libros de Alexandre* (estr. 935–940) y *Alexandreis*, II 308–318, de Gautier de Châtillon." *Berceo* 122 (1992): 45–51.

Pereira Mira, Carlos Benjamín. *El "Codex Miscellaneus Ovetensis" (Ms. Esc. R.II.18: Fuentes y bibliografía, Estado de la cuestión)*. Oviedo, Spain: Universidad, Departamento de Historia, 2001.

– *Éxodo librario en la biblioteca capitular de Oviedo: El Codex miscellaneus ovetensis: Manuscrito escurialense R. II. 18*. Oviedo, Spain: Trea/Ediuno, 2006.

Pinet, Simone. "Babel historiada, traducida: Un episodio del Libro de Alexandre." In *Literatura y conocimiento medieval: Actas de las VIII Jornadas Medievales*, ed. Lillian von der Walde Moheno et al., 371–89. Mexico: Universidad Nacional Autónoma de México-Universidad Autónoma Metropolitana-El Colegio de México, 2003.

– "Toward a Political Economy of the *Libro de Alexandre*." *diacritics* 36.3 (2006): 44–63.

– "Walk on the Wild Side." *Medieval Encounters*, 14.2–3 (2008): 368–89.

Plato. *Republic*. Translated by G.M.A. Grube. Indianapolis: Hackett, 1992.

Rashdall, Hastings. *The Universities of Europe in the Middle Ages*. Vol. 2, part 1. London: Oxford University Press, 1936.

Reilly, Bernard. "The Chancery of Alfonso VII of León-Castile: The Period 1116–1135 Reconsidered," *Speculum* 51 (1976): 246–57.

Rico, Francisco. "La clerecía del mester." *Hispanic Review* 53 (1985): 1–23, 127–50.

– *El pequeño mundo del hombre: Varia fortuna de una idea en las letras españolas*. Madrid: Castalia, 1970.

Rodamilans Ramos, Fernando. "La moneda y el sistema monetario en la Castilla medieval." *Ab Initio* (2010): 22–83.

Rodríguez Velasco, Jesús. *Ciudadanía, soberanía monárquica y caballería: Poética del orden de caballería*. Madrid: Akal, 2009. Translated by Eunice Rodríguez Ferguson as *Order and Chivalry. Knighthood and Chivalry in Late Medieval Castile*. Philadelphia: University of Pennsylvania Press, 2010.

– "Theorizing the Language of the Law." In "Theories of Medieval Iberia," ed. Oscar Martín and Simone Pinet, special issue, *diacritics* 36 (2006): 64–86.

Romm, James S. *The Edges of the Earth in Ancient Thought: Geography, Exploration and Fiction*. Princeton: Princeton University Press, 1992.

Rossi, Teresa María. "Los sustitutos nominales de 'nada' como índice del vulgarizamiento en el *Libro de Alexandre*." In *Del tradurre*, vol. 1, 9–23. Rome: Bulzoni, 1992. Also published as "De un pepión a un pepino en el refuerzo enfático de la negación," *Rassegna Iberistica* 53 (1995): 39–42.

Round, Nicholas G. "Juan Ruiz and Some Versions of 'Nummus.'" In *The Medieval Mind: Hispanic Studies in Honour of Alan Deyermond*, ed. Ian Macpherson and Ralph Penny, 381–400. London: Tamesis, 1997.

Rucquoi, Adeline. "La double vie du *studium* de Palencia." In "Homage à Antonio García y García," special issue, *Studia Gratiana* 29 (1998): 723–48.

– "La royauté sous Alphonse VIII de Castille." *Cahiers de linguistique hispanique médiévale* 23 (2000): 215–41.

Rueda, Mercedes. *Primeras acuñaciones de Castilla y León*. Salamanca: Junta de Castilla y León / Asociación Española de Arqueología Medieval, 1991.

Sáenz López-Pérez, Sandra. "Imagen y conocimiento del mundo en la edad media a través de la cartografía hispana." PhD diss., Universidad Complutense de Madrid, 2007.

– *Los mapas de los Beatos: La revelación del mundo en la Edad Media*. Madrid: Siloé, Arte y bibliofilia, 2014.

Sánchez Jiménez, Antonio. *La literatura en la corte de Alfonso VIII de Castilla*. PhD diss., Universidad de Salamanca, 2001.

Sargent, Thomas J. *The Big Problem of Small Change*. Princeton: Princeton University Press, 2002.

Sas, Louis Furman. *Vocabulario del Libro de Alexandre*. Madrid: Academia Española, 1976.

Scafi, Alessandro. *Mapping Paradise: A History of Heaven on Earth*. Chicago: University of Chicago Press, 2006.

Schmitt, Jean-Claude. *Le Corps des images: Essais sur la culture visuelle au Moyen Âge*. Paris: Gallimard, 2002.

Severin, Dorothy S. "No vale un dinero." In *Studies in Honor of Bruce W. Wardropper*, ed. Dian Fox, Harry Sieber, and Robert Ter Horst, 267–78. Newark, DE: Juan de la Cuesta, 1989.

Shell, Marc. *Money, Language, and Thought: Literary and Philosophical Economies from the Medieval to the Modern Era*. Berkeley: University of California Press, 1982.

Spufford, Peter. *Money and Its Use in Medieval Europe*. Cambridge: Cambridge University Press, 1989.

Steiner, Emily, and Ransom, Lynn. *Taxonomies of Knowledge: Information and Order in Medieval Manuscripts*. Philadelphia; University of Pennsylvania Press, 2015.

Such, Peter. "The Origins and Use of School Rhetoric in the *Libro de Alexandre*." PhD diss., University of Cambridge, 1978.

Surtz, Ronald. "El héroe intelectual en el mester de clerecía." *La Torre: Revista de la Universidad de Puerto Rico* 1.2 (1987): 265–74.

Terry, Helen, V. "The Treatment of the Horse and Hawk Episodes in the Literature of Fernán González." *Hispania* 13 (1930): 497–504.

Tibbets, Gerald R., "The Balkhī School of Geographers." In Harley and Woodward, eds., *The History of Cartography*, vol. 2, bk. 1: *Cartography in the Traditional Islamic and South Asian Societies*, 108–36.

– "The Beginnings of a Cartographic Tradition." In Harley and Woodward, eds., *The History of Cartography*, vol. 2, bk. 1: *Cartography in the Traditional Islamic and South Asian Societies*, 90–107.

Tilliette, J.-Y. "La chambre de la comtesse Adèle: Savoir scientifique et technique littèraire dans le c. cvcvi de Baudri de Bourgueil." *Romania* 102 (1981): 145–71.

Townsend, David. *The Alexandreis: A Twelfth-Century Epic*. Peterbobough, ON: Broadview, 2006.

Ubieto Arteta, Antonio. *Ciclos económicos en la Edad Media española*. Valencia: Anúbar, 1969.

Uría Maqua, Isabel. "El *Libro de Apolonio*, contrapunto del *Libro de Alexandre*." *Vox romanica* 56 (1997): 193–211.

– *Panorama crítico del mester de clerecía*. Madrid: Castalia, 2000.

Vicens Vives, Jaime. *An Economic History of Spain*. Princeton: Princeton University Press, 1969.

Vidier, M.A. "La mappemonde de Théodulfe et la mappemonde de Ripoll (IXe–XIe)." *Bulletin de géographie historique et descriptive* 3 (1911): 295–313.

Vinsauf, Geoffrey of. *Poetry Nova of Geoffrey of Vinsauf*. Trans. Margaret F. Nims (1967); reprint, Toronto: Pontifical Institute of Medieval Studies, 2007.

Walsh, John K., "Obras perdidas del mester de clerecía." *La corónica* 28.1 (1999): 147–66.

Weiss, Julian. "Apolonio's Mercantile Morality and the Ideology of Courtliness." In *The Medieval Mind: Hispanic Studies in Honour of Alan*

Deyermond, ed. Ian Macpherson and Ralph Penny, 501–16. London: Tamesis, 1997.

– *The Mester de Clerecía: Intellectuals and Ideologies in Thirteenth-Century Castile.* London: Tamesis, 2007.

Williams, John. *The Illustrated Beatus: A Corpus of the Illustrations in the Commentary on the Apocalypse.* London: Harvey Miller, 1994.

– "Isidore, Orosius and the Beatus Map." *Imago Mundi* 49 (1997): 7–32.

Willis, Raymond S. *The Debt of the Spanish* Libro de Alexandre *to the French* Roman d'Alexandre. Princeton: Elliot Monographs 33, 1935 [New York: Kraus Reprint, 1965].

– "Mester de clerecía: A Definition of the *Libro de Alexandre*." *Romance Philology* 10 (1957): 212–24.

– *The Relationship of the Spanish* Libro de Alexandre *to the* Alexandreis *of Gautier de Châtillon.* New York: Kraus Reprint, 1965.

Wood, Diana. *Medieval Economic Thought.* Cambridge: Cambridge University Press, 2002.

Woodward, David. "Medieval *Mappamundi*." In Harley and Woodward., eds., *The History of Cartography*, vol. 1: *Cartography in Prehistoric, Ancient and Medieval Europe and the Mediterranean*, 286–370.

Wright, Roger. "Bilingualism and Diglossia in Medieval Iberia (3050–1350)." In *A Comparative History of Literatures in the Iberian Peninsula*, vol. 1, ed. Fernando Cabo Aseguinolaza et al., 333–350. Amsterdam: John Benjamins, 2010.

– "Latin and Romance in the Castilian Chancery (1180–1230)." *Bulletin of Hispanic Studies* 73 (1996): 115–28.

– *El Tratado de Cabreros (1206): Estudio sociofilológico de una reforma ortográfica.* London: University of London, Queen Mary and Westfield College, 2000.

Zumthor, Paul. *Babel ou l'inachèvement.* Paris: Seuil, 1997.

Index

abbreviatio: as rhetorical figure in cartography, 17, 24; as rhetorical figure in the *Libro de Alexandre*, 91, 151n47, 155–6n70; as strategy, 135; as technique, 9, 33

administration: as Apollonius's negotiation of morality and ethics, 129; as bureaucracy, 96; as definition of *mester*, 60; as trait of *magister*, 68

adventure: Alexander's, 48; in contemporary deferrals of mortality, 103; as experience (Apollonius's), 117; as experience (Alexander's), 122; knightly (Alexander's), 112; in the sea, 171n34

Alexander: as character in Libro de Alexandre, 8, 10, 12–13, 32, 34, 38, 42–3, 48–9, 51–2, 56, 74–6, 82–3, 91, 111–16, 122, 124–5, 129–30, 132, 144n4, 151n48, 153n53; 155n66, 168n81; as hero, 5, 7, 58, 71, 117, 120, 131; legend of, 3, 9, 33, 37, 48, 67, 117, 144–5n1, 154n63, 165n61; in Spain's vernacular version, 7, 38, 78, 81, 83, 94

Alexandre, Libro de, 3, 5–12, 13–14, 21, 26, 32–6, 38, 42, 44, 46–7, 52–3, 56–8, 59, 61–74, 77–8, 81–93, 95, 97, 100–4, 107, 110–12, 115–16, 120–2, 127, 129, 132, 134–5, 143n1, n3, 144n4, 150n34, 151n47, 151n48,153n57, 155n68, 155n70, 158n4, 161n35, 162n48, 163n49, 168n81, 169n17, 171n29, 171n30, 172n47; poet, 7–10, 13, 33–5, 38–9, 41–5, 47, 49, 52–3, 56, 60–2, 67, 72–3, 76–8, 85–6, 89–92, 93, 101–2, 111, 115–19, 122, 130, 151n48, 153n57, 155n66, 155n70, 156n74, 157n82, 158n5, 162n36

Alexandreis. See under Châtillon, Gautier de

Alfonso III, 26, 28, 138

Alfonso VI, 96, 99, 104–5

Alfonso VIII, 3, 5, 11, 60, 62–4, 66–8, 70, 97, 98–9, 159n12, 161n35

Alfonso X, 4, 6, 10–11, 16, 62, 69, 83, 88–9, 98, 132, 169n22, 171n32

Ancos, Pablo, 4, 143n2, 143–4n3, 144n4, 157n3, 158n4, 161n27, Apelles: 36–44, 77–8

Apolonio or Apollonius: as hero or
    protagonist, 117–29, 131–2; *Libro
    de*, 3, 5–6, 10–11, 64, 67, 69, 97,
    110, 116–17, 121, 126, 132, 134–5,
    144n1, 169n17, 171n34
archive: clerical, 57–8; of knowledge,
    4, 20; maps as, 32; as memory, 134;
    written, 58
Arizaleta, Amaia, 38, 63–4, 66–71, 78,
    144n6, 158–9n12, 161n35, 162n48,
    163n51, 172n40

Babel: as metaphor, 9–10, 44, 47, 82–
    3, 87–8, 90–2, 94, 163n51, 167n75;
    as motif, 10, 46, 68–9, 79, 81–4, 86,
    89, 91, 135, 155n66, 162n48; Tower
    of, 11, 47, 54, 78, 79, 81, 86, 135,
    164n54, 166n63. *See also* Babylon
Babylon, 9, 35–8, 44–9, 78, 80–2,
    84–6, 92, 94, 111, 140, 155n66,
    155n68, 164n54
Bataille, Georges, 12, 103, 106
Beatus (of Liébana), 18, 25–6, 39, 141,
    146n9, 148n26, 149n28, 150n32,
    150n35, 150n36
Biglieri, Aníbal, 41, 69, 164n59
body: as building, 79; as commodity,
    128; as geography, 51–3; of God,
    17, 52; hair, 75; mortal, 23, 107,
    126, 145n1, 172n47; of the text, 9,
    52, 77, 92, 101. *See also* Ebstorf;
    maps
build/building: of culture, 18, 23,
    26, 42–3, 74, 136; related to Babel,
    47, 78–80, 82, 85–6, 89, 94, 163n54;
    related to maps, 37, 72, 73; related
    to memory, 20, 72–3; related to
    sovereignty, 69, 74, 94, 125, 136,
    161n22

Cam, Ham, or Cham (son of Noah),
    15–16, 39, 84, 86, 139. *See also*
    Noah: sons
Carruthers, Mary, 20, 73
cartography: as discipline, 4, 6, 8–12,
    14, 16, 18–21, 23, 24–5, 72, 134–5,
    150n32, 150n35; operations or fig-
    ures of, 17, 19, 24, 26, 39, 73, 135;
    and pedagogy, 33–4, 72; as source,
    13, 21, 35–6, 53, 150n40, 152n51,
    154n63; as tool or instrument for
    knowledge, 13, 17, 21, 23–4, 53, 72,
    78. *See also* maps
Casas Rigall, Juan, 77, 89, 151n47,
    151n48, 152n49, 153n59, 155n70,
    156n73, 156n74
Castile, 7, 12, 23, 33, 62, 65, 67–8, 70,
    90, 96–100, 103, 108–10, 127, 141,
    159n13, 160n14
Châtillon, Gautier de, 7, 32, 34, 39,
    46, 52, 60, 77, 172n47; *Alexandreis*,
    7, 32–5, 41, 44, 46, 49, 52, 60, 77,
    81, 134, 155n70
Cid: hero or protagonist, 5, 104–6,
    109; *Poem of the*, 5–6, 11, 97, 102,
    104–6, 108, 110, 135
classification: device for, 21, 23, 31–2;
    and knowledge, 32, 44
clerecía: *mester de*, 4–5, 7, 9, 23, 54,
    59–61, 63, 88, 90, 94, 95–8, 100, 104,
    107, 109, 143n1, 147n20, 150n32;
    as mode, 166n66; and sovereignty,
    166n68, 171n32. *See also* cleric; com-
    position; didacticism; labour; task
cleric: clerical culture, 8, 11, 13,
    17–18, 24, 26, 33, 44, 57, 61, 69,
    88, 95, 110, 135, 158n12; clerical
    knowledge, 7, 10, 19, 21, 29, 34,
    54, 76, 101, 117–22, 128, 172n38;

figure of, 3–6, 9, 11–12, 17, 20, 26, 28, 35, 38, 41, 43–4, 57–8, 62, 64, 66–7, 70–3, 78, 107, 116–17, 134, 143n1, 159n14, 161n35; task of, 10–12, 20–1, 23, 44, 58, 62, 76, 90, 94, 101–2, 116, 123, 135–6, 144n4, 158n12

coins: coinage, 96, 98–9; *dinero*, 97–100, 107, 113; general, 96–7, 154n63; *maravedí*, 98–9; *meaja*, 97, 100, 113; *pepión*, 97–8, 100, 112; small, 96–9, 101, 107, 113, 136, 169n11; *sueldo*, 97, 99

commerce. 18, 44–5, 96, 98, 103, 127–8,

community, 10, 45, 47, 67, 80, 86–7, 90, 92–4, 103, 106, 108, 116, 134

composition, 3–5, 7–12, 14, 20–1, 24, 30, 33, 42, 53, 57–8, 60–4, 67, 69, 74, 76, 78, 88–90, 95, 100–1, 134, 143n2, 144n4, 149n30, 157n3, 159n14

conversion, 34, 117, 120, 127, 171n33, 171n34

Copeland, Rita, 7, 10, 32, 61, 153n56

court: Alexander's, 39; and behaviour, 67–9, 108, 110, 118, 126–8; and clerics, 5, 66, 68, 70–1, 94, 110, 160n20; and commerce, 128; culture, 7, 33; and king, 4, 63, 68–9, 104–5, 118, 128, 132, 169n17; and politics, 11–12, 67, 70, 171n32; and *studium*, 43, 64, 134

craft, 3–4, 8, 10–11, 20, 37–8, 40, 49, 52, 59–60, 71–2, 76, 79, 86, 89–90, 95, 102, 107, 116, 132, 135, 145n1, 165n54. *See also* labour; mester; task

credit, 5, 68, 106, 108–9, 111–15, 119, 122, 127

curialitas, 67–9, 118, 129

curriculum, 7–10, 12, 14, 19, 21–3, 27, 32–3, 38, 61–2, 65, 73, 76, 144n9, 148n25, 158n4, 158n5, 159n14, 160n15

Darius, 10, 36–9, 44, 46–7, 77, 83–4, 89, 111–15, 122, 155n66, 169n19

deixis, 9, 33, 78

de Man, Paul, 87, 88

description, 14, 16, 21, 23–4, 26, 32–6, 38–9, 41–6, 49, 52–4, 567, 71, 75–6, 78, 81–4, 92, 95, 107, 131, 147n23, 148n27, 151n48, 152n51, 153n59, 156n78, 169n19. *See also* ekphrasis

diagram, 9, 16–18, 20, 22, 27–8, 30–2, 34–5, 52, 58, 73, 137–42, 149n30, 152n49, 154n63

didacticism, 3, 18, 21–3, 30, 53, 147n20

Diego de Campos, 78, 81, 162n48. *See also* Planeta

digression/digression, 8–9, 29, 33–6, 42–4, 52, 56–7, 78, 81–2, 84, 91, 120, 122, 124, 131, 135, 151n48, 152n49

Ebstorf, 17–8, 52–3, 81, 146n8

Eco, Umberto, 82, 92

economy: of desire, 120, 169n17; general, 16, 98–9, 101, 104, 109; gift, 11, 97, 105, 108–9, 135; of grace, 120, 126–7; literary, 105; monetary, 96, 99; political, 11, 12, 103, 115, 136; profit, 11, 97, 105, 108–9, 135; seigneurial, 106

ekphrasis: 38, 42–3, 84, 91–2, 152n51, 154n62, 155n70. *See also* description

empire, 4, 37, 43–4, 48, 55–7, 133,
    149n30, 154n63, 166n68; imperial/
    imperialism, 3, 42, 44, 48, 67, 69,
    115, 131–2, 156n73, 165n61
encyclopaedic, 18, 20, 22. *See also*
    archive; Isidore of Seville
Etymologies, 8, 14–15, 22, 29, 41, 65,
    78, 81, 138–40, 146n12, 148n26,
    151n40, 168n1, 172n47
exchange, 9, 11, 86, 97–8, 100–1,
    103–6, 108–111, 115–16, 127–9, 132,
    169n17

Fernán: character/protagonist, 5,
    108–9; *Libro de Fernán González*,
    5–6, 11, 64, 67, 97, 102, 104, 106–10,
    135, 143n1, 170n24, 170n26
Fernando III, 62, 66–7, 70, 98, 161n35
fiction: as bookish, 13, 67, 70; and
    cartography, 20, 32–3, 58; and
    economics, 97, 104, 106, 109, 135;
    invention of, 8, 21, 33, 58, 70, 136,
    150n32; production or composi-
    tion of, 5, 9–10, 14, 33, 57–8, 63;
    and sovereignty, 64; vernacular
    learned, 4, 20, 23, 58, 71–2, 110

Gautier Dalché, Patrick, 19, 23–4, 29,
    33, 99, 146n10, 146n12, 149n32,
    150n35
Genesis, 79, 81–3, 89, 91, 163n52,
    165n56
geography, 9, 17, 19–20, 21–4, 26, 30,
    35, 37–8, 52–3, 58, 146n12, 147n23,
    150n40, 156n70
gift: *don* 104–5, 110; as present,
    103–6, 108, 111, 120, 126, 170n24;
    as talent, 78. *See also* economy
grammar, 7, 10, 23, 61, 65, 70–1, 76,
    158n5

Guijarro González, Susana, 65, 66,
    159n13, 160n14, 160n15

harangue, 70, 74, 107, 155n66,
    171n29, 172n40
history: cartography, 18, 135, 150n40;
    and cartography, 152n48, 153n53,
    156n70; as discipline, 6, 8, 12,
    19, 23, 26, 30, 33, 43–4, 52, 57, 69,
    82, 90, 94, 127, 166n70; divine,
    54, 58; economic, 95–6, 98, 104;
    human, 30, 52, 56, 64, 79, 83, 90,
    94, 156n70; of literature, 6; moral,
    47; as practice or historiography,
    5, 19, 32, 57, 58, 63–4, 69–72, 92,
    158n12; Spanish, 5
horseshoe arches, 27, 31–2, 73,
    139–41, 148n26
Hugh of Saint Victor, 22, 26, 73,
    148n27, 154n59, 157n3, 160n15

interest, 104, 109–10, 133, 170n25. *See
    also* economy; profit
interpretation, 5, 9, 14, 33–4, 38, 42–4,
    52–4, 61, 67, 71–2, 74, 79, 82–3,
    85, 92, 105, 115–16, 134, 149n30,
    149n32, 151n48, 163n51
inventio, inventional, 4, 7, 20–1, 33,
    48, 72–4, 104, 135
Isidore of Seville, 7, 14–15, 19, 22, 25,
    28–30, 36, 38, 41, 65, 74, 78, 81–3,
    139–40, 146n12, 148n26, 149n30,
    168n1, 172n47

Jacob, Christian, 17, 58
Japheth or Japhet, 15–6, 84, 86, 139.
    See also Noah: sons
Jiménez de Rada, Rodrigo, 5, 10,
    66–9, 78, 81–2, 90, 117, 161n22,
    162n48

Kellog, Judith, 103, 106
knowledge, 3, 13, 15, 17, 9, 22, 32, 35, 41–3, 54, 58, 61, 82, 122 , 125, 131; organization of, 17, 23–4, 27, 30–2, 44, 56, 73; archive/storage/pres-ervation of, 4, 17, 19–20, 32, 44, 58; clerical, 7, 21–2, 60–1, 65, 70, 76, 101–2, 111, 117, 119–22, 124–5, 171n33, 172n38; fragmentation of, 15; production of, 17, 56, 76, 82, 101, 111; scientific, 152n49, 154n59; transmission/dissemination of, 3, 15, 32, 58, 102; vision and, 13, 18, 33, 41–2, 54, 57–8, 73, 150n34

labour, 4, 10–11, 15–16, 43, 67, 71, 76, 85–6, 90, 92–3, 135–6, 166n64, 170n27. *See also* clerecía; task
Libro de Alexandre. See *Alexandre, Libro de*
Libro de Apolonio. *See under* Apolonio or Apollonius
Libro de Fernán González. *See under* Fernán
literature, 3–8, 14, 19–20, 22, 25, 38, 62, 66, 69, 71, 76, 87–8, 94, 95–7, 101, 104, 107, 109, 114, 145n2, 159n14
Lucas de Tuy, 5, 10, 66

Macrobius, 21–2, 141. *See also* maps
maps: as device or instrument or tool, 9, 13, 24, 73; Isidorian or T/O maps, 14–20, 24, 27–34, 36, 41, 52, 56, 86, 150n35–6, 151n48; Macrobian or zonal or climatic, 15, 21–2, 27, 29; *mappamundi, mappaemundi*, 17–20, 24–8, 30, 32, 36, 43–4, 52, 54–6, 58, 72, 81, 123–4, 148n26, 150n32, 150n35, 151n48, 153n52, 156n79, 168n81;

monumental and mural, 26, 53–6, 58, 148n27, 149n28–9; verbal, 8–9, 26, 32, 34–5, 37–58, 72, 123–4, 148n27, 149n30–1, 153n53, 154n59, 156n73; visual or drawn, 8–9, 12, 24, 27, 48–9, 56, 72, 146n9, 146n10, 147n23, 152n49. *See also* cartog-raphy; diagram; geography; *and appendix, p. 137*
market: related to, 127, 132; space of, 100–2, 105, 108, 112, 115, 127, 131
Mauss, Marcel, 11, 103, 105–6
memory: clerics and, 17, 27, 35, 63, 76, 78, 134–5, 152n48; and maps, 15, 20, 30, 32, 72–3; in medieval pedagogy, 19–20, 23, 72; and place, 20, 31, 41, 73, 155n66; role of, 4, 26, 46, 72
Menéndez Pidal, Gonzalo, 14–15, 25, 28–9, 137–8, 150n35
Michael, Ian, 67, 152n52, 168n1
monk: figure of, 23–4, 31; monastic, 7, 19, 60, 65, 73–4, 159n13, 160n15. *See also* cleric

Nimrod, Nembrot, 83, 88, 89, 164n64, 165n57, 166n63, 166n70
Noah: Ark of, 16, 35, 39, 84; sons, 15–16, 27–8, 39, 84, 86, 88, 137–42, 151n48, 157n82

Orosius, 19, 25, 140, 146n12, 148n26

Palencia, 60–1, 65–6, 158n5, 159n14, 161n22
pilgrim: figure of, 37, 40–1, 127, 132; pilgrimage, 38, 41, 132, 96
Planeta, 63, 67–8, 78
profit, 102, 104–5, 116–17, 119, 125–7, 129, 131–2; profit economy, 11, 97,

108, 109, 115, 135. *See also* economy; risk

reading: close, 19, 61, 64, 74; interpretation, 12, 23, 70, 87, 107,
119, 127–8, 143n2, 145n2, 157n81,
169n17; as labour, 76, 119; out loud
or public, 3, 51, 61, 63, 157n3; road
of, 38, 42, 153n56
representation, 8, 12, 14, 16, 19,
23–4, 34, 39, 42, 49, 63–4, 67,
69–70, 72, 81, 103–4, 131, 140,
145n2, 156n79
rhetoric, 3–12, 19–20, 23–4, 32, 42, 52,
57, 58, 61–5, 69–72, 76, 78, 93–4,
96, 129, 159n14, 165n54, 171n29;
related to economics, 102, 105,
10–8, 110–12, 115, 123, 128; related
to maps, 14, 16–17, 26, 28–9, 33–4,
78, 135
Rico, Francisco, 49, 156n75
risk, 52, 117, 119, 123–4, 126, 129,
131–2. *See also* economy; profit
Rodamilans Ramos, Fernando, 96, 99
rondel, 30–1, 141
rotae, 27, 30–2, 73, 138–41
Rucquoi, Adeline, 66–9, 161n22,
171n32

Shell, Marc, 101, 103, 120, 126
Shem or Sem, 15–16, 39, 84, 86, 88–9,
139
shield: Achilles's, 42–4; Alexander's,
36–8, 42–3, 50, 152n52, 153n53,
153n57, 157n81; Darius's, 46, 83;
map on, 37, 42, 153n54
sovereignty, 3, 5, 10–11, 64, 67–9, 88,
90, 116, 118–20, 127–8, 131–2, 135,
166n68, 171n32

space, 9, 17, 25, 29, 38, 52, 57, 61,
80, 94, 116, 127, 131–3, 144n10,
171n34; of the page, 24, 27, 31; of
the court, 67–8, 128
speculation, 105–6, 110–12, 115, 133,
135, 162n45. *See also* economy;
profit; risk
speculum principum, 54, 65, 67
Such, Peter, 7, 10, 151n47
Surtz, Ronald, 120–1, 171n34, 172n38
symbol, 14, 27, 42, 52–3, 78, 81, 154n63

task: of cleric, 3, 5, 10–12, 21, 23, 44,
58, 62, 71, 76, 78, 89, 90, 93, 101,
102, 116, 123, 135, 144n4; as craft,
10–11, 42, 57, 71, 76, 89, 90, 115;
as labour, 3, 64, 67, 71, 76, 89, 121,
135, 158n12; related to translation,
87, 89, 93–4, 135. See also *clerecía*;
labour
technique, 8–9, 11, 89–90, 58, 90, 92,
95, 104, 140; of memory, 20–1,
31–3, 78; *technè*, 10–11, 86, 89–90,
92–4, 135, 167n75; technology
(aircraft), 13
tent, Alexander's, 36, 38, 43, 53–4, 56,
156n70
trade, 86, 101, 126–9, 132, 136. *See
also* economy; exchange; market
translation, 4, 6–12, 19, 21–5, 32–5,
38, 41, 58, 61–2, 67, 69, 72, 74,
76–8, 84, 86–91, 93–4, 104, 110, 129,
134–5, 144n10, 146n10, 165n54,
165n55, 166n66, 167n79
travel, 8, 14, 32, 48, 53, 60, 68, 82, 116,
119, 121–4, 126, 128–9, 132, 171n34

Uría Maqua, Isabel, 10, 61, 117,
143n1, 171n34

value: economic, 100–1, 103–6, 113,
    115, 118, 126; moral, 103–5, 107,
    112, 115, 126; symbolic, 68, 101,
    106–7, 115
vision: related to knowledge, 42–4,
    53, 57, 150n34; religious, 24; as
    sight, 37, 50; of world, 13, 43, 52–3,
    156n76

Weiss, Julian, 62, 67, 78, 127–8,
    143n1, 61n28, 166n66, 168n17
Willis, Raymond, 46, 56, 60, 144n10,
    152n52, 168n1

Zumthor, Paul, 81, 91, 166n63